Prioritising Wellbeing and Self-Care in Higher Education

This book illuminates international voices of those who feel empowered to do things differently in higher education, providing inspiration to those who are seeking guidance, reassurance, or a beacon of hope.

Doing things differently comes with an awareness and curiosity to explore what can be. Increasingly, more and more professionals in higher education are choosing themselves, happiness, families, relationships, kindness, and compassion over arbitrary notions of institutional prestige, continuous pressure to overwork, and competitiveness with others. The chapters in this book do more than highlight flaws in the system, they call for proactive engagement in interrupting and reimagining what is broken. The authors share their own experiences as a way of encouraging readers to take small steps towards self-care, to notice their surroundings, and to embrace change as an empowering tool. The focus is on becoming the change we aspire to see, with a collective readiness to instigate positive transformations.

Sharing ambitious ideas to encourage change, this book is a valuable resource for those seeking to enhance their self-care and wellbeing in the higher education context, and for those seeking to engage with others in support of these efforts.

Narelle Lemon, VC Professoriate Research Fellow at Edith Cowan University in Perth, Australia, is an interdisciplinary scholar specialising in arts, education, and positive psychology. Her research focuses on enhancing wellbeing literacy in K-12 schools, teacher education, higher education, and community settings, emphasising evidence-based practices for proactive flourishing.

Wellbeing and Self-care in Higher Education
Editor: Narelle Lemon

For more information about this series, please visit: www.routledge.com/Wellbeing-and-Self-care-in-Higher-Education/book-series/WSCHE

Prioritising Wellbeing and Self-Care in Higher Education

How We Can Do Things Differently to Disrupt Silence

Edited by Narelle Lemon

Routledge
Taylor & Francis Group

LONDON AND NEW YORK

Designed cover image: © Getty Images

First published 2025
by Routledge
4 Park Square, Milton Park, Abingdon, Oxon OX14 4RN

and by Routledge
605 Third Avenue, New York, NY 10158

Routledge is an imprint of the Taylor & Francis Group, an informa business

British Library Cataloguing-in-Publication Data
A catalogue record for this book is available from the British Library

ISBN: 9781032600895 (hbk)
ISBN: 9781032600888 (pbk)
ISBN: 9781003457510 (ebk)

DOI: 10.4324/9781003457510

Typeset in Galliard
by KnowledgeWorks Global Ltd.

Contents

Images and tables

Images

Tables

Notes on contributors

Sarah Barradell is a senior lecturer at Swinburne University of Technology, Australia. Sarah's academic work connects the areas of teaching, research, and leadership. Her efforts and expertise in curriculum, teaching, and learning have resulted in numerous awards at local, national, and international level. Her research interests are centred around: health professional education; helping students learn for changing practice and with more influence; staff–student partnerships; and the scholarship of teaching and learning. Sarah is also a registered physiotherapist with extensive expertise in public and private sectors both in Australia and overseas.

Lauren Black (they/them) is a PhD candidate in the Faculty of Education and Social Work, University of Auckland and Teaching Assistant at Auckland University of Technology. Their current doctoral research considers how young people are engaging with health and sexuality education, both within and outside of the classroom. Their work draws on embodied understandings of lived experiences, particularly relating to issues of queer in/visibility in spaces of education.

Shaun Britton is an academic director and lecturer in the Film, Games and Animation department at Swinburne University in Melbourne, Australia. An animator, character, and product designer, he was past president of Illustrators Australia and a former Walt Disney and Warner Bros. senior creative. His practice-led research has been published in MIT's *Design Issues* and in *Visual Communication Quarterly*, other creative outcomes, including the graphic novel *Snip-and-Chu*, are developed through his boutique design agency, Squidinc Studio.

Emily Brownell (she/her) is a mother, an M.Sc. student in Community Health Sciences at the University of Manitoba, a student research assistant at the Manitoba Centre for Health Policy, and a SPECTRUM Fellow. Her thesis focuses on using Indigenous methodologies to learn about the perinatal care experiences of First Nations women in Northern Manitoba with the goal of contributing to more women- and family-centred healthcare.

She has been a SPECTRUM fellow since 2019 and has worked on a wide variety of tasks and projects as part of the partnership. Her research interests include parent–child health, Indigenous health and research methodologies, and substance use and addiction services. She has lived on Treaty 1 Territory and the homeland of the Red River Métis all her life. She loves spending time at the lake with family, playing tennis, reading and listening to audiobooks, and attending concerts.

Hera J. M. Casidsid (she/her) is a M.Sc. Community Health Sciences student at the University of Manitoba. She has a background Psychology and has various research and extra-curricular experiences. Hera is currently one of Manitoba Centre for Health Policy's (MCHP) Student Co-Lead, a Student Fellow for Social Policy Evaluation Collaborative Team Research at Universities in Manitoba (SPECTRUM), and a Research Assistant at MCHP. She is also working as a Vocational Evaluator (Psychometrist) at Manitoba Possible, conducting vocational assessments for people with disabilities. Hera's research interest is in social determinants of health as well as health services research, particularly in the area of mental health. For her Master's thesis, she will evaluate whether participation in the Manitoba Healthy Baby programme is associated with a reduced risk of developing postpartum depression among mothers using the linkable routinely collected data housed at MCHP. In her spare time, she enjoys travelling and exploring new restaurants.

Bertha Chin is Senior Lecturer at the Department of Communications and New Media, NUS Singapore. She has published extensively on transcultural fandom, fan labour, subcultural celebrity, anti-fandom and fan-producer relationships. She is co-editor of *Crowdfunding the Future: Media Industries, Ethics and Digital Society* (2015, Peter Lang) and *Eating Fandom* (2020, Routledge). She is also co-Editor-in-Chief of Popular Communication.

Nyla Comeau (she/her) is a master's student in the Indigenous Knowledge (MSW) Program. She holds a bachelor's degree in social work and her interest lies in psychology, Indigenous studies, and creative arts. Nyla's area of research is focused to the medicine wheel and creative arts as a source of wellness. She aspires to work with those who manage mental illness to find balance and wellness in their lives. Nyla has written poetry published in University of Manitoba *Feminist and Queer Review* and since has aspired to contribute through written word. Her desire is to work alongside those in community to empower individuals to remember their unique gifts and to inspire connection to community. She has worked alongside various populations and has a passion for working with women in confidence building, and their personal healing. In her leisure she enjoys checking out different cafes, traveling, and spending time with her loved ones.

Anita Durksen (she/her) is a doctoral candidate in the department of Community Health Sciences at the University of Manitoba. She holds a BSc in Physiology and Physics (2000) and a MSc in Physiology (2003) from McGill University. Anita has experience in academic and government environments, having worked as a research assistant, research coordinator, a data manager and analyst, a teaching assistant, a policy intern, and an epidemiologist. Anita's research interests lie in harnessing the power of administrative data to understand areas of society where we see success and areas in which change is needed, particularly when considering the healthy development of our children. Anita and her husband have two teenage children whom they are probably failing miserably but nonetheless trying to raise into solid human beings using techniques of love and grace. Anita enjoys time spent outdoors, gardening, food preparation, running after a frisbee, and making music.

Jennifer E. Enns, PhD, is a research scientist at the Manitoba Centre for Health Policy, University of Manitoba, with expertise in quantitative methods for administrative data research. Over the last several years, she has been engaged in a series of community-partnered research projects focused on health equity and the social determinants of health. In recent collaborative projects, she has used the administrative data in the Manitoba Population Research Data Repository to examine Indigenous maternal and child health outcomes, education and justice system outcomes of children and youth involved in Boys and Girls Clubs of Winnipeg programming, and mental health outcomes associated with methamphetamine use. Dr. Enns has an extensive knowledge translation portfolio, which includes knowledge products tailored for policy-makers, academics, community partners, and lay audiences. She also serves as a writing mentor to undergraduate and graduate students and to research support staff at the Manitoba Centre for Health Policy.

Tracy Fortune is an occupational therapy educator and researcher. Her interests and research are focussed on doctoral education and development, academic identity, curriculum development, project based learning, and education for global citizenship. Tracy currently coordinates the Graduate Research and Master of Occupational Therapy Practice programmes at La Trobe University in Melbourne, Australia. Tracy is a Fellow of the Higher Education Research & Development Society (HERDSA) and a Senior Fellow, UK Higher Education Academy (SFHEA).

Mark Freeman is a Lecturer in the Department of Film, Games and Animation at Swinburne University of Technology, Melbourne Australia and spent a year as a Chair of that Department in 2022. His research ranges from an interest in national cinema, cultural representation and archetypes to reality television and narratology. He has published work on the aesthetics of found footage horror and the improvisational comedy of Elaine May, and worked as editor on the journal *Senses of Cinema*.

Jeanette Fyffe is an Honorary Senior Lecturer at La Trobe and the Director, Researcher Development and Training at Deakin University. Jeanette started her academic life as a physicist before turning towards researcher and academic development. Her broad research interests lie in higher education, most especially the role of intellectual climate in the formation of scholars, doctoral supervision, and academic judgment. She is actively and collegially studying the "idea of the university".

Louise Grimmer is a retail marketing scholar and Associate Head Research in the Tasmanian School of Business and Economics at the University of Tasmania. Her research focuses on small stores, local shopping, and how independent retail stores improve physical spaces and contribute to local economies and communities. Her research has been published in leading international retail marketing journals and she is Associate Editor of the *Journal of Consumer Behaviour* and *The International Review of Retail, Distribution and Consumer Research*. Louise is a Fulbright Scholar and Senior Fellow of the UK's Institute of Place Management. She writes the 'Retail Therapy' column for *The Mercury*, hosts the 'Shopology' retail podcast, and is a regular contributor to 'The Conversation'. She has provided commentary for hundreds of media interviews on retailing, marketing, and consumer behaviour.

Alice J. Hovorka completed her PhD at Clark University in Massachusetts. Her research programme broadly explores human–environment relationships and is theoretically informed by feminist, poststructuralist, and posthumanist philosophical perspectives. She focuses on three specific research areas: lives of animals in Botswana; urbanisation, gender, and everyday life in Botswana; teaching and learning in higher education. She has also worked as a gender analysis and adviser with the International Development Research Centre (IDRC) in Ottawa, the Resource Centres on Urban Agriculture and Food Security (RUAF) in the Netherlands, and with the Government of Botswana. Dr. Hovorka served as a Professor at the Department of Geography & School of Environmental Studies, Queen's University, Ontario. Before joining Queen's, she worked as a faculty of Geography at the College of Social and Applied Human Sciences of University of Guelph. Currently, Alice is the Dean of the Faculty of Environmental and Urban Change at York University in Toronto.

Mikayla Hunter (she/they) is a M.Sc. Community Health Sciences student at the University of Manitoba. She completed her undergraduate studies at the University of Winnipeg, obtaining a double major in Rhetoric, Writing, & Communications and Psychology. Mikayla's master's thesis research focuses on exploring the primary healthcare needs and experiences of underrepresented members of the 2SLGBTQIA+ community. They hope that their work can inform the development of culturally appropriate clinical guidelines and improve the quality of care that 2SLGBTQIA+ patients receive from primary healthcare providers. In addition to her thesis work, Mikayla is the Lead Fellow for SPECTRUM. She is also the research coordinator for *Larry Saves the Healthcare System*, an evidence-informed, arts-based approach to explaining Canadian healthcare bureaucracy. They work on the MEGAN-CAN (Measuring Equity and Generating Action in Cancer) project, investigating the cancer care continuum experiences of sexual and gender minorities. Mikayla has two cats and is an avid gardener.

Khairunnisa Haji Ibrahim is a lecturer under the Geography, Environment and Development (GED) programme at the Faculty of Arts and Social Sciences, Universiti Brunei Darussalam. She researches and teaches a range of topics covering the social, cultural, and technical aspects of geography. Currently, she researches and teaches topics under three strands: women's and gender studies, spatial analysis, and popular culture. She is particularly interested in gender politics in knowledge production.

Narelle Lemon is a Professor and VC Professoriate Research Fellow Edith Cowan University, Perth, Australia. She is also an Adjunct Professor at Victoria University of Wellington, New Zealand. Narelle is an interdisciplinary scholar across the fields of arts, education, and positive psychology. Her research expertise is in fostering wellbeing literacy in the contexts of K-12 schools, initial teacher education, higher education, and community education – that is, capacity building in wellbeing and self-care of proactive action across diverse areas of evidence-based wellbeing science in order to flourish. Narelle is interested in the lived experience of being an academic – care, collaboration, mindful, and supportive practices. She is series editor for *Wellbeing and self-care in higher education: Embracing positive solutions* (Routledge) that is attracting much attention and supporting the dialogue of self-care being worthy of our attention. Narelle's contribution to the field of education has also been acknowledged through a 2019 National Teaching Citation, awarded by Australian Awards for University Teaching (AAUT), in scholarship of learning and teaching for sustained development of curricula and resources to support the integration of social media into initial teacher education to benefit student learning and engagement. Narelle blogs, posts, grams, and podcasts as a part of her networked scholar practices.

Yuqi Lin is a doctoral researcher at the Melbourne Centre for Study of Higher Education, Graduate School of Education, University of Melbourne. Her research interests lie in the sociology of education, particularly higher education policy, internationalisation of higher education, the wellbeing of international students and student experiences. Her works have appeared in international journals and books, including *Higher Education Quarterly*, *Journal of International Students*, and for Springer publishing. She specialised in qualitative research and promoting the use of autoethnography to amplify student voices. She has advocated for international students' rights, working as a youth representative and student leader in multiple organisations. Meanwhile, she has been working to improve the doctoral student experience, leading the interdisciplinary doctoral student collaboration programmes at the University of Melbourne.

Christopher Little currently teaches as a Senior Lecturer in the University Teaching Academy at Manchester Metropolitan University. This role encompasses lecturing and tutoring on postgraduate qualifications in teaching and learning, as well as co-leading MMU's AdvanceHE professional recognition route. Prior to this Chris worked as a Learning Developer and Teaching Fellow at Keele University. His research interests lie in inclusive education, undergraduate research, academic practices and literacies, and youth inclusion.

Kirsten Locke is an educational theorist and philosopher. Her teaching and research interests include key thinkers and themes in continental and feminist philosophy (such as Nietzsche, Lyotard, and Cixous; affect, the sublime, infancy). She is interested in working with art and music to explore philosophical questions, and the intersections of feminist and critical philosophies to issues of gender and equity in education. Kirsten serves on the National Council of the New Zealand Association for Research in Education and is an Associate Editor for *Educational Philosophy and Theory*. Her 2022 monograph entitled *Jean-François Lyotard: Pedagogies of Affect* was published by Springer.

Katrina McChesney is a senior lecturer in education at the University of Waikato, New Zealand. Her research centres on people's lived experiences in educational spaces and places, with a commitment to inclusive, socially just, person-centred educational Katrina is currently leading or co-leading several projects related to equity and inclusion in higher education, exploring doctoral research by distance; trauma-informed postgraduate supervision; and the visibility of parents in higher education. Katrina serves on the National Council of the New Zealand Association for Research in Education and is co-editor of *Studies in Graduate and Postgraduate Education*.

Megan McPherson is a settler artist, educator, and researcher based at the Wilin Centre for Indigenous Art and Cultural Development, The University of Melbourne. Megan's overarching creative practice research emphasis is in printmaking, textiles, and installations. She publishes in the areas of the academic identity, social media use, Indigenous knowledges and pedagogies, and student success in the creative arts. She explores her focus in the intersections of pedagogical and material engagements in artistic, social, and cultural productions using ethnographic, sociological, and creative practice methodologies to explore identity, subjectivities, affect, and agency.

Linda Noble and **Malgorzata Powietrzynska** have a shared passion for teaching and learning. They are teacher educators, co-teaching graduate level courses in the School of Education at Brooklyn College, CUNY. In recognition of their work they received an Award for Excellence in Teaching. While Linda teaches in a NYC public high school, Malgorzata is a manager in a post-secondary educational institution. Linda and Malgorzata co-engage in research focusing on infusing contemplative practices into education and they collaborate on providing professional development workshops in self-care and mindfulness to in-service public-school teachers.

Abdul Qawi Noori is an active researcher and reviewer of six international journals. He is a PhD candidate at the Monash University of Australia and obtained an M.Ed. in Educational Management and Administration from the Universiti Teknologi Malaysia and a B.A. in English Language and Literature from Takhar University. He has worked as an Assistant Professor at the English Department of Takhar University, Afghanistan and published over 17 research papers in prestigious international journals and presented papers at four international conferences in different countries. His research areas are inclusive leadership and sense of belonging, data-driven decision-making, teacher education, school effectiveness, quality assurance, technology in teaching and learning, and quality management in higher education.

Tiriki Onus (Yorta Yorta and Dja Dja Wurrung) is a successful visual artist, curator, performance artist, opera singer, and lecturer in Indigenous Arts and Culture at the Victorian College of the Arts. At the Wilin Centre, he fosters innovation in research, development, advocacy, and presentation of Indigenous arts and cultural practice. In 2015 he was the inaugural Hutchinson Indigenous Fellow, and is Deputy Dean, Place and Associate Dean, Indigenous in the Faculty of Fine Arts and Music and co-Director of the Research Unit for Indigenous Arts and Cultures.

Julia Ouzia is a Lecturer in Psychology (Education) at King's College London. Originally trained as a cognitive scientist/psycholinguist conducting research in the area of multilingual cognition, Julia is currently retraining as a Gestalt psychotherapist at the Metanoia Institute in London. She has a special interest in relational aspects of Gestalt Therapy and actively conducts research in this area. As an educator, Julia is also passionate about ensuring high quality education as well as wellbeing within the Higher Education community. As a result, she champions a variety of inclusive education initiatives at King's College London.

Stephaney Patrick (she/her) is a doctoral candidate in the Peace and Conflict Studies Program at the University of Manitoba. She holds an MA in Coexistence and Conflict and an MA in Sustainable Development, both from the Heller School of Social Policy and Management at Brandeis University, as well as an honours BSc in Political Science from the University of the

West Indies and is a Joint Japan World Bank Scholar. Stephaney's career has spanned over ten years as a civil servant working with the Government of Jamaica as a Development Specialist and Policy Analyst. Her work involved approaching violence as a public health issue and using a cross-sectoral collaboration approach to strengthen the country's crime and violence prevention strategies. She is passionate about creating spaces for the inclusion of young peoples' voices in decision-making. In her spare time, she likes to counsel young people, teach Bible study sessions, dance, and sing.

Jamie Pfau (she/her) is a PhD student in Community Health Sciences at the University of Manitoba. She holds a Master's degree in social work and an honours degree in psychology. For years, Jamie's research has focused on child welfare, promoting better outcomes for apprehended children, and being a social justice advocate. Her research focus has led her to becoming a Fellow with SPECTRUM since 2019. Her passion can be easily explained through her journey of infertility that led to her becoming a treatment foster parent. Jamie and her partner are raising five children. She is also the co-founder of Peace For All of Us, a non-profit that houses youth who have aged out of foster care, and female survivors of domestic violence and their children. Jamie is a Senior Policy Analyst with the Manitoba Government in the Education Department. In her spare time, Jamie enjoys travelling and hand building pottery.

Raine Melissa Riman is currently a PhD candidate in media anthropology at Swinburne University of Technology, Malaysia. Her PhD research explores the (re)production of national identity across postcolonial media spaces in response to the COVID-19 crisis. She has guest lectured on several international food system forum and co-founded the EAT Borneo Conference and the Sarawak Coffee Culture research network.

Emily Rooney is a clinical psychology PhD candidate at the University of Toledo and has her master's in psychology from The Citadel. Her research interests include trauma-related psychopathology, subsequent risk/protective factors, and transdiagnostic mechanisms, specifically emotion regulation. She is also interested in multidisciplinary areas that intersect with trauma psychopathology, such as technology and culture. She is continually inspired by her clients especially their resilience and courage to be vulnerable. Emily's desire for connection fuels her patient-centred approach to therapy. When she is not practising psychology, Emily enjoys trying out new coffee shops, clumsily practising yoga, making day trips to explore nearby towns, and (after a fulfilling work week), winding down on Friday evenings and sharing a bottle of wine with her husband.

Deena Kara Shaffer (she/her), PhD, MDes (candidate), MEd, BEd, BA, OCT. Deena is the Director, Office of Student and Academic Services, Faculty of Environmental and Urban Change, at York University in Toronto.

Prior, at Toronto Metropolitan University (formerly Ryerson), she served as Manager of Thriving Innovations in Student Wellbeing, as Adjunct Faculty in the Sociology Department, and as Lecturer in the Psychology Department. Deena is also the founder of Awakened Learning, designing compelling learning experiences for parents, leaders, and students of all ages, and the President of the Learning Specialists Association of Canada. Deena is the creator of the #LearnThat movement, co-founder of the now international Thriving in Action resilience intervention, and co-author of *Thriving in Action Online* and *Thriving in the Classroom*. Deena holds a doctorate in nature-based pedagogy and learning strategies; is a trained yoga, restorative, and meditation teacher; is a published poet; and, is a public speaker on learning and well-becoming. Deena's ideal day is spent outdoors tobogganing, or getting muddy, with her two kids.

Estrella Sendra is a creative researcher, award-winning educator, and practitioner working as Lecturer in Culture, Media and Creative Industries Education (Festivals and Events) at King's College London. Drawing on her work as a film festival curator, organiser, and filmmaker, she is particularly interested in innovative education and research methods. This includes the design of creative assessment methods, such as video essays and festivals, the publication of creative research, articles, and toolkits sharing and reflecting on pedagogy. She is co-author of the open access *Introductory Guide to Video Essays* (Learning on Screen, 2020) and author of the journal article 'Video essays: Curating and transforming film education through artistic research' (2020). In 2020 she was awarded the SOAS Director's Teaching Prize for Inspirational Teaching. She is the co-principal investigator of the New Frontiers in Research Fund project 'Decolonising Film Festival Research in a Post-Pandemic World'. She is Associate Editor in Screenworks.

Yue Xu is a PhD student and qualitative researcher in the Faculty of Education, Monash University. The context of her research focuses on identity work and intercultural studies, with concerns about teaching/learning authenticity and the development of professional/academic identities of educators as well as graduate students. Some of her relevant research outputs can be found in *International Journal of Inclusive Education*, and a recently published book *Research and Teaching and a Pandemic World*. After completing her master's degree in Australia and prior to further pursuing a doctorate, she had worked in multiple professions in the field of education and beyond, including as an EAL teacher for learners of different ages and editorial assistant for several ACS journals. Such interdisciplinary experiences have equipped her with a unique lens to look at the different roles that have shaped and reshaped her professional identity down her career path, and to empathise with the broader international doctoral researcher's cohort on a global scale.

Series preface

As academics, scholars, staff, and colleagues working in the context of universities in the contemporary climate we are often challenged with where we place our own wellbeing. It is not uncommon to hear about burnout, stress, anxiety, pressures with workload, having too many balls in the air, toxic cultures, increasing demands, isolation, and feeling distressed (Berg & Seeber, 2016; Lemon & McDonough, 2018; Mountz et al., 2015). The reality is that universities are stressful places (Beer et al., 2015; Cranton & Taylor, 2012; Kasworm & Bowles, 2012; Mountz et al., 2015; Ryan, 2013; Sullivan & Weissner, 2010; Wang & Cranton, 2012). McNaughton and Billot (2016) argue that the "deeply personal effects of changing roles, expectations and demands" (p. 646) have been downplayed and that academics and staff engage in constant reconstruction of their identities and work practices. It is important to acknowledge this, as much as it is to acknowledge the need to place wellbeing and self-care at the forefront of these lived experiences and situations.

Wellbeing can be approached at multiple levels including micro and macro. In placing wellbeing at the heart of the higher education workplace, self-care becomes an imperative both individually and systemically (Berg & Seeber, 2016; Lemon & McDonough, 2018). Self-care is most commonly oriented towards individual action to monitor and ensure personal wellbeing, however it is also a collective act. There is a plethora of different terms that are in action to describe how one approaches their wellbeing holistically (Godfrey et al., 2011). With different terminology comes different ways self-care is understood. For this collection self-care is understood as "the actions that individuals take for themselves, on behalf of and with others in order to develop, protect, maintain and improve their health, wellbeing or wellness" (Self Care Forum, 2019, para. 1). It covers a spectrum of health-related (emotional, physical, and/or spiritual) actions including prevention, promotion, and treatment, while aiming to encourage individuals to take personal responsibility for their health and to advocate for themselves and others in accessing resources and care (Knapik & Laverty, 2018). Self-love, -compassion, -awareness, and -regulation are significant elements of self-care. But what does this look like for those working in higher education? In this book series authors respond to the questions: *What do you do for self-care? How do you position wellbeing as part of your role in academia?*

In thinking about these questions' authors are invited to critically discuss and respond to inspiration sparked by one or more of the questions of:

- How do we bring self-regulation to how we approach our work?
- How do we create a compassionate workplace in academia?
- What does it mean for our work when we are aware and enact self-compassion?
- What awareness has occurred that has disrupted the way we approach work?
- Where do mindful intentions sit?
- How do we shift the rhetoric of "this is how it has always been" in relation to over working, and indiscretions between workload and approaches to workload?
- How do we counteract the traditional narrative of over work?
- How do we create and sustain a healthier approach?
- How can we empower the "I" and "we" as we navigate self-care as a part of who we are as academics?
- How can we promote a curiosity about how we approach self-care?
- What changes do we need to make?
- How can we approach self-care with energy and promote shifts in how we work individually, collectively, and systemically?

The purpose of this book series is to:

- Place academic wellbeing and self-care at the heart of discussions around working in higher education.
- Provide a diverse range of strategies for how to put in place wellbeing and self-care approaches as an academic.
- Provide a narrative connection point for readers from a variety of backgrounds in academia.
- Highlight lived experiences and honour the voice of those working in higher education.
- Provide a visual narrative that supports connection to authors' lived experience(s).
- Contribute to the conversation on ways that wellbeing and self-care can be positioned in the work that those working in higher education do.
- Highlight new ways of working in higher education that disrupt current tensions that neglect wellbeing.

References

Beer, L. E., Rodriguez, K., Taylor, C., Martinez-Jones, N., Griffin, J., Smith, T. R., Lamar, M., & Anaya, R. (2015). Awareness, integration and interconnectedness. *Journal of Transformative Education, 13*(2), 161–185.

Berg, M., & Seeber, B. K. (2016). *The slow professor: Challenging the culture of speed in the academy*. Toronto: University of Toronto Press.

Cranton, P., & Taylor, E. W. (2012). Transformative learning theory: Seeking a more unified theory. In E. W. Taylor & P. Cranton (Eds.), *The handbook of transformative learning* (pp. 3–20). San Francisco, CA: Jossey-Bass.

Godfrey, C. M., Harrison, M. B., Lysaght, R., Lamb, M., Graham, I. D., & Oakley, P. (2011). The experience of self-care: A systematic review. *JBI Library of Systematic Reviews*, *8*(34), 1351–1460. Retrieved from http://www.ncbi.nlm.nih.gov/pubmed/27819888

Lemon, N., & McDonough, S. (Eds.). (2018). *Mindfulness in the academy: Practices and perspectives from scholars*. Singapore: Springer.

Kasworm, C., & Bowles, T. (2012). Fostering transformative learning in higher education settings. In E. Taylor & P. Cranton (Eds.), *The handbook of transformative learning* (pp. 388–407). Thousand Oaks, CA: Sage.

Knapik, K., & Laverty, A. (2018). Self-care individual, relational, and political sensibilities. In M. A. Henning, C. U. Krägeloh, R. Dryer, F. Moir, D. R. Billington, & A. G. Hill (Eds.), *Wellbeing in higher education: Cultivating a healthy lifestyle among faculty and students*. Oxon, UK: Routledge.

McNaughton, S. M., & Billot, J. (2016). Negotiating academic teacher identity shifts during higher education contextual change. *Teaching in Higher Education*, *21*(6), 644–658.

Mountz, A., Bonds, A., Mansfield, B., Loyd, J., Hyndman, J., & Watton-Roberts, M. (2015). For slow scholarship: A feminist politics of resistance through collective action in the neoliberal university. *ACME: An International E-Journal of Critical Geographies*, *14*(4), 1235–1259.

Ryan, M. (2013). The pedagogical balancing act: Teaching reflection in higher education. *Teaching in Higher Education*, *18*, 144–155.

Self Care Forum (2019). Self Care Forum: Home. Retrieved 27 July 2019, from http://www.selfcareforum.org/

Sullivan, L. G., & Weissner, C. A. (2010). Learning to be reflective leaders: A case study from the NCCHC Hispanic leadership fellows program. In D. L. Wallin (Ed.), Special issue: *Leadership in an era of change. New directions for community colleges*, No. 149 (pp. 41–50). San Francisco, CA: Jossey-Bass.

Wang, V. C., & Cranton, P. (2012). Promoting and implementing Self-Directed Learning (SDL): An effective adult education model. *International Journal of Adult Vocational Education and Technology*, *3*, 16–25.

International reviewers

Ines Alves, University of Glasgow, Scotland, UK
Sarah Barradell, Swinburne University of Technology
Eric Bel, Teesside University, United Kingdom
Lauren Black, University of Auckland, New Zealand
Destini Braxton, Virginia Commonwealth University, Richmond, VA, USA
Shaun Britton, Swinburne University of Technology, Melbourne, Australia
Emily Brownell, University of Manitoba, Manitoba, Canada
Hera J. M. Casidsid, University of Manitoba, Manitoba, Canada
Urmee Chakma, La Trobe University, Melbourne, Australia
Bertha Chin, NUS, Singapore
Timothy Clark, University of the West of England, Bristol, United Kingdom
Nyla Comeau, University of Manitoba, Manitoba, Canada
Catelijne Coopmans, Independent scholar, Girona, Spain
Dangeni, Newcastle University, UK
Mandy Dhahan, University of Arizona, Tucson, Arizona
Aine Dolin, University of Saskatchewan, CA
Anita Durksen, University of Manitoba, Manitoba, Canada
Bronwyn Eager, The University of Tasmania, Australia
Dely Lazarte Elliot, University of Glasgow, Scotland, UK
Jennifer E. Enns, University of Manitoba, Manitoba, Canada
Aslı Ermiş-Mert, Koç University, Turkey
Zyra Evangelista, University of Glasgow, Scotland, UK
Tracy Fortune, La Trobe University
Akiko Fujii, International Christian University, Tokyo, Japan
Jeanette Fyffe, La Trobe University and Deakin University
Louise Grimmer, University of Tasmania, Tasmania, Australia

Kay Hammond, Auckland University of Technology, New Zealand

Lauren Hansen, Deakin University, Burwood, Australia

Chiyo Hayashi, International Christian University, Tokyo, Japan

Catherine Hill, Te Herenga Waka Victoria University of Wellington, New Zealand

Mikayla Hunter, University of Manitoba, Manitoba, Canada

Miriam Jaehn, Centre for Southeast Asian Studies, Kyoto University, Japan

Imene Zoulikha Kassous, University of Glasgow, Scotland, UK

Yoko Kobayashi, International Christian University, Tokyo, Japan

Narelle Lemon, Edith Cowan University, Perth Australia

Catherine Lido, University of Glasgow, Scotland, UK

Yuqi Lin, The University of Melbourne, Australia

Chris Little, Manchester Metropolitan University, Manchester, United Kingdom

Kirsten Locke, University of Auckland, New Zealand

Patricia Lucas, Auckland University of Technology, Auckland, New Zealand

Danni McCarthy, Deakin University, Burwood, Australia

Katrina McChesney, University of Waikato, Tauranga, New Zealand

Sharon McDonough, Federation University, Ballarat, Victoria, Australia

Megan McPherson, The University of Melbourne, Australia

Nicole Melzack, University of Southampton, United Kingdom

Felicity Molloy, Independent Scholar, New Zealand

Rahmila Murtiana, Swinburne University of Technology, Melbourne, Australia

Alla Al Najim, University of Glasgow, Scotland, UK

Linda Noble, Brooklyn College, New York, United States of America

Julia Ouzia, King's College London, London, United Kingdom

Stephaney Patrick, University of Manitoba, Manitoba, Canada

Jamie Pfau, University of Manitoba, Manitoba, Canada

Thinh Ngoc Pham, Solent University, UK

Malgorzata Powietrzynska, Brooklyn College, New York, United States of America

Meenal Rai, Auckland University of Technology, Auckland, New Zealand

Melanie Reaves, Montana State University Billings in Billings, Montana

Iona Burnell Reilly, University of East London, UK

Raine Melissa Riman, Swinburne University of Technology, Sarawak, Malaysia Borneo

Emily Rooney, University of Toledo, Toledo, Ohio, United States of America
Estrella Sendra, King's College London, London, United Kingdom
Melanie Shoffner, James Madison University, Harrisonburg, VA, USA
Linus Tan, Swinburne University of Technology, Melbourne, Australia
Johanna Tomczak, Independent Scholar, United Kingdom
Yao Wang, Newcastle University, UK
Izumi Watenabe-Kim, International Christian University, Tokyo, Japan
Angela W. Webb, James Madison University, Harrisonburg, VA, USA
Minoli Wijetunga, Monash University, Melbourne, Australia
Yue Xu, Monash University, Australia
Sunyee Yip, La Trobe University, Melbourne, Australia
Sharon Zumbrunn, Virginia Commonwealth University, Richmond, VA, USA

Chapter 1

Unmasking wellbeing

Voices redefining self-care and wellbeing in higher education

Narelle Lemon

Introduction

I think of self-care as proactive actions we take to support, grow, maintain, and protect our health, wellness, and wellbeing while drawing on diverse areas of wellbeing science. We need to draw on many areas of wellbeing science to form what can be considered as a toolbox of strategies or practices, aka tools. These tools come together to support being one's best self and selection is influenced by our access, knowledge, capacity, stage of maintaining, protecting, or growing our wellbeing. Our toolbox will and can change, be extended, can be added to, can be sharpened, or adjusted depending on the context. As such self-care is multidimensional and multifaceted; it is not the same for each of us, it is complex, however it does need to be purposeful (Dorociak et al., 2017; Lemon, 2021b, 2021a). Imagine it as a menu of self-care practices empowering us to be the best version of ourselves. In higher education, achieving this equilibrium or mental calmness in self-care (Cordaro, 2020) is possible but demanding. It requires effort, dedication, and collective commitment to reshape self-care as something deserving of our attention – not an afterthought for times when we are exhausted and told to reconsider our wellbeing choices by professionals or loved ones.

Within the literature on self-care, an interesting perspective emerges, suggesting that there are two distinct approaches: a personal mindset and a professional mindset. The personal mindset revolves around practices that enhance individual wellbeing, prompting questions like, "What do I personally need right now?" On the other hand, the professional self-care mindset requires attention to what is necessary to maintain a healthy professional self, posing questions like, "What do I need to care for myself in the workplace?" Combining both mindsets empowers individuals to take a more holistic approach to wellbeing within a system associated with caring for others (Lee & Miller, 2013). This is a consideration worth deliberating on in the context of higher education.

In either approach, and particularly in their convergence, the role of self-compassion emerges as a pivotal positive emotion as we navigate self-care and

DOI: 10.4324/9781003457510-1

wellbeing. It invites us to embrace "being kind and understanding toward oneself during instances of pain or failure, rather than being harshly self-critical, and recognizing that one's own experience of imperfection is a part of the human experience" (Neff, 2003, p. 224). Notably, self-compassion stands out as one of the most influential predictors of both personal and professional self-care practices (Jay Miller et al., 2019). In the field of higher education, considering self-care and self-compassion as inseparable allies is crucial (Lemon et al., 2023).

The expectation to do more with less with decreased perceptions of autonomy and job security, increasing student numbers and teaching quality focus, and greater emphasis on high-quality research outputs has been a sustained throughline of negative impact on academic wellbeing globally (Catano et al., 2010; Fontinha et al., 2019; Johnson et al., 2019; Kenny, 2018). We are also

Image 1.1 Unmasking for ripples

wearing the merge of the boundary between work and non-work domains (Fetherston et al., 2021). This is exhausting.

Can we be the change we want to see? I hope we can be. I think it is time that the pendulum swung back into our favour; we are ready to shift things and interrupt from a space of compassion, kindness, and careful consideration. And most significantly, the most important reason for me to lead this edited book is to honour the empowerment, agency, and darn hard work, personal battles, peer pressure, tears, appreciation, compassion, and every other emotion that has come with realising and being proactive in doing things differently when it comes to our wellbeing. This book is about honouring and promoting these voices – to celebrate and to pass on to others who need some help or want to be inspired or feel like there is no hope. I really want there to be hope for our sector, for us. So, let's begin now to interrupt, flip, disrupt, and to raise the voices of our peers and colleagues who are doing things differently. I invite you to unmask, to facilitate the ripple(s) of change.

More than just a one-off programme

As the sector begins to move forward and do things differently, it is important to acknowledge the work and approaches that are being explored, put out into the community, and are impacting positively, to provide models to build from. One that is sparking interest at the moment is occurring at The University of British Colombia (UBC). UBC Thrive (UBC Wellbeing Design Lab, 2023b) is a mindset and a month-long series during the month of November with a programme of events focused on helping everyone at UBC explore their path to mental health. The areas of learn, talk, and explore within the programme brings together students, faculty, staff, and community; illuminating an interesting holistic approach. The programme is aligned to a bigger strategic policy in health literacy (UBC Wellbeing Design Lab, 2023a) and to strategic long-term, university-wide goals being pursued through initiatives that advance wellbeing in six key focus areas: Collaborative Leadership, Mental Health & Resilience, Food & Nutrition, Social Connection, Built & Natural Environments, and Physical Activity. The establishment of a Wellbeing Strategic Framework was a response to UBC's Strategic Plan, delineating its unified strategy for integrating wellbeing into organisational plans, policies, practices, work plans, and decision-making processes (UBC Wellbeing Design Lab, 2023c). Of interest here are the strategic milestones around mental health and resilience literacy with a commitment to wellbeing, and "take action" goals. The language used has a "moving forward" framing, something which is refreshing in policy documentations for systems approaches aligned to milestones, and toolkits, slides, and resources are provided to assist in achieving a holistic approach across all teams within the university.

The sector have numerous examples of university frameworks and plans that focus on the students' mental health, wellbeing, or wellness to support academic success. Furthermore there has been development of frameworks and plans to provide national guidance for universities to support mental health and wellbeing such as The Australian University Mental Health Framework (Orygen, 2020) and Real Talk Framework (Universities Australia, 2023). There are co-designed strengths-based examples (University of Western Australia, 2023), systems approaches that look at diverse areas of wellbeing (The University of Queensland, 2023), and the scaffolding of mental health training for the academic community (Edith Cowan University, 2021). What we now need to see is a framework for academic and professional staff, not just students. Some universities are leading in this area (Charles Sturt University, 2023) but more is required, lots more! As we embrace a doing things differently approach we must be careful not to "do" to each other or create programmes, interventions, or policy that are one offs, do more damage, impede staff, or place staff against students (Brewster et al., 2022). We also need to be aware that wellbeing and self-care are more than one-off programmes, career literacy, or health literacy that focus on no smoking and vaping, access to sports and recreational facilities, lunch time yoga, workplace accident risk management, supporting attendance on campus, healthy eating, and flu shots. We need to draw on wellbeing science and the diverse areas to think through what I, we, and us wellbeing, wellness, and self-care look like. We need to:

> look beyond the provision of reactive services or isolated individual interventions, to proactively and cohesively embed cultural and structural change across the whole institution [to support] positive wellbeing outcomes for the whole university community.
>
> Brewster et al. (2022, p. 548)

A collective response

This book collection is a pivotal contribution to the book series "Wellbeing and Self-Care in Higher Education: Embracing Positive Solutions", and its title is intentional for several crucial reasons that merit early clarification. Firstly, it underscores the imperative for the higher education sector to re-evaluate its approach to valuing wellbeing and self-care. The existing dynamics of blame between individuals and the sector are unsustainable, prompting the need for a shift away from this counterproductive blame game. Secondly, the contributors, comprising scholars, researchers, teachers, administrators, policymakers, and leaders, advocate for a departure from merely acknowledging the system's flaws. Instead, they call for proactive engagement in interrupting and reimagining what is broken. The focus is on *becoming* the change we aspire to see, with a collective readiness to instigate positive transformations. The contributors express their desire for change in favour of the academic community fostering this through compassion, kindness, and careful consideration. Most significantly, the driving force behind proposing this edited book is to pay homage to the empowerment, agency, and strenuous efforts – both personal and professional – involved in reshaping perspectives on wellbeing. The contributors acknowledge the spectrum of emotions, from battles and pressures to tears and compassion, that accompany the journey of doing things differently in the realm of wellbeing. The book serves as a platform to honour and amplify these diverse voices, celebrating the resilience and hard work of those who have ventured into new territories. It aims to inspire and provide a beacon of hope for individuals within the sector who may be seeking guidance, inspiration, or reassurance. As the contributors advocate for a collective beginning, the book encourages readers to interrupt the status quo, flip perspectives, disrupt norms, and elevate the voices of peers and colleagues who are pioneering innovative approaches to wellbeing in higher education. The goal is to cultivate a sense of hope and optimism for the future of the sector and its individuals.

In the series to date we have a marvellous collection that is drawing attention to wellbeing and self-care in higher education from the perspectives of academics, leaders, researchers, and educators (a list of which can be found at the front of the book). With each of these books, narrative, proactive strategies and visual narratives feature. We have collectively been coming together to define wellbeing and self-care. Insights and problems within the sector have been shared across emerging to experienced scholars internationally. As the series grows in popularity and draws attention to wellbeing and self-acre in higher education, it is important to continue to push the boundaries of the place of wellbeing and self-care. With this comes a need for a book in the series that calls this out in a language that is relatable for our peers and colleagues and connectable for leaders, policymakers, and administrators who are yet to land the importance, significance and need.

As such this edited book aims to empower colleagues to share how they are approaching their wellbeing and self-care, what this looks and sounds like, and to inspire a shift in the sector with what can be possible. This is accomplished specifically by:

- Showcasing the empowerment that comes from doing things differently from peers and colleagues globally across various career trajectories.
- Illuminating the value of wellbeing and self-care in higher education from individual and collective voices that drill down deeply to personal and relatable and/or resonating experiences.
- Highlighting the need to interrupt current sustained unproductive, overwhelming, and simply compassion lacking ways that the sector continues to roll out to represent wellbeing and self-care that are disempowering, insulting, and not of worth.
- Providing an opportunity for peers and colleagues who engage with this book (and the series) to connect with proactive solutions and possibilities that value wellbeing and self-care.

- Supporting a movement of shifting the higher education sector's notions of wellbeing and self-care, including practice action, evidence-based research, case studies, in-depth narratives and visual narratives, and disruption to deficit or negative focus on language, practice, and embodiment.
- Extending conversations and actions forward as we move from the third to fourth year of the pandemic and the rise of exhaustion, cancel culture, quiet quitting, hustle culture, vulnerability, the place of humanising our experiences, and the place of languishing and flourishing continue to feature in our discussions, lived experiences, and workplaces.

In this collection we are empowered to think about our work, identity, collaboration, impact, and engagement differently. Doing things differently comes with an awareness and curiosity to explore what can be. It can be about reaffirming a way of being, seeing, or understanding our self and the contexts we work in, or it can be about growing, changing, adapting, and developing something in ourselves. As we navigate the higher education space we are forever (re)negotiating who we are. In relation to our self-care and wellbeing this rings true for so many of us, especially concerning raising our own and others' awareness of wellbeing and self-care as a priority. Small steps are powerful. Noticing is refreshing. Change can be challenging. Imagining and putting this into action is empowering. Reflection is required. With doing things differently comes amazing rewards in who we are, what we do, and how we engage with our self and others.

The book consists of chapters that respond to a single word chosen by the author(s) In relation to self-care and wellbeing in higher education. The authors assert that self-care is imperative both individually and systemically for those working in higher education, including academics, learning designers, researchers, scholars, and professional staff members. As the higher education sector is constantly changing, the authors propose that highlighting lived experiences and doing things differently can illuminate what is working, what is not, and what is possible. The menu of words explored in this book to think about self-care and wellbeing in higher education are:

Rethink
Laughter
Visibility
Place
Confront
Transformation
Awareness
Hope
Place
Heterotopia
Balance

Connection
Belonging
Boundary
Awe
New
Kindness
Expansive
Balance

The authors encourage readers to take small steps towards self-care, to notice their surroundings, and to embrace change as an empowering tool. Reflection is also pointed out as a necessary component of self-care and personal and professional growth. Ambitious ideas are shared that provide insights into proactive actions, offering transferability, affirmation and/or inspiration. Ultimately, the book serves as a valuable resource for those seeking to enhance their self-care and wellbeing in the higher education context, and for those seeking to engage with others in support of these efforts.

Across five sections we hear from 33 international scholars from various disciplines and career trajectories. Each is vulnerable in the sharing of a lived experience and their proactive actions. In this next section I introduce each section with a collective poem, and then give an insight into each author's (or group of authors') perspective.

The setting

In academia's realm, expectations unfold,
Rooted in history, where pressures prevail.

Roots run deep, tangled with society's ties,
A complex connection, where my spirit lies.
Queer identities, a complex fight.
Identity, culture, a nuanced theme

Silence, laughter, rethink, disrupt
A tapestry of stories, a realm that conceives.
Identity, laughter, and visibility's quest,
A commentary on academia, time to shift.

Rethink

Louise Grimmer in her chapter opens this collection with a visual narrative that aligns powerfully with the exploration of the deeply ingrained culture of high expectations in academia, emphasising its historical roots and the associated pressure for rigorous standards, achievement, and competition. The author shares a personal transformation in approaching academic work by challenging the norm of overexertion and perfectionism, opting instead to lower expectations for oneself and others. This shift involves prioritising wellbeing over relentless pursuit of promotion, leading to a more sustainable and fulfilling approach to academic life. The chapter delves into the paradox of perfectionism, the impact of high expectations on mental health and burnout, and the need for a balance that redefines success beyond traditional markers in academia. The author proposes solutions, including forming supportive networks like the "Promoting Academic Women" initiative. The chapter concludes by advocating for transformative shift in academia towards a more compassionate and balanced approach that fosters holistic wellbeing for individuals in the academic community.

Laughter

In this chapter, Katrina McChesney and Kirsten Locke explore the challenges faced by women in academia, highlighting the intense pressures, expectations, and potential consequences associated with academic life. They highlight the overwhelming nature of academic careers, characterised by extensive teaching loads, research commitments, and the need to navigate complex institutional structures. To cope with this environment, the authors turn to the concept of laughter as a form of survival, self-care, and resistance, drawing inspiration from feminist writer Hélène Cixous. They delve into Cixous's characterisation of laughter, particularly in relation to the myth of Medusa, and discuss how laughter can serve as a means of reclaiming agency, perspective, and voice in the face of oppression. The chapter incorporates humour through deliberately inserted jokes, acknowledging the liberating potential of laughter in navigating the seriousness and challenges of academic life. The authors conclude by encouraging readers to consider the role of laughter in academia, its diverse forms, and its potential for fostering wellbeing, solidarity, and resistance.

Visibility

Lauren Black writes a powerful chapter that delves into the intersection of personal and professional identities for queer individuals within the academic setting. It explores the complexities of maintaining visibility while also using silence as a strategic tool for self-care in the face of discrimination and marginalisation. The narrative employs narrative and poetic inquiry to unravel the contradictions and constraints of queer visibility in the neoliberal university, illuminating the importance of collective action. The chapter challenges normative individualised resilience strategies prevalent in academia and calls for a reimagining of self-care as a personal, political, and collective endeavour, urging a shift from individualistic notions to shared, reciprocal care within academic institutions.

Place

Raine Melissa Riman embarks on a poignant journey through the complexities of identity, culture, and place. The author, a self-identified hybrid navigating between academia and industry, intricately weaves personal narratives with reflections on the nuances of being a product of diverse backgrounds. The chapter unfolds as a narrative of struggle, negotiating the expectations of conforming to predefined identities while embracing the fluidity of a hybrid self. The chapter confronts the paradoxical nature of diversity in the author's home, Sarawak. It challenges the superficial celebration of diversity, urging a deeper recognition of the hybrids existing within. The essay concludes with a reflection on growth, acknowledging the possibility that the familiar may not always be conducive to personal and academic development. The author embraces the role of a "diversity killjoy," confronting the paradoxes of diversity and aspiring to align with authentic aspirations.

Repositioning learning and teaching for self and others

Confront the stage where lessons sway,
Embrace failure's dance, in the pedagogic array.

Awe's fabric woven with collaborative thread,
Sustained bond, where self and other are wed,
    a transformative spread.

Awareness, a bridge across the design expanse.
Bridging gaps for self and others' enhanced.

Students co-create, a transformative sensation.
Hope, an ally for self and others' liberation.

Place, a repositioning, a conscious quest,
Indigenous knowledge, the curriculum's zest.
    a significant embrace,
    a curriculum's trace for self and others' shared space.

Confront

Embracing failure in a higher education context is rarely spoken about. In this chapter Chris Little shares the experience of confronting learning on the spot and failing forward with his pedagogical decisions despite meticulous planning for an inclusive, authentic, and active session. Instead of continuing and analysing later, the author took the bold step of stopping the seminar, engaging students in a real-time discussion about the challenges, and co-creating a new, more effective approach. This act of critical honesty served as an act of self-care, relieving the author of the burden of failure, transforming their teaching philosophy, and fostering a pedagogy of compassion and openness. The chapter uses a reflective model to explore the incident and emphasises the importance of embracing uncomfortable moments in teaching for better outcomes and wellbeing. Through this narrative, the author highlights the transformative power of vulnerability and critical self-reflection in creating a more equitable and compassionate learning environment.

Awe

In this chapter, the Linda Noble and Malgorzata Powietrzynska celebrate their sustained collaboration while underscoring the vital role of awe in weaving individual values into the shared fabric of humanity, particularly within the challenges of socio-economic-environmental distress. Illuminating the need for teacher candidates to adopt asset-based approaches, they draw on the works of various scholars to support the cultivation of self-efficacy for a better future. The authors share a seven-year collaborative journey, advocating for contemplative pedagogy that integrates practices like mindfulness and meditation to enhance self-care and creative crisis response. The chapter explores awe in diverse contexts such as nature, visual design, music, and the life cycle, proposing that fostering awe in higher education can alleviate stress, promote empathy, and instil a sense of interconnectedness.

Awareness

This chapter explores the central role of awareness in tertiary design education, accentuating the importance of understanding both learning material and students. Shaun Britton introduces a novel pedagogical framework, the Depict, Collect, Select (DCS) system, designed to support staff and students in character design classes. The framework consists of a visual model illustrating iterative design activities, task forms for personalised progress tracking, and a specific teaching delivery approach. The DCS aims to bridge the awareness gap between students' current abilities and the skills needed for professional practice, promoting wellbeing, self-care, and effective learning in the context of design education.

Hope

In this chapter, Julia Ouzia and Estrella Sendra explore the intersection of bell hooks' pedagogy of hope and Gestalt philosophy, emphasising the role of hope as a liberating force in education. They focus on a specific third-year undergraduate module, "Events and Festivals: From Conception to Realization", at King's College London, where students co-curate and co-produce the CMCI Winter Festival. The authors argue that a practice-led learning and assessment method can break the boundaries of traditional classrooms and empower students as co-creators who can creatively transform the world. They introduce a seven-element model encompassing community care, embodied lived experience, creative and experiential learning, active listening, horizontal collaboration, contextual consideration, and hope. The authors demonstrate how the festival, as a student-led creative project, exemplifies the integration of hooks' pedagogy of hope and Gestalt philosophy, fostering a hopeful and creative learning environment that contributes to sustained wellbeing in higher education.

Place

The challenges and strategies for indigenising the curriculum in Australian art education are presented in a heartfelt chapter written by Megan McPherson and Tiriki Onus in this chapter with an invitation to reposition art education and how it intends to position itself; recognising and acknowledging settler colonisation governances within long and continuing First Peoples' histories. It introduces the subject "Stories of Place", designed to ground students in Indigenous knowledges and creative practices, highlighting its significance through a smoking ceremony. The geographical and historical context of Melbourne, acknowledging the displacement of First Nations Peoples, becomes a focal point. Navigating between worlds in the university studio is explored, stressing the complexity of artistic practice and reflection on one's purpose. The concept of "research-creation" is introduced, emphasising the transformative potential of artistic practices. The chapter concludes by reiterating the importance of acknowledging Aboriginal Land and fostering allyship to integrate Indigenous knowledges within the university curriculum.

Connection, interconnection, and companions

Self-care, a political act, relational base,
Courage, collaboration, vulnerability they chase.

Cherish, protect, celebrate, a collective trace,
Transformative potential, the modern university's face.

Navigating challenges, wellbeing's embrace,
In heterotopic spaces, positive change takes place.

Healthy relationships, a vital line,
Wellbeing flourishes, human connections align.

Authentic connections, warmth, empathy shine,
A lifeline in crises, connections redefine.

Companionship tangible, as the story moulds,
Belonging transcends, the narrative unfolds.

Heterotopia

This chapter reflects on the changing landscape of academia, comparing the nurturing environment of the past with the contemporary entrepreneurial university. The authors, Sarah Barradell, Tracy Fortune, and Jeanette Fyffe, share their experience of a mentoring project that unintentionally created a heterotopic space – a transformative refuge acknowledging difference and offering hope. Using Foucault's principles of heterotopia, the chapter examines the contrasts between the past university, the present neoliberal institution, and the authors' created heterotopia. Drawing out the importance of self-care as a relational and political act, the authors advocate for courage, collaboration, vulnerability, and the recognition of such heterotopic spaces as legitimate in fostering wellbeing and positive change. The chapter concludes by encouraging academics to cherish, protect, and celebrate the transformative potential of collective efforts in navigating the challenges of the modern university.

Balance

This chapter explores the innovative fellowship model of SPECTRUM, a research collaborative in Manitoba, Canada, challenging the traditional top-down structure in academia. Graduate student Fellows are considered equal partners, fostering a proactive work–life balance. The chapter highlights the importance of addressing mental health concerns in graduate students, especially those with intersecting marginalised identities. SPECTRUM's non-hierarchical and flexible fellowship model aims to support student Fellows, acknowledging the high risk of adverse mental health outcomes. The Fellows, Hunter, Pfau, Casidsid, Patrick, Brownell, Durksen, Comeau, and Enns, discuss how the model helps balance life by allowing them to pursue passions, navigate personal challenges, and engage in research aligned with their values. The collaborative nature of SPECTRUM provides a supportive environment, enabling Fellows to balance emotional resources, contributing to their overall wellbeing. The chapter concludes by suggesting strategies, such as personal check-ins and diversity in teamwork, to proactively support wellbeing within academia.

Connection

Here, the author uses the ecosystem of the oak tree as a metaphor for interconnected relationships in higher education. Drawing parallels between the relationships of organisms within the oak's ecosystem and human connections in academia, the author emphasises the importance of fostering healthy relationships while being mindful of potentially harmful ones. The narrative delves into the Emily Rooney's personal experiences as a clinical psychology graduate student, highlighting the challenges of higher education and the crucial role that meaningful connections played in their wellbeing. The chapter discusses the prevalence of mental health issues in higher education, especially among college students, and underscores the impact of the COVID-19 pandemic on social connections. The author shares insights into the power of authentic connection, referencing the principles of warmth, empathy, and genuineness as essential components. The narrative also explores the lifeline that connection provided during moments of crisis, discussing the author's own experience with mental health challenges and the pivotal role played by reaching out to a supportive brother. Additionally, the chapter touches upon the role of pain and compassion in strengthening relationships, using examples such as the aftermath of 9/11. It highlights the need to be cautious of parasitic relationships that can drain energy, drawing parallels with mistletoe and oak trees. The author provides practical steps for fostering connections, including being true to oneself, reaching out for help, turning pain into compassion, seeking small opportunities to connect, and practising warmth, empathy, and genuineness. The chapter concludes with the hope that readers will find guidance for navigating the challenges of higher education and flourishing in their own ecosystems of connection.

Belonging

Bertha Chin explores the role of pets, particularly cats, in the lives of academics. Using the example of a cat named Jiji, the author discusses the tangible connection and sense of belonging that pets provide to academics, especially in the face of isolation, cultural displacement, and the challenges of academic life. Jiji's story unfolds from her adoption in London to becoming a constant companion through the author's academic journey, providing emotional support during the ups and downs of research and career uncertainties. The chapter delves into the impact of the COVID-19 pandemic on academic life, including the shift to virtual conferences and the challenges faced by diasporic academics. The loss of Jiji becomes a focal point, prompting reflections on identity, cultural displacement, and the complexities of belonging in both the academic and personal spheres. The narrative underscores the significance of pets as companions that go beyond the academic network, offering solace and a constant presence amid the uncertainties of the academic profession.

Emerging Researchers, mentoring and finding one's self

In academia's quiet dance,
Emerging Researchers face boundaries like shadows.
A metamorphosis unfolds,
> *a journey of self-discovery,*
> *transforming darkness into a new scholarly light.*
> *Mentors guide with wisdom, breaking through limits,*
> *and self-care becomes a gentle melody, soothing the academic soul.*
In pages turned and challenges met, a resilient spirit arises,
> *and wellbeing blooms. Transformation whispers in every lesson learned,*
> > *as Emerging Researchers find their radiant light*
> > *in the garden of scholarly growth.*

Boundary

In the chapter, "Listening to the Stillness and Darkness of Academia: Boundaries that Encircle International Emerging Researchers", Yue Xu and Yuqi Lin, international emerging researchers based in Australia, employ a collective autoethnographic approach to unravel the intricate dimensions of their academic journey. Addressing the challenges faced by international doctoral students, the authors explore protective and harmful academic boundaries, emphasising the need for self-awareness and self-emancipation. They delve into the dual nature of expectations, acknowledging their role as catalysts for success while becoming burdens impacting wellbeing. A specific incident unveils the darker side of academia, highlighting power dynamics and ethical considerations. The authors stress the importance of acknowledging these facets and cultivating discernment. The narrative concludes with the authors' self-discovery, recognising their value as researchers, and envisions a more inclusive academic ecosystem through the dismantling of boundaries, inspiring colleagues to confront and overcome similar challenges.

Transformation

In academia, the pursuit of knowledge and professional growth can sometimes intertwine with personal challenges, and thus the act of self-care becomes a vital cornerstone for navigating the complex landscape. Khairunnisa Haji Ibrahim, in her chapter, shares her transformative journey through the practice of Morning Pages – a daily journaling ritual that goes beyond mere documentation. In her chapter, she takes us on a poignant exploration of how this introspective habit became a linchpin in her battle against feelings of inadequacy, the discovery of ADHD, and the intricacies of balancing motherhood and career. As we delve into her narrative, we witness the profound impact of journaling on fostering self-awareness, acceptance, and overall wellbeing.

Against the backdrop of the pandemic, Khairunnisa not only found solace in her Morning Pages but also uncovered a powerful tool for managing fear and uncertainty. This chapter not only advocates for the therapeutic benefits of journaling but also provides insights into the scientific underpinnings, practical strategies, and a compelling case for how acts of self-care, such as daily journaling, can be transformative in the challenging landscape of academia.

New

The chapter by Abdul Qawi Noori delves into the vital human need for belonging and its impact on wellbeing, particularly in the context of researchers. The autoethnographic exploration focuses on a researcher's journey from a conflict-affected country to Australia, investigating the quest for belonging. By comparing the sociocultural and educational landscapes of Afghanistan and Australia, the study provides valuable insights for academic institutions, policymakers, and individuals supporting the integration and wellbeing of individuals from diverse backgrounds. The information is relevant for students considering international study opportunities.

Taking a closer look at leadership

In the realm of leadership, expansive and wide,
A journey unfolds with a mindful stride.
>*Contrasting with constriction,*
>*embracing the vast,*
>*Not more tasks added,*
>*but a shift unsurpassed.*
Dialogues open, inclusivity embraced,
Encounters bring lessons, of pushback and heal,
In moments of conflict, empathy to feel.
Spacious leadership, uncertainty's dance,
Humility, openness, in each circumstance.
In the academic dance, a leader ascends,
Intrapersonal echoes, where true strength blends.
Reconciliation found, wellbeing is graceful, soothing, healing.

Expansive

The chapter delves into the dimensions of expansive leadership, exploring the term "expansive" by contrasting it with its opposite – constriction, compaction, and containment. The authors emphasise that expansive leadership is not about adding more tasks to leaders but cultivating a qualitative shift in leadership approaches and actions. The narrative introduces the authors, Alice Hovorka and Deena Kara Shaffer, both engaged in educational leadership roles. They contend that leadership, particularly in educational administration, can be a site for social justice, dismantling hierarchies, and reimagining structures. The dichotomy between traditional educational administrators and leaders for social justice is discussed, with the authors positioning themselves as advocates for the latter. Hovorka reflects on her leadership journey as a Dean, highlighting the importance of embracing an interactive and participatory approach. She values collaboration, inclusivity, and open dialogue, seeking to create a leadership style that is inherently expansive. Shaffer, on the other hand, shares her journey as a Director, Past President, and Founder. She challenges traditional notions of leadership, expressing her discomfort with hierarchical climbs and illuminating lateral impact, shared programmes, and ethical entrepreneurship. The chapter unfolds through encounters in expansive leadership, illustrating instances where both authors navigate challenges. Expansive leadership is presented as collaborative, humane, welcoming pushback, and even healing. The authors stress the significance of leaders embracing competing desires and acknowledging the relational aspects of leadership. They suggest that expansive leadership is not a one-size-fits-all concept and should be rooted in feminist values. They argue for a care-filled leadership approach that fosters authentic relationships, understands subjective experiences, and works toward equity.

Balance

Mark Freeman in his chapter reflects on his unexpected shift from what he calls a modest academic position to a role with significant leadership responsibilities. The chapter explores the challenges of adapting to this rapid change, highlighting the need for self-reflection, negotiation, and a deep understanding of one's identity in the academic community. Freeman introduces the metaphor of a reverse bungee, symbolising the stasis on firm ground followed by a disorienting ascent, highlighting the necessity of finding balance and perspective. The narrative delves into the internal and external dynamics of leadership, addressing issues like imposter syndrome, the alignment of personal and professional schemas, and the four domains of effective workplace leadership proposed by Hogan and Warrenfeltz: Business, Intrapersonal, Interpersonal, and Leadership. Freeman shares practical insights on navigating these domains, emphasising the importance of seeking support, maintaining personal credibility, fostering interpersonal relationships, and employing effective leadership strategies. The chapter concludes with Freeman's personal experience of reconciling his academic identity with the demands of leadership, highlighting the process of internalisation and the alignment of private self-concept with public behaviour.

One more thought

This edited collection offers a unique perspective on self-care and wellbeing in the context of higher education, contributing to a set of varying books within a book series. The international authors showcase the importance of doing things differently and exploring new possibilities. The act of doing things differently involves reaffirming one's way of being, understanding the self and the contexts in which we work, and adapting to change. The authors argue that self-care is not only an individual action, but also a relational one, requiring support and inspiration from others. We invite you to also be a part of doing things differently.

References

Brewster, L., Jones, E., Priestley, M., Wilbraham, S. J., Spanner, L., & Hughes, G. (2022). 'Look after the staff and they would look after the students' cultures of wellbeing and mental health in the university setting. *Journal of Further and Higher Education*, 46(4), 548–560. https://doi.org/10.1080/0309877X.2021.1986473

Catano, V., Francis, L., Haines, T., Kirpalani, H., Shannon, H., Stringer, B., & Lozanzki, L. (2010). Occupational stress in Canadian universities: A national survey. *International Journal of Stress Management*, 17(3), 232–258. https://doi.org/10.1037/a0018582

Charles Sturt University. (2023). *Staff Wellbeing Framework and Plan 2023–2025*. https://cdn.csu.edu.au/__data/assets/pdf_file/0003/4180017/2023_2025-Staff-Wellbeing-Framework-and-Plan.pdf

Cordaro, M. (2020). Pouring from an empty cup: The case for compassion fatigue in higher education. *Building Healthy Academic Communities Journal*, 4(2), 28. https://doi.org/10.18061/bhac.v4i2.7618

Dorociak, K. E., Rupert, P. A., Bryant, F. B., & Zahniser, E. (2017). Development of a self-care assessment for psychologists. *Journal of Counseling Psychology*, 64(3), 325–334. https://doi.org/10.1037/cou0000206

Edith Cowan University (2021). *ECU's Mental Health and Wellbeing Strategy 2021–2024* (Australia). https://www.ecu.edu.au/about-ecu/commitment-to-mental-health-and-wellbeing

Fetherston, C., Fetherston, A., Batt, S., Sully, M., & Wei, R. (2021). Wellbeing and work-life merge in Australian and UK academics. *Studies in Higher Education*, 46(12), 2774–2788. https://doi.org/10.1080/03075079.2020.1828326

Fontinha, R., Easton, S., & Van Laar, D. (2019). Overtime and quality of working life in academics and nonacademics: The role of perceived work-life balance. *International Journal of Stress Management*, 26(2), 173–183. https://doi.org/10.1037/str0000067

Jay Miller, J., Lee, J., Niu, C., Grise-Owens, E., & Bode, M. (2019). Self-compassion as a predictor of self-care: A study of social work clinicians. *Clinical Social Work Journal*, 47(4), 321–331. https://doi.org/10.1007/s10615-019-00710-6

Johnson, S. J., Willis, S. M., & Evans, J. (2019). An examination of stressors, strain, and resilience in academic and non-academic U.K. university job roles. *International Journal of Stress Management*, 26(2), 162–172. https://doi.org/10.1037/str0000096

Kenny, J. (2018). Re-empowering academics in a corporate culture: An exploration of workload and performativity in a university. *Higher Education*, 75(2), 365–380. https://doi.org/10.1007/s10734-017-0143-z

Lee, J. J., & Miller, S. E. (2013). A self-care framework for social workers: Building a strong foundation for practice. *Families in Society: The Journal of Contemporary Social Services, 94*(2), 96–103. https://doi.org/10.1606/1044-3894.4289

Lemon, N. (2021a). Self-care is worthy of our attention: Using our self-interest for good in higher education. In N. Lemon (Ed.), *Creating a place for self-care and wellbeing in higher education* (pp. 1–9). Routledge. https://doi.org/10.4324/9781003144397-1

Lemon, N. (2021b). Vulnerability, self-care, and the relationship with us and others in higher education. In N. Lemon (Ed.), *Healthy Relationships in Higher Education: Promoting Wellbeing Across Academia* (pp. 1–9). Routledge. https://doi.org/10.4324/9781003144984-1

Lemon, N., Harju-Luukkainen, H., & Garvis, S. (2023). Caring for self and others through challenging times: Interrupting the pandemic with compassion and kindness in higher education. In N. Lemon, H. Harju-Luukkainen, & S. Garvis (Eds.), *Practising compassion in higher education: caring for self and others through challenging times* (pp. 1–15). Routledge.

Neff, K. D. (2003). The development and validation of a scale to measure self-compassion. *Self and Identity, 2*(3), 223–250. https://doi.org/10.1080/15298860309027

Orygen (2020). *Australian University Mental Health Framework.* https://www.orygen.org.au/Orygen-Institute/University-Mental-Health-Framework/Framework/University-Mental-Health-Framework

The University of Queensland (2023). *Wheel of wellbeing.* https://staff.uq.edu.au/information-and-services/health-safety-and-wellbeing/personal-health-and-wellbeing/uq-wellness-program/wheel-wellbeing

UBC Wellbeing Design Lab (2023a). *Health literacy: Mental health + resilience.* University of British Columbia. https://wellbeing.ubc.ca/mental-health-resilience

UBC Wellbeing Design Lab (2023b). *Thrive.* University of British Columbia https://wellbeing.ubc.ca/campaigns-initiatives/thrive

UBC Wellbeing Design Lab (2023c). *Wellbeing Strategic Framework.* University of British Columbia. https://wellbeing.ubc.ca/framework

Universities Australia (2023). *Real Talk Mental Health Framework.* https://universitiesaustralia.edu.au/publication/real-talk-framework/

University of Western Australia (2023). *UWA Mental Health and Wellbeing Framework.* https://www.uwa.edu.au/about-us/leadership-and-strategy/uwa-mental-health-and-wellbeing-framework

Section 1

The setting

Chapter 2

Rethinking expectations in academia

How lowering expectations of ourselves and others improves wellbeing

Louise Grimmer

Introduction

If I'd been writing this chapter last year, I'd have been pictured on that bike with my feet firmly on the pedals, hands strongly grasping the handlebars, head down, pedalling determinedly towards my destination.

I have so much to do, to achieve, to perfect, and I need to do it all at once and as quickly as possible. I have to say "yes" to every single request made of me – yes to joining this committee, yes to mentoring that person, yes to taking on another PhD student or research project, yes to a leadership role, yes to committing to writing papers with others, yes to help organise conferences and seminars, yes to anything and everything so that I can be 'perfect' and then I'll be 'allowed' to apply for promotion. Getting to Associate Professor is all that matters, it is everything to me.

I work from early in the morning until late at night. I work on weekends. I set myself high targets for publishing, I say yes to everything that will advance my career. I play 'the game'.

What a waste. A waste of effort. A waste of time. A waste of emotion.

I am sluggish and tired, my body aches from my sedentary academic posture, and I am angry, furious in fact, and frustrated, so very frustrated.

Working so hard, giving so much, missing out on weekends and family time, only to come to the realisation that, in many instances, all the hard work and effort was for nothing. I am not really getting anywhere in terms of career progression. It doesn't matter how many journal articles, how much funding I receive, how many committee positions, how much I contribute to the academy, how many public talks and community presentations I give, how often I help and mentor colleagues and junior academics, how much media coverage I secure – even with my Fulbright scholarship – if those in positions of power decide that you will stay at a particular level, it's very difficult to advance without their encouragement and support.

I've spent the earlier part of this year speaking with other women whose experiences mirror mine. The feeling of betrayal is palpable in everyone who shares their story. Smart women, committed women, loyal women, creative and innovative

DOI: 10.4324/9781003457510-3

Image 2.1 I took my feet off the pedals

women, often juggling children or caring for partners or parents, and never feeling quite good enough; being 'blocked' from applying for promotion, or told they need to wait a few more years when it's clear this is not the case. At the same time they often see male colleagues getting ahead, being promoted, lauded for outputs and achievements, while cleverly dodging the emotional labour that falls disproportionately on their female colleagues at work (Walsh & Baker, 2022).

Regarding academic promotion, friends and colleagues from outside the 'academic bubble' are astonished and perplexed by the academic promotion system. It just doesn't exist outside academia. Non-academics don't have to constantly prove themselves, document every activity and achievement, volunteer for more and more work, and then spend hours and hours preparing their case to be considered for promotion. There is no other system like it, and with good reason.

Anyway, back to my original story. I decided things couldn't continue as they were. I was exhausted, my bones ached, and I was angry at work and at home. All. The. Time.

Something had to change, and only I could make that change. My university wasn't going to change, my colleagues weren't going to change, and my bosses certainly weren't going to change. It was up to me.

So, just like the picture, I decided to let go. I took my feet of the pedals, I relaxed my grip on the handlebars, I slowed down, and no longer had a set destination. The feeling of release, of freedom, was palpable. I dropped my shoulders, I relaxed my jaw, and smiled.

I decided to lower the expectations I had of myself. I started by asking myself "What would happen if I decided not to apply for promotion at all?" and "How would that feel?". I wondered what would happen if I did things that I actually enjoyed (my own research, industry engagement, media communication, helping others) instead of being on administrative committees or in leadership roles that have no real value or consequence? Instead of striving to do 'everything' just so I could make the case that I deserved the opportunity to apply for promotion, what would happen if I stepped back and took promotion off the agenda? How would that feel emotionally and physically?

So I started to experiment. It wasn't easy at first. I had to start saying "no" to requests, and I withdrew from research projects and committees and a leadership role. People advised me that I was putting my career in jeopardy because without all these things I wouldn't be able to apply for promotion. I replied I no longer cared about promotion; at first I didn't really believe it, but the more I kept saying it, the more it became true. Promotion had been a monkey on my back for too long. I cast it off and I felt euphoric. Actual, real euphoria. I put my wellbeing, and my family, at the centre of everything for the first time in my academic career.

At the same time as lowering expectations of myself, I realised I would also have to lower the expectations I had of managers and colleagues. I realised some of the problems arose when my expectations of others weren't met. When I felt they let me down, when they didn't praise my work or effort, when they failed to highlight the positives and instead focussed on the negatives, when they ignored me or when they reprimanded me. I expected they would behave in a certain way, and when they didn't, I felt baffled and betrayed. I decided to change the way I thought about expectations, expectations of myself and others. I lowered them. I lowered them so low, they barely existed. It no longer mattered to me what other people thought or did at work. I would no longer allow it to affect me – I took the power of 'expectation' away.

But how did I get here? And why did I allow it to go on so long? Of course, academia is characterised by its pursuit of excellence, intellectual growth, and the advancement of knowledge. But the very same characteristics that make it a stimulating environment for so many, also contribute to an atmosphere of high expectations and relentless demands. There is growing recognition of the toll these expectations can take on the mental and emotional wellbeing of academics. In this chapter I want to delve into the concept of rethinking expectations in academia, exploring the benefits of lowering expectations of ourselves and others, for the sake of improved wellbeing. And I'm doing it from the perspective of an academic staff member. There is much written about undergraduate, postgraduate students as well as PhD candidates and their experiences in academia. There are far fewer studies or literature focussing on academic staff experiences.

But before I delve into it, I want to acknowledge I am privileged to have a job as an academic. I am well-paid, I was able to work during the COVID-19 pandemic, I am tenured and have good working conditions. I also want to acknowledge, however, that the academic system is set up to encourage perfectionism, competition, imposter phenomenon, disappointment, and criticism, which can lead to toxic cultures, burnout, and poor physical and mental wellbeing. And women are more at risk than their male colleagues.

And finally, I acknowledge, my approach won't work for everyone. Most of us still want to get promoted! Yes, maybe some of my reflections, conclusions, and strategies might be beneficial, even in a small way, in helping you take a step back, assess, and approach your academic work and contribution with lowered expectations – of yourself and others.

The culture of high expectations

The culture of high expectations in academia has deep historical roots. Traditionally, academic success has been closely tied to notions of rigorous standards, achievement, and competition. This culture has fostered an environment where overexertion, perfectionism, and burnout are often seen as badges of honour. How many of us have had conversations with colleagues about just how super busy they/we are? How many LinkedIn posts espouse the 'virtue' inherent in being busy? We feel we must fill our days with activity and achievement and record it all on social media. This oversharing of activity and busy mindset can lead to detrimental consequences for mental and emotional health and wellbeing. We need a paradigm shift – one that emphasises balance and moves away from the busy = success mentality.

Another compounding issue is academics work in an environment where we are constantly critiqued, measured, and criticised – our work, and by extension, ourselves, is held up and, more often than not, torn down; mostly privately, but sometimes very publicly.

While some might argue this offers a robust environment for the best work to emerge, I think it's now got to a point where it's no longer healthy or warranted. How many times have we been at conferences where junior, female or minority delegates are belittled and criticised by senior (usually male) academics? How many of us have felt confident enough to intervene? How many of us have instead approached the presenter afterwards and assured them they did a great job and to try and ignore the grumpy professor?

Our research projects, publications, grants, and ethics applications are constantly criticised too. Our papers are reviewed anonymously, with some subjected to the very worst type of feedback. Often the people reviewing our work show they don't understand the field or the approach. Nevertheless, we have to make changes to our work to accommodate unknown reviewers who

Table 2.1 The perfectionist and the pursuer of excellence

The pursuer of excellence	The perfectionist
Sets high but flexible standards, that can be adjusted based on experience	Sets excessively high, rigid standards that are not adjusted regardless of experience
Focuses on the process and the outcome	Focuses only on the outcome
Is driven by positive motivation	Is driven by fear
Can be satisfied by a range of outcomes	Can only be satisfied by one improbable outcome
Views mistakes as inevitable learning opportunities	Views mistakes as unacceptable failure

Source: Zebrowski and Pollard (2022, n.p.).

always know better. Or worse, our papers are rejected outright, and that feeling of total deflation is experienced again. Because it's personal. It's always personal. For most of us in academia, it's hard to separate the person from the work. And constant criticism and rejection just feeds feelings of inadequacy.

The paradox of perfectionism

Perfectionism, often regarded as a driving force for success, can paradoxically hinder both personal and professional development (see Table 2.1). The unrelenting pursuit of flawlessness can lead to chronic stress, anxiety, and a fear of failure. Lowering the bar of perfectionism can liberate us from self-doubt and create an atmosphere conducive to experimentation, creativity, and genuine engagement and collaboration. Embracing mistakes as learning opportunities, rather than signs of inadequacy, is an essential step toward a healthier academic experience.

Shafran, Egan, and Wade (2019 [2010]) describe a type of perfectionism as "dysfunctional perfectionism" – the relentless pursual of self-imposed demanding standards, in spite of the pursuit causing problems.

Expectations and burnout

Symptoms of burnout include:

- Not sleeping properly or feeling exhausted no matter how much sleep you get, resulting in fatigue and insomnia;
- Lacking motivation to attend work, go to meetings or to start projects and other activities;
- Lashing out at others irritably due to frustration;
- Lacking inspiration and creativity;

- Loss of confidence in academic abilities;
- Incapable of meeting important deadlines;
- Increased pain and tension in your body, which can be manifested as headaches, sore muscle aches, or jaw tension;
- Higher frequency of illness due to stress and exhaustion;
- Increase in bad habits such as overeating, staying up too late, nail biting, or any other habit you tend to acquire when you are stressed or not taking care of yourself;
- Inability to concentrate on routine tasks;
- Feeling bored or uninterested in activities or hobbies you used to enjoy, and
- Feelings of anxiety or depression.

Educators, as both transmitters of knowledge and role models, play a pivotal role in shaping the academic experience. However, they too are subject to the pressures of high expectations. The 'publish or perish' culture and the demand for constant innovation can leave educators feeling overwhelmed and burnt out. By re-evaluating the metrics of success and recognising the importance of teaching and mentorship alongside research, institutions can empower educators to prioritise their wellbeing without compromising their impact.

Impacts on mental health

The pressure to meet high expectations in academia can contribute to a range of mental health challenges. Anxiety, depression, imposter phenomenon (it's not a 'syndrome'), and feelings of isolation are prevalent among academics. Through recalibrating expectations, institutions can create an environment where individuals feel safe to seek help without stigma. Emphasising mental health resources, counselling services, and peer support networks can dismantle the notion that seeking help is a sign of weakness, promoting a culture of empathy and understanding.

Prior to the pandemic, research on the impact of the university environment on the mental health of academics was lacking (Urbina-Garcia, 2020). Solutions identified in earlier studies on academic burnout and stress include cognitive reappraisal, social-self comparison, problem-directed action, recalling positive events, and showing gratitude (Talbot & Mercer, 2018); accepting responsibility, seeking social support, and using cognitive/emotional reappraisal or giving a different meaning to stressful situations (Mohamed & Abed, 2017); supportive colleagues and time management (Darabi, Macaskill, & Reidy, 2017). Some of these are similar to my lowering expectations approach, but others are, in my view, not that helpful. Accepting responsibility and time management, for example, are methods that don't go to the core of the problems academics face.

In the wake of COVID-19, scholarly research on the impact of the pandemic on students and PhD candidates have proliferated. At the same time, there is a general acknowledgement that academic staff were also negatively impacted, but again, the studies are few and far between.

Striking a balance

Lowering expectations does not equate to lowering standards. I haven't let my work slip in terms of effort and aiming for excellence. It's not about slouching off. Instead, it entails recognising the difference between healthy striving and toxic overexertion. I believe striking a balance between ambition and self-care is crucial for sustained academic and personal growth. Institutions can play a pivotal role by encouraging a diverse range of achievements beyond academic excellence alone. Recognising the value of personal growth, community engagement, and interdisciplinary exploration can alleviate the pressure to excel in a narrow field and contribute to a more well-rounded and fulfilled academic journey.

Nurturing intrinsic motivation

Relying solely on external expectations can lead to a sense of emptiness and detachment from work. Embracing intrinsic motivation – the inherent satisfaction derived from the work activities and responsibilities we enjoy – can foster better mental health and wellbeing. Institutions can promote intrinsic motivation by offering opportunities for self-directed learning, interdisciplinary collaboration, and research driven by personal curiosity. This approach not only enhances the quality of academic output but also contributes to a more fulfilling and sustainable academic journey.

Redefining success

The traditional markers of success in academia, such as publications and grants, are important but limited indicators of the value an individual brings to the academic community. Redefining success to encompass personal growth, community engagement, and a commitment to ethical research can shift the focus from competition to collaboration. Celebrating diverse achievements and acknowledging the effort invested, regardless of immediate outcomes, can cultivate a culture of appreciation and mutual support.

By lowering expectations of immediate and uniform success, institutions can create a more inclusive environment that acknowledges diverse pathways to achievement. Cultivating mentorship programmes, providing targeted resources, and celebrating a spectrum of accomplishments can empower underrepresented groups and enhance their overall sense of belonging.

Solutions

Lowering or letting go of expectations is not a simple process and it can take some time to 'de-programme' the way we think about people, about institutions, and about ourselves. It's also a little more complicated if you are still planning to go for promotion! But I believe it can be achieved to varying degrees, depending on your goals and objectives for your career, and for your wellbeing.

Here are some suggestions for getting started:

1 Seek out colleagues and friends who are striving to make the same changes.
2 Surround yourself with supportive, rather than competitive, peers. You'll be surprised at the instant difference this makes to your mindset and your enjoyment at work.
3 Join the Promoting Academic Women network (see below), or set up your own group with like-minded colleagues.
4 If you can, try to extricate yourself as much as possible from unhealthy work environments and relationships. Limit the time spent in the company of toxic colleagues and negative managers. If this means sometimes not attending meetings, or withdrawing from committees, then so be it.
5 Try removing social media apps from your mobile phone home screen. It's super tempting to check LinkedIn, Facebook and 'X' – 'doomscrolling' – where you're bombarded with other people's achievements (small and large). Constantly being exposed to what others are doing, achieving, and celebrating is not that great for mental wellbeing. It makes us feel inadequate and that we aren't doing enough to get ahead. That we must work harder! Those who've taken a break from social media report feeling refreshed, less stressed and harried, and many have permanently left social sites. Others are strict on when and for how long they access their accounts – and this approach can work for those who don't want to give up connections made on social platforms.
6 Get amongst the greenery. I'm not a bushwalker or a beach person, but I am a gardener. I find being amongst plants one of the most enjoyable things to do. I immediately feel calmer and happier when I am surrounded by greenery. Whatever your outdoor fun is – beach, mountain, bush, etc. – try to get out in the fresh air and sunshine as much as possible. We all know the benefits and many of us need to break away from the desk more often and recharge outside.
7 And finally, find joy in helping others. I end this chapter with some revealing (and shocking) statistics about women in higher education and how I and a small group of female colleagues set about trying to address the issue.

It all started in 2022 when I read two articles about the lack of women at senior level in Australian universities and the gender pay gap in academia.

Despite relatively even numbers of men and women employed in higher education, the disparity between the sexes is stark, and unacceptable.

Men [also] dominate the upper levels of Australian academia. The latest available figures (from 2019) show:

- 86% more men than women at associate professor and professor levels D and E (10,363 men, 5,562 women)
- 11% more men than women at senior lecturer level C (6,355 men, 5,724 women)
- 25% more women than men at lecturer level B (7,428 men, 9,253 women)
- 15% more women than men at associate lecturer level A (4,426 men and 5,093 women).

Overall, the numbers of men and women employed as academics aren't very different. In 2019, Australian universities employed 54,204 full-time and fractional full-time academics: 28,572 men (53%) and 25,632 (47%) women. It's the seniority of the positions they hold that differs starkly.

(Devlin, 2021a, n.p.)

Devlin (2021b, n.p.) also argues:

Universities – and other workplaces full of educated, insightful people – are well equipped to lead and make changes to enable gender equality. But they haven't. And I haven't seen any credible, funded, adequate plans for any workplace to do so in the near future.

Until recently, women have been too busy and tired doing most or all of the childcare, housework and elder care to have time to do much about the blatant inequality we all experience. But somehow, despite the extra burdens COVID-19 has placed on us, we've reached a tipping point. Perhaps the extremity of the inequality – laid bare during COVID-19 – has pushed us to the edge. Whatever the reason, we've somehow found the impetus to take action.

Women have waited long enough for things that "should" happen to happen. We've waited long enough for the people with power – mostly men – to do the right thing. We've followed the rules, done as we've been asked to do, helped out, worked hard, kept quiet and generally been very good girls.

This evidently hasn't worked in our favour, nor in the favour of women worldwide. And so, for the sake of growth, competitiveness, society and the future readiness of businesses and economies, as well as our own advancement, we must take matters into our own hands.

Personally, I'm starting with the sector I have worked in for three decades – universities. Despite being home to some of the country's brightest minds, we have some of the most sexist practices and embarrassing gender inequality figures a developed nation could have. The result is a workplace with 86% more male than female professors, as one example of many.

Devlin's analysis was both shocking and enlightening to me. It also explained a lot about my own experiences in academia. I wanted to do something to try and address the issues. I put out a tweet about the problems women were facing in the higher education sector and said I was starting a network called 'Promoting Academic Women' (www.promotingacademicwomen.com). The tweet gained traction and I was invited on local ABC radio to talk about the issue and the objectives of the new network. I joined with a female colleague Dr Bronwyn Eager who is expert in website design among other things (as well as her own excellent research in entrepreneurship) and purchased a domain name. Bronwyn set up the website and we started to promote the network on (then) Twitter and LinkedIn. The response was incredible. Women (and even a couple of men) signed up to our mailing list. The network was free to join and we planned on running events with guest speakers, panels, and support and mentoring.

Our launch event featured a brilliant session on Imposter Phenomenon by an expert in the field – Associate Professor Terri Simpkin. This was a face-to-face event at the University of Tasmania and a terrific way to launch the network. I had assumed our members would just come from the University of Tasmania where I was based, but it was soon evident that female academics from institutions around Australia, as well as abroad, were just as keen to be involved. At the time of writing, we have 380 members, and growing.

We realised we needed to move everything online and use Zoom to connect with our community. In one year, we've provided two panel presentations with female Level D academics sharing their journey in academia, a second session on Imposter Phenomenon, Virtues and Leadership – Crafting a Legacy of Character, Using ChatGPT for Career Advancement, How to Communicate Research and Staying True to You. At the end of the year we were incredibly fortunate to have presentations from Professor Inger Mewburn ('The Thesis Whisperer') and Professor Marcia Devlin – who started this all!

The feedback from network members has been incredible. So many women value the network and what we are trying to do, in a very small way, to provide community and networking and information. Just hearing from other women telling their stories, sometimes of adversity, as well as different approaches, insights, and solutions have provided support and encouragement for members. So many women have emailed me about the positive benefits of our network, and some have shared their stories of success in being promoted – which makes everything worthwhile!

I share this story of the Promoting Academic Women network to show that lowering expectations doesn't mean doing nothing. It means directing your energy where you feel it can make the best impact (for you and others) and engaging in meaningful and enjoyable activity. While our network can't (and won't) solve the bigger problems women face in academia, if we can help just a few women rise up the ranks, as well as providing support and community for others, that is more than enough.

Conclusion

The journey of rethinking expectations in academia is a profound one, requiring a shift in mindset at both individual and institutional levels. By recognising the limitations of unrelenting perfectionism, valuing mental health, fostering inclusivity, and nurturing intrinsic motivation, academia can evolve into a space where individuals thrive holistically. Lowering expectations does not imply compromising on quality or ambition; rather, it signifies embracing a more compassionate and balanced approach to education and research. As academia moves toward this transformative shift, the wellbeing of students, educators, and researchers will undoubtedly flourish, creating a more sustainable and vibrant intellectual landscape.

References

Darabi, M., Macaskill, A., & Reidy, L. (2017). A qualitative study of the UK academic role: Positive features, negative aspects and associated stressors in a mainly teaching-focused university. *Journal of Further and Higher Education, 41*(4), 566–580.

Devlin, M. (2021a). No change at the top for university leaders as men outnumber women 3 to 1. *The Conversation.* https://theconversation.com/no-change-at-the-top-for-university-leaders-as-men-outnumber-women-3-to-1-154556

Devlin, M. (2021b). Time to gender parity has blown out to 135 years. Here's what women can do to close the gap. *The Conversation.* https://theconversation.com/time-to-gender-parity-has-blown-out-to-135-years-heres-what-women-can-do-to-close-the-gap-160253

Mohamed, S. A., & Abed, F. (2017). Job stressors, burnout levels and coping strategies among faculty members and assistants: A comparative study. *Journal of Nursing and Health Science, 6*(1), 22–36.

Shafran, R., Egan, S., & Wade, T. (2019 [2010]). *Overcoming perfectionism: A self-help guide using scientifically supported cognitive behavioural techniques* (2nd edition). Robinson Publishing.

Talbot, K., & Mercer, S. (2018). Exploring university ESL/EFL teachers' emotional well-being and emotional regulation in the United States, Japan and Austria. *Chinese Journal of Applied Linguistics, 41*(4), 410–432.

Urbina-Garcia, A. (2020). What do we know about university academics' mental health? A systematic literature review. *Stress & Health, 36*(5), 563–585.

Walsh, M. J., & Baker, S. A. (2022). What is emotional labour and how do we get it wrong? *The Conversation.* https://theconversation.com/what-is-emotional-labour-and-how-do-we-get-it-wrong-185773

Zebrowski, K., & Pollard, C. A. (2022). *10 tips for treating academic perfectionism.* International OCD Foundation. https://iocdf.org/expert-opinions/10-tips-for-treating-academic-perfectionism/

Chapter 3

Flourishing in academia
Laughter as survival, self-care, solidarity, and resistance

Katrina McChesney and Kirsten Locke

Introduction

Academia demands our best thinking, our deepest commitments, and the furthest reaches of our time and service. It's serious stuff, and we are never far from a reminder that the stakes are high. Long lists fill our diaries. Ever-expanding collections of evidence fill our professional portfolios. How do we feel as we attempt to juggle everything that makes up our academic careers? In a word – breathless. How can we capture that in our text? Summoning long lists, long sentences, endless commas and qualifiers, and additional thoughts, we cram this paragraph full of the stuff of our lives in academia: intensive teaching loads, productivity expectations, research completion timelines, obligations to funders, student perceptions, and our obligations to colleagues and students overlaid with the mechanisms of promotion rounds, research evaluation regimes, progress reports, university calendars, restructures, redundancy rounds, and fixed-term contracts. To survive, we must learn the rules of the game; relate pleasantly and collegially to others; prove ourselves to be both productive team players and initiative-filled, self-driven exceptional performers. Should we diverge from or fail to meet the expectations that sometimes seem to crush us, punishment awaits in a range of obvious and less obvious forms: exclusion; silencing; dismissal (contractually or inter-personally); criticism; gossip; assumptions and pervasive narratives constructed about our work; 'wrap-around support' and review interventions from our managers; student disrespect or obstruction; complaints; failure to renew contracts; 'not yet ready – premature application' decisions in promotion rounds; rejection of proposals or papers; selection for redundancy or enhanced retirement. We are exhausted even writing this. It must be time for a joke …

> *What do you call an academic who's on top of their to-do-list?*
> *If we ever find one, we'll let you know.*

Against this landscape of pressure and overwhelm, we are learning to harness the power of laughter as a means of survival, self-care, and resistance. Inspired by the writings of Hélène Cixous, we are coming to understand laughter as

DOI: 10.4324/9781003457510-4

a form of feminine (or, more inclusively, non-masculine, non-normative, and non-dominant) dis-order that reclaims agency, perspective, and voice in the face of oppression and all that is supposedly so very serious.

This chapter shares our reflections on Cixous's characterisation of laughter and its function within the academy. We probe the complexities of walking with integrity and wisdom through the minefields of demands placed upon us as academics, and we invite others to explore the release and political possibilities offered by choosing to laugh at the absurd and even nonsensical within an academy supposedly full of the brightest minds on the planet.

We are both women, Cixous is a feminist writer, and the myth we explore in this chapter is fundamentally linked to gender. Self-care itself also emerges from feminist thought, where it is recognised as "an act of political warfare" (Lorde, 1988, p. 131; see also Lipton, 2020). Nonetheless, we are not wanting to centre questions of gender here (we have explored these elsewhere; see Locke & McChesney, 2023). We value the feminist lens that allows us (all) to consider the power of laughter as a disruptive form of resistance and self-care. However, we hope that this chapter transcends gender-based starting points and that our ideas around laughter may be liberating for more groups than only women. Here, we want to think mostly about laughter *itself*, rather than the *people* who laugh.

Here and in our past work (Locke & McChesney, 2023), we seek to enact aspects of what Cixous (1981, 1986) termed *écriture féminine*. Écriture féminine challenges dominant writing norms in a form of feminist resistance and liberation (Lipton, 2020), echoing the disruption that laughter can also offer us. Recognising the irony inherent in the many texts on laughter that fail to actually invite or cause anyone *to laugh*, we have sought to offer a text that in its very nature engages with lightness, humour, and play. Thus, we have deliberately inserted jokes into our text as small disruptive interludes, riffing around our themes of laughter, wellbeing, self-care, and (to a lesser extent) gender in academia. We don't promise they'll be brilliant, but we hope the jokes invite you to some form of laughter – ironic, despairing, delighted, groan-laden, or the laughter that recognises shared experience.

Three feminists walk into a bar.
They whoop with delight and congratulate themselves on taking over
a male-dominated form of humour.

We begin below by reviewing literature on laughter, first broadly and then within educational contexts. We then draw on Cixous's treatment of the Medusa and feminine dis-order to consider the role of laughter for wellbeing and self-care in today's neoliberal higher education environments. We conclude this chapter by considering both the complexities of, and some practical possibilities for, summoning laughter as self-care in higher education settings.

Understandings of laughter

Laughter is a universal element of human wellbeing (Lindquist, 2016). It is mentioned in the Bible, the Qur'an, the earliest texts of the Ancient Greeks, and the oral traditions of many Indigenous cultures (Ben-Moshe, 2023). Today, laughter is studied within affective, discursive, philosophical, business, sociological, psychological, medical, and cultural disciplines as well as being harnessed in therapeutic techniques such as Laughter Yoga and Laughter Wellness (Ben-Moshe, 2023).

Laughter has much to offer us. It can promote healing, connection, life lessons, belonging, and perspective. In serious times, laughter offers "a way to understand and heal from personal or historical trauma, as well as a way to fight adversity" (Lindquist, 2016, p. 28).

Despite its 'everyday-ness', however, laughter is a complex phenomenon. There are a wide range of radically different scholarly and philosophical understandings of laughter's meaning and function. For example,

> Thomas Hobbes and René Descartes … believed that we laugh because we feel superior; Immanuel Kant and Arthur Schopenhauer … argued that comedy stems from a sense of incongruity; and Herbert Spencer and Sigmund Freud … suggested that comedians provide a form of much-needed relief (from, respectively, 'nervous energy' and repressed emotions).
>
> Herring (2020, para. 3)

Bergson (1911) outlined three important features of laughter. First, laughter is a human endeavour: What makes us laugh are human qualities and characteristics (in other humans, but in non-humans as well – think of cat videos!). Second, laughing requires a sense of detachment from other more melancholic or 'sad' emotions. These other emotions can stop us laughing at something that we would otherwise find funny – it's really hard to laugh when in a state of rage or despair. And third, laughter comes more effortlessly in the company of others. It is a social and human activity and therefore has social meaning; as such, laughter has as much place in the social milieu of the academy as in any other place where humans interact.

Nietzsche (1999) provides a more 'ironic' perspective, seeing laughter as inextricably linked to tragedy. For Nietzsche, laughter and joy are philosophical and psychological responses to the inevitable darkness and difficulty that accompany the human condition. Nietzsche also considered laughter's role in simultaneously allowing our limits to be made visible whilst also providing a strategy to overcome these limits – or at least to overcome the terror associated with our limits. Finally, Nietzsche discussed laughter in relation to critique. In this, he could be seen as the ultimate jokester philosopher, always poking fun and needling any tendency toward taken-for-granted conventions and traditions – a precursor, in one sense, to Cixous's representation of laughter as subversion and dis-order.

Why did the philosophy lecturer request a standing desk for her office?
So she could stand to reason.

Bryant and Bainbridge (2022) argue that the production and perception of laughter are universal yet also culturally contingent. While all laughter is fundamentally a social practice, the ways in which laughter is engaged serve an endless array of sociological functions and purposes. Bryant and Bainbridge note the divergences and convergences across different cultures' engagement with laughing, and the surprisingly few academic studies attempting to make sense of this phenomenon.

Billig (2005) provides a sociocritical examination of contemporary understandings of laughter, calling on philosophers including Bergson and Freud to explore the darker potentialities of laughter and humour. He highlights the role of laughter and humour as an important disciplinary device, suggesting that humour's most powerful form may be as "the darker, less admired practice of ridicule" that ensures "members of society routinely comply with the customs and habits of their social milieu" (Billig, 2005, p. 2). This disciplining function of laughter may resonate with the pressure, social comparison, and drive for self-protection that often characterise academic settings.

Pailer et al. (2009) position the theorisation of laughter at the "intersection between gender theories and theories of laughter" (p. 7): an interesting perspective given our use of a feminist thinker's work to underpin this chapter. Pailer et al.'s edited book questions the extent to which humour (and by proxy, laughter) can be considered subversive. The collection concludes in an ambivalent position, recognising that when juxtaposed with gender, the subversive qualities of humour and laughter can be variously empowering or minimised.

Laughter in education and the academy

Laughter serves a variety of functions in educational contexts (Banas et al., 2011). It may embody relief, release, or an enjoyment of the unexpected or imperfect (Morreall, 2014); it may build bridges between people through a shared and essentially human experience (Vlieghe, 2014). It may enhance teaching and learning through encouraging student engagement and making learning experiences more memorable (Ellingson, 2018) or by helping us "brea[k] through" moments of difficulty to enable growth (Stengel, 2014, p. 200).

On the other hand, laughter in educational settings may be (or may be seen to be) "hostile and irresponsible" (Morreall, 2014, p. 121) or "inherently antisocial" (p. 123). Interestingly, Vlieghe (2014) suggests that in some educational contexts, laughter has lost its "inherent equalizing and communizing potential" because it "forms a threat to any organization of social existence according to similarities and differences in identity and position" (p. 148). This potential for laughter to dismantle structures of oppression and difference can lead to laughter being suppressed, frowned upon, and avoided (see also Morreall, 2014). In neoliberal contexts, in particular, emotional responses are carefully regulated such that only those emotional performances that are perceived as benefiting the institution are rewarded (Lipton, 2020).

In higher education specifically, researchers have explored laughter's pedagogical (Chowdhury, 2022), discursive (Hah, 2021), socio-political (Bloch, 2012), solidarity (Dynel, 2020), and leadership (Grace-Odeleye & Santiago, 2019) functions. Researchers have also explored how laughter in higher education settings influences outcomes such as student engagement, wellbeing, and affect (Erdoğdu & Çakıroğlu, 2021; Sharma et al., 2022). And while the outcomes of the aforementioned studies are largely positive, there are also accounts of harmful manifestations of laughter within the academy. Examples include racial (Cabrera, 2014) and gender-based (Kanyemba & Naidu, 2022) forms of joking as well as the use of pejorative or mocking laughter to belittle entire fields of scholarship (Pereira, 2013).

And yet — and crucially for our purposes – laughter can also liberate or mediate difficult experiences in the academy. Grosland (2019), for example, highlights both laughter and tears as examples of the intense emotional responses that arise when studying race and racism in higher education, while Lipton (2020) highlights the role of laughter as a strategy for resistance, survival, and wellbeing among women in the neoliberal academy. These more emancipatory possibilities for laughter's role resonate with the literature reviewed earlier around laughter, life, and wellbeing.

What do you get if you cross an academic with a yoga instructor?
Flexible office hours.

We now follow Lipton's (2020) lead and turn to the work of feminist writer Hélène Cixous to reflect further on laughter in relation to higher education.

Cixous, the Medusa, and laughter as feminine dis-order

Cixous's essay *The Laugh of the Medusa* (1976) positions laughter within a broader argument about feminine power that disrupts patriarchal norms and order. As a whole, the text does not focus on either laughter or the Medusa character. Rather, Cixous summons the spectre or "evocative symbol" (Lipton, 2020, p. 211) of Medusa only through her choice of title and very brief explicit mentions in the text. This strategy is an intentional writerly device: in Cixous's (1976, p. 875) words, "woman must put herself into the text—as into the world and into history—by her own movement". The whole essay sits in the shadow of the Medusa, but readers must complete the interpretation for themselves.

Medusa appears in both Ancient Greek and Roman mythology. Although descriptions differ, she was often depicted as either beautiful or grotesque, and in most representations she was a female creature with snakes for hair.

She turned all who looked upon her to stone, a power that endured even after Perseus cut off her head. Medusa thus represents the feminine as both powerful and dangerous, yet in most tellings of her story, her very monstrosity was created by the ways she was oppressed and abused by men.

What song would Medusa sing at karaoke night?
'At first I was afraid, I was petrified ...'

Cixous (1976) takes this myth and reframes Medusa. While the dominant or masculine gaze had never been able to truly *see* Medusa (being immediately turned to stone), Cixous's feminine gaze offers a new insight: "You only have to look at the Medusa straight on to see her. And she's not deadly. She's beautiful and she's laughing" (p. 885). Cixous's Medusa is active, agentic, powerful, and free. She may still be dangerous, but she is her own woman. With her many snakes, Medusa is also inherently *multiple*, linking to wider feminist projects around performance, identity, spirit, plurality, and complexity (Valiquette, 2019). She is powerful, resistant, uncapturable, indefinable, and irreducible despite others' attempts to tame her.

Elsewhere, Cixous (1981) writes about the ways women can be "completely crushed, especially in places like universities" (p. 51). For us, Cixous's laughing Medusa brings affective, embodied, dis-ordered, and emotionally resonant dimensions into our scholarly beings. Further, with a Nietzschean and firmly unapologetic affirmation of laughter amid imperfect circumstances, Cixous and her Medusa say *yes* to life. Their example calls us, in our lives and academic careers, to be open to what is possible and to seek joyful, full-bodied expressions of who we are. Cixous's Medusa offers us permission to stand against hegemonic and patriarchal norms and to embrace being women, writers, and fully human beings. This Medusa is neither crumbling under the weight of oppression nor cowering in fear to avoid critique. Hear Cixous's joyful description once more: "She's beautiful and she's laughing" (p. 885).

Cixous shows us that laughter can be a form of resistance and dis-order. As Brabazon (2022, p. 25) puts it, "laughter is powerful. It rebukes. It ridicules. It frightens. It creates a community. It recalibrates power relationships, even temporarily ... Laughter makes trouble and creates instability". Through her laughter, Cixous's Medusa dismantles oppressive power structures, calling out their nonsensicality and showing herself to be independent of their attempts to define her. Medusa laughs – in the face of her tormentors, but also in response to the attempts to discipline, tame, categorise, and blunten her desires and her body – and thus she transcends the "masculine economy" (Cixous, 1981, p. 42). As she disrupts binaries, she is rendered agentically promiscuous: capable of occupying multiple identities, roles, and ways of being according to her own pleasure.

The snakes that Medusa embodies in her hair are, for Cixous, the physical traits of this multiplicity. They may well be venomous and her piercing gaze may well turn her aggressors to stone, but Cixous subverts expectations, positioning these 'monstrous' tentacles and powers as the literal manifestations of the power of woman to resist, move, evade capture, and write herself into being rather than being defined by any other voice.

Me, Medusa, and I

The image below, which we commissioned for this chapter, simultaneously represents each of us, academic women in general, and Cixous's laughing Medusa. We are two women in permanent academic positions in New Zealand. We are also wives/partners (not each other's!), mothers, friends, musicians, ~~slow~~ methodical or 'aspirant' runners, Pākehā (of New Zealand European heritage, although Kirsten also has Māori whakapapa/heritage), ambitious,

Image 3.1 The Laugh of the Medusa

idealistic, capable, busy, and joyful. We're sensitive, fragile, concerned for the wellbeing of others, and concerned with being good, ethical academic citizens. And we share a propensity to critique academia and wider social ideologies; to question norms; to chew over meaty topics; to pierce uncritical or poorly thought through positions held by ourselves or others; and to insist that things can and must get better.

The brief we gave Andrew, our illustrator, was:

An image of Medusa laughing. Looking empowered, strong. Surrounded by things that somehow signify academic and feminine pressures. Books, deadlines, children, family, home, expectations, compliance, 'be good', 'succeed', 'perform', writing, conventions. Medusa as an academic woman, and laughing (rather than being overwhelmed/downtrodden). Something playful, clever/quirky. We also discussed having glasses on the snakes!

When we received Andrew's illustration, we laughed in delight! The bespectacled face of the Medusa somehow encapsulated the fact that this Medusa is each one of us personally. The many entangled snakes and juggling balls surrounding the Medusa captured our busy lives and the multiplicity of our academic and personal experiences. We recognised the snakes' outward, firm, and steely gazes, communicating the seriousness of academia and the responsibilities of parenting. And in the illustration as in our lived experiences, the individual obligations and elements of our identities intersect making a whole that is greater than the sum of the parts. We are each multiple – inhabiting complex identities and positions and positionalities and obligations. Without a doubt, we are this Medusa.

Seeing ourselves and our snakes in Andrew's illustration gave us much pause for reflection. We realised that whereas in the original myth the snakes functioned to protect Medusa by scaring and if necessary attacking others, in our Medusa story it is *we* who need some level of protection *from* the snakes that surround us. And it is *laughter*, Cixous teaches us, that can offer such protection. Laughter neutralises some of the venom and makes our 'snakes' more buoyant and less heavy to wear. Laughter thus offers:

a means of expressing our humanity in an empathetic and kind way. As Robin Williams put it, 'With comedy you are allowed to laugh about the insanity, you realise how absurd it all is, the painful stuff and the wonderful stuff too. For a brief moment everyone is connected, and you all go "Hey, we're human"'.

Ben-Moshe (2023, p. 88)

In the moment captured by the illustration, this/our Medusa has agentically closed her eyes and thrown her head back, releasing an unguarded, liberating belly laugh. She is free; complete in herself; joyful; powerful. We can also choose to have moments of levity and lightness and joy. For us, our shared writing – even writing this chapter – is one of those moments. We can come from the stresses associated with deadlines, meetings, colleagues, complex projects, or dysfunctional institutional processes and relax into this joyful form of writing/sense-making of our respective experiences. This, too, links to Cixous's wisdom and her invitation to reimagine writing through écriture féminine.

> *What was Medusa's favourite type of art?*
> *Still life.*

Flourishing in academia: Laughter as survival, solidarity, self-care, and resistance

It is important to recognise that laughter itself – like the Medusa and like our complex lives – is multiple in nature, taking many forms. As Ben-Moshe (2023, pp. 95–96) reminds us:

> A degree of sensitivity and common sense is needed when sharing or inviting humour with individuals in the wake of pain, trauma or grief. The two-faced nature of humour calls for constant assessment and reflection to ensure its appropriate and timely use.

Some laughter is spiky and edgy. It can cut, hurt, and diminish either ourselves or those around us. Laughter can also be a non-response; an awkward nothing that reflects a lack of engagement, care, or competence to move into a situation that requires courage and change. Neither of these forms of laughter can enrich our lives, our work, or the academy itself.

Cixous's feminine version of laughter, in contrast, liberates. It slices through the walls of expectation, the straitjackets that constrain our freedom of movement or thought, and the mountains of obligations. It is generative and reproductive. This form of laughter has political power that gives it sharp edges and hence power and precision. Deployed wisely, it offers us a way to stay healthy and well; connect and nourish bonds with others; and resist the oppressive seriousness that so often seeks to diminish our voices, lives, and wellbeing – all things that are deeply needed in the context of academia today (Cox et al., 2023; Mason & McChesney, 2023). We have learned that (Locke & Mc-Chesney, 2023, p. 4):

> There is a critical perspective to take even in academia's power-laden halls. Sometimes smart people do not-very-smart things; sometimes the intensity and conscientiousness needs to be tempered with the relief of a letting-go, this-is-ridiculous, hold-on-just-a-moment-and-think-about-this sort of laugh … there's a sense of relief in being able to see something in all its imperfection and a sense of solidarity in knowing someone else sees it that way too.

Learning from Cixous, we have come to increasingly value laughter as a possible response to the neoliberal, performative, reaching, slick, deficit-oriented academic machine. We believe that laughter can give us back our voices and offer an accessible, freeing response to the relentlessness of academic life. We want to preserve the possibility for a space to emerge in academia where laughter is possible, recognising that at present this is often not the case.

Making laughter possible means *choosing*, at least sometimes, to laugh. Choosing to resist the dehumanising narratives with which universities continually call for more outputs, more excellence, more funding, more productivity, more students, more speed, more efficiency. Choosing to disrupt the power of these narratives that seek to mould us into shiny, efficient, silver bullets lined up in the universities' arsenals. Choosing to laugh at such dehumanising, misguided constructions of reality. Choosing to return to the starting point of our shared humanity – seeing the academy instead as a social institution, a community of scholars (the *universitas*) established to enrich people's individual and collective lives through the pursuit, creation, and sharing of knowledge.

Below, we offer some prompts for thinking around laughter in academic settings. Every reader will have a different personality, cultural background, work experience, and wider life landscape, but we hope some of these questions will be helpful for tuning into criticality, joy, possibilities, and ways of doing things differently.

- How can you bring laughter into your workplace? Your writing? Your collaborations? Your teaching? Your leadership?
- What are your 'snakes'? Which of them have you chosen? Why? What delights you about your snakes?
- Where are the moments in your academic life when you can pause, close your eyes against the 'snakes', and take a moment of release?
- Recognising that academic careers are long and oftentimes slow, can you imagine 'future you' looking back on your current situation? What might 'future you' be able to laugh at, with the benefit of hindsight or distance?
- If a time comes when you can no longer laugh, might it be time to take action toward reconfiguring the snakes you wear, or causing one or more of your snakes to somehow shed its skin?
- Where are the contradictions in your context or experience? Can you laugh at the absurdity or irony as well as trying to think seriously or walk diligently through the situations you encounter?
- How can you ensure that laughter is healthy and does not cause harm to others? How can you stand up against cruel, belittling, or power-laden laughter but invite positive, standing-shoulder-to-shoulder, perspective-giving laughter?

- What (or who) are the 'monsters' that loom large and threaten in your academic setting? (Perhaps promotion criteria, Reviewer 2, contract renewals, funding panels, or restructuring …) How might laughter offer a way to shrink these down to size, even for a moment, offering you an alternative perspective?
- Who are the people you can safely laugh with? Whose laughter builds you up, encourages you, warms you, and offers solidarity or helpful perspective? And whose ways of laughing cut into others or deliver disguised attacks, which you need to be careful not to get drawn into?
- What might it look like to place laughter (and/or related experiences such as joy, positivity, inhibition, liberation …) at the centre of your academic identity? What might be the risks and affordances of such a step?
- How might you incorporate laughter across the wider landscape of your life? When and where can you laugh with family, friends, neighbours, children, and others you care about? How might this enhance your overall health and wellbeing?
- How could laughter be called upon as a means of resisting oppression and injustice in your setting?

Ultimately, the time we have spent thinking with Cixous has affirmed for us that academia and its 'snakes' do not need to be heavy and menacing. Although it's easy to be drawn into dark, oppressive views of academia, we believe that in order for things to become better it is essential that we create space to value and enact laughter and all that it offers us. As laughter infiltrates the structures of academia – be they social, political, managerial, or otherwise – there are opportunities for disruption, deconstruction, and delight.

How many feminists does it take to change a lightbulb?
None – it's not the lightbulb that needs to be changed.

References

Banas, J. A., Dunbar, N., Rodriguez, D., & Liu, S. (2011). A review of humor in educational settings: Four decades of research. *Communication Education*, *60*(1), 115–144. https://doi.org/10.1080/03634523.2010.496867

Ben-Moshe, R. (2023). *The laughter effect: How to build joy, resilience and positivity in your life*. Nero.

Bergson, H. (1911). *Laughter: An essay on the meaning of the comic* (C. Brereton & F. Rothwell, Eds.). Macmillan.

Billig, M. (2005). *Laughter and ridicule: Towards a social critique of humour*. SAGE.

Bloch, C. (2012). *Passion and paranoia: Emotions and the culture of emotion in academia*. Taylor & Francis.

Brabazon, T. (2022). *12 rules for (academic) life: A stroppy feminist's guide through teaching, learning, politics, and Jordan Peterson*. Springer.

Bryant, G. A., & Bainbridge, C. M. (2022). Laughter and culture. *Philosophical Transactions of the Royal Society B, 377*, 20210179. https://doi.org/10.1098/rstb.2021.0179

Cabrera, N. L. (2014). But we're not laughing: White male college students' racial joking and what this says about 'post-racial' discourse. *Journal of College Student Development, 55*(1), 1–15.

Chowdhury, F. (2022). Can laughter lead to learning? Humor as a pedagogical tool. *International Journal of Higher Education, 11*(1), 175–186. https://doi.org/10.5430/ijhe.v11n1p175

Cixous, H. (1976). The laugh of the Medusa (trans. K. Cohen & P. Cohen). *Signs: Journal of Women in Culture and Society, 1*(4), 875–893.

Cixous, H. (1981). Castration or decapitation? (trans. A. Kuhn). *Signs: Journal of Women in Culture and Society, 7*(1), 41–55. https://doi.org/10.1086/493857

Cixous, H. (1986). *The newly born woman.* University of Minnesota Press.

Cox, B., Locke, K., Sharp, E., Rayne, A., Walker, L., & Steeves, T. (2023). Doing leadership differently as resistance: Care-fully reworking Aotearoa New Zealand's research system. *New Zealand Geographer.* https://doi.org/10.1111/nzg.12379

Dynel, M. (2020). Laughter through tears: Unprofessional review comments as humor on the ShitMyReviewersSay Twitter account. *Intercultural Pragmatics, 17*(5), 513–544. https://doi.org/10.1515/ip-2020-5001

Ellingson, L. (2018). Pedagogy of laughter: Using humor to make teaching and learning more fun and effective. In C. Matthews, U. Edgington, & A. Channon (Eds.), *Teaching with sociological imagination in higher and further education* (pp. 123–134). Springer. https://doi.org/10.1007/978-981-10-6725-9_8

Erdoğdu, F., & Çakıroğlu, Ü. (2021). The educational power of humor on student engagement in online learning environments. *Research and Practice in Technology Enhanced Learning, 16*, 9. https://doi.org/10.1186/s41039-021-00158-8

Grace-Odeleye, B. E., & Santiago, J. (2019). Utilizing humor to enhance leadership styles in higher education administration. *International Journal of Educational Leadership and Management, 7*(2), 171–202.

Grosland, T. J. (2019). Through laughter and through tears: Emotional narratives to antiracist pedagogy. *Race Ethnicity and Education, 22*(3), 301–318. https://doi.org/10.1080/13613324.2018.1468750

Hah, S. (2021). 'Why did you become a linguist? Nobody reads your work!'– Academic struggles constructed through humour and laughter. *Studies in Higher Education, 46*(8), 1518–1532. https://doi.org/10.1080/03075079.2019.1692196

Herring, E. (2020). *Laughter is vital.* Aeon. https://aeon.co/essays/for-henri-bergson-laughter-is-what-keeps-us-elastic-and-free

Kanyemba, R., & Naidu, M. (2022). 'Sexist humour' towards female students in higher education settings. *International Journal of African Higher Education, 9*(1), 53–72. https://doi.org/10.6017/ijahe.v9i1.15233

Lindquist, C. (2016). Very good medicine: Indigenous humor and laughter. *Journal of American Indian Higher Education, 27*(4), 28–31.

Lipton, B. (2020). *Academic women in neoliberal times.* Palgrave Macmillan.

Locke, K., & McChesney, K. (2023). The sex or the head? Feminine voices and academic women through the work of Hélène Cixous. *Educational Philosophy and Theory, 55*(13), 1537–1549. https://doi.org/10.1080/00131857.2023.2219841

Lorde, A. (1988). *A burst of light: Essays.* Firebrand Books.

Mason, S., & McChesney, K. (2023). Exclusion through (in)visibility: What parenting-related facilities are evident on Australian and New Zealand university campus maps? *Higher Education Research and Development*. https://doi.org/10.1080/0729436 0.2023.2258824

Morreall, J. (2014). Humor, philosophy and education. *Educational Philosophy and Theory*, *46*(2), 120–131. https://doi.org/10.1080/00131857.2012.721735

Nietzsche, F. W. (1999). *The birth of tragedy and other writings* (R. Geuss & R. Speirs, Eds., R. Speirs, Trans.). Cambridge University Press.

Pailer, G., Böhn, A., Horlacher, S., & Scheck, U. (2009). *Gender and laughter: Comic affirmation and subversion in traditional and modern media*. Brill.

Pereira, M. D. M. (2013). Dangerous laughter: The mocking of Gender Studies in academia. *Open Democracy*. https://www.opendemocracy.net/en/5050/dangerous-laughter-mocking-of-gender-studies-in-academia/

Sharma, E., Sharma, S., Gonot-Schoupinsky, X. P., & Gonot-Schoupinsky, F. N. (2022). The impact of a laughter prescription on creativity, well-being, affect, and academic efficacy in university students. *Journal of Creative Behaviour*, *56*(3), 344–361. https://doi.org/10.1002/jocb.533

Stengel, B. S. (2014). After the laughter. *Educational Philosophy and Theory*, *46*(2), 200–211. https://doi.org/10.1080/00131857.2012.721729

Valiquette, R. A. (2019). *An ecology of immanent otherness: The onto/eco-poethics of Hélène Cixous*. [Doctoral thesis, York University]. York Space Institutional Repository. https://yorkspace.library.yorku.ca/xmlui/handle/10315/36789

Vlieghe, J. (2014). Laughter as immanent life-affirmation: Reconsidering the educational value of laughter through a Bakhtinian lens. *Educational Philosophy and Theory*, *46*(2), 148–161. https://doi.org/10.1080/00131857.2012.721733

Chapter 4

Queer visibility and self-care in academia

Exploring the contradictions of identity, activism, and silence

Lauren Black

Introduction

Queerness is more visible in society than perhaps ever before, owing in part to the increase in diverse knowledge sharing and language use. It is important to recognise that diverse sexualities and gender identities are not a new phenomenon. These identities have always existed; however, the language we use to describe them is new. Nowadays, many people recognise the fluidity of their own identity, and some explore this fluidity through performance and expression. The increasing diversity of sexuality and gender, amongst other intersections, offers a need to reconceptualise what inclusivity means and looks like within institutions. While universities are leaning into discussions of intersectionality, these discussions tend to be about diversity, rather than for diversity. Issues of gender and sexuality are certainly on global and political agendas, and have been for some time, although this increased visibility is not always productive. In allowing tensions and conflict to emerge, queer bodies are both seen and silenced. Put another way, there is an element of unsafety in visibility.

Often those who do not fit into or align with the cis-heteropatriarchy model of the university are deemed disruptive, regardless of political intentions (Murray, 2018). When the personal is political, as is the case for queer and other marginalised bodies, maintaining a professional identity has implications both for and against wellbeing. Many queer staff and students use silence as a tool of self-care by concealing one's identity (or difference) as a strategic action of complicity (Ferfolja, 2018). While I attempt to weave my identity and beliefs into my scholarly activism (and arguably these can never be separate), I also use forms of silence in certain spaces. Silence is used by queer bodies for a variety of reasons, particularly as a tool for wellbeing. Within the university both real and perceived discrimination engenders queer voices and bodies to remain silent as an act of self-protection (Ferfolja et al., 2020). As a researcher, I look to enhance and enable queer visibility in education for young people. As a queer student and staff member, I protect my own embodied knowledge and identity in the spaces deemed too risky. Exclusionary practices felt by both queer staff and students function to erase diversity and foster dominance of cis heteropatriarchy in the institution.

DOI: 10.4324/9781003457510-5

Through narrative and poetic inquiry, this chapter will explore the constraints and contradictions of queer visibility within the neoliberal university. I draw upon queer debates to highlight how silence can be used as a tool of wellbeing in response to the limitations of diversity and professional identity. I focus on the potentials of collective action, as resistance to normative individualised resilience strategies relied upon and projected in neoliberal academia while writing through my own experiences as a queer PhD student, and casualised academic staff member.

Writing precarity through poetry

Poetry has been realised as a powerful and adaptive tool in qualitative research. It allows researchers and writers to articulate lived experiences in depth, and offers both concealment and revealment of deep ideas, emotions, and experiences. Poetry has been used reflectively and reflexively by researchers to represent and realise ideas (Moore, 2018; Prendergast, 2009). Poetry challenges the absence of voice and representation and provides accessible modes of communicating. Voices and stories are heard in different ways, allowing for new, and potentially unexpected, insights into the world of experiences (Adams, 2020). In this, poetry allows one to become visible within the story (M. Richardson, 1998).

Poetry in this chapter is used as a pre-enquiry pause, a way to locate myself inside the context and signal my position within it (Adams, 2020). Using poetry as an expression, or perhaps a departure point, I unpack the complexity of identity in academia within multiple contexts and across complex layers. Poetry, for me, allows a glimpse into embodied thoughts drawn from spaces of passion, perception, and angst, to explore the messiness, pluralities, and contradictions of being in spaces that I may not belong.

Turning inward though poetry allows for an addressing of silence. The embodied positioning of thought though lived experience offers new insights to being where knowledge is generated against the imposition of structural oppression and alienation (Prendergast, 2009). It is from here we work to reform knowledge and knowledge production on our own terms, rather than within frames of oppression (Lorde, 1984).

Precariously queer

The language used to describe lives and communities matters. These words have the potential to affirm and validate identities but can also function as tools of exclusion and disempowerment. I use the term queer throughout this chapter to refer to individuals who reject heterosexuality and heteronormativity, with an awareness of the shifting contexts of queerness throughout time. I use the term as one of empowerment and fluidity, to highlight multiplicity and to avoid fragmenting identity akin to an acronym. I use the term queer as a rejection to the assumption that diverse bodies are fully accepted in society (Ghaziani, 2011) and to refute the idea that mere tolerance with heteronormativity is the goal of social change. Queerness highlights a desire to build upon the past, recognising the collective historical and present-day struggles. Importantly though, language does not create social reality; it creates meaning for social reality (L. Richardson, 2001).

> i write each paper with a disclaimer
> of my identity
> as if each time
> i have to reclaim it
> i have to give it power
>   warning
> coming out
> over   and over again

Queer as a term of identity encompasses a diversity of sex, gender, and sexuality and allows for an expansive description of an individual's sense of self while leaving breathing room for interpretation. Queer is a way of describing, without *describing*. It is from this embodied queer position that I work, study, write, and exist. The poem above was formed out of frustration, of frustration for myself, for theory, for academic standards, and for mere tolerance of diversity. The language of queerness is often invalidated in academia through heteronormative structures of marginalisation and othering (Breeze & Taylor, 2018).

The temporary, insecure, short term, and casualised employment modes have come to be defined by insecurity, disposability, and marginalisation.

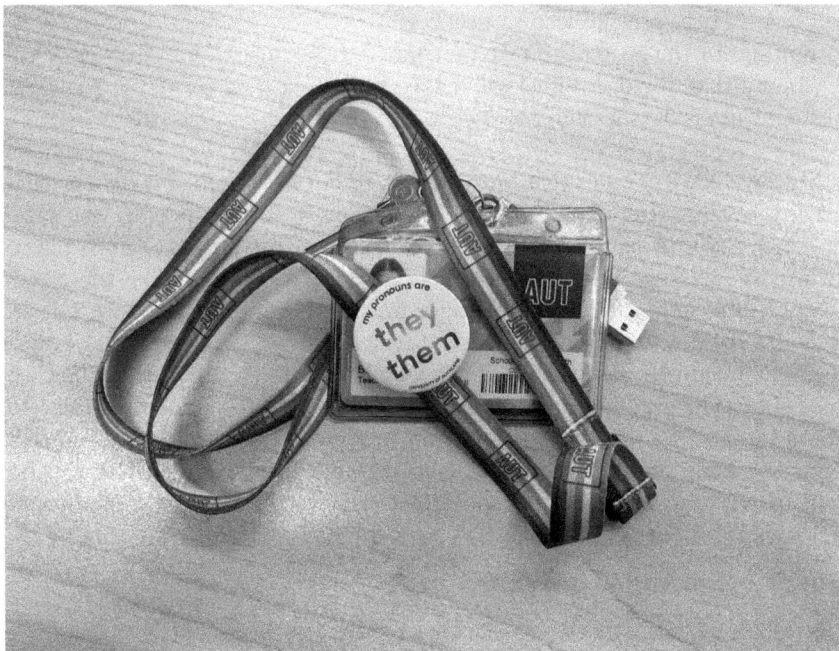

Image 4.1 The issue of (in)visibility in education

The unsustainable and exploitative nature of precarious employment has downstream consequences for already marginalised communities. As short-term, casual contracts are increasingly used by universities, the rise of precarious employment impacts conditions of belonging and wellbeing. Casual work creates a divide amongst collectives, underpinned by precarious pay and working conditions (Costa, 2020) whereby precarious workers often find themselves voiceless in the workplace. Precarity is an ontological condition of vulnerability (Butler, 2009). We tip-toe around carefully, for what feels stable now is not guaranteed at any future point in time.

As I reflect on my personal, political, and pedagogical identities, I question where I belong in the university. Like many, I sit in the blurry domain somewhere between student-teacher. Though arguably we are all student-teacher, existing somewhere in the hyphenated between. The visual narrative speaks to the issue of (in)visibility in education. I both reveal and conceal my identity in the classroom, a place I simultaneously belong and do not belong, depending on which hat I am wearing.

> our bodies float
> drifting through shadows
>   seen but unseen
> in a room of black and white
> there is little room for colour.
>
> i float in between the seams of success
> waiting for the current to take me away
> hoping that one day things will make sense
> the future is days learning to fly.

Murray (2018) argues that "just being present in academia is seen as challenging because it is a space that was not made by, or for, people 'like you'" (p. 163). I wear a signifier of diversity, the rainbow lanyard, as a subtle hint of inclusivity. But this well-intentioned display means nothing when there is an absence of meaningful policy, action, or practice beyond the symbols. Calvard et al. (2020) posit for a university to be truly inclusive, overt symbols of queer visibility must form part of a culture that celebrates diversity and genuine engagement. The visibility of queer staff in universities is vital for those who do not fit in, or those who are othered. I try to avoid the silent presence and challenge the assumptions of heterosexuality, though there are undoubtedly conflicts between my own personal and professional values within the institution.

Queer belonging in academia

Like all fields, academia is constantly shifting, evolving, and changing. The meaning associated with being in academia and doing academic work is always in process. The non-static nature allows academia to be dynamic and non-linear. This intention is to allow diversity in understanding, culture, and relations. This position is inattentive to power relations, whereby knowledge and power operate as preservation of the status quo. The predetermination of social roles, or social inequalities, is endemic to the university, where issues of power, knowledge, and status prevail throughout the institution. Those who lack knowledge or power thus operate from a position of oppression; an inferior role that lacks status to challenge normality. Wellbeing is a systemic and structural political factor, though often relegated to the fault of the individual. Queer communities have long known the personal is political, as our bodies, sexualities, relationships, and desires have been at the centre of public debates throughout time. The relegation of wellbeing as something done by individuals necessitates the concept of self-care.

In neoliberal academia, structural failures are often realised as individual faults (Oliver & Morris, 2020). This shapes the rules, norms, and practices that inform the social and political productions of the university. To belong in these spaces, individuals must take up these norms performatively. Bodies perceived as outsiders are expected to re-shape themselves to fit; there is no room for pushing the boundaries.

Queer (in)visibility

In response to invisibility, queer movements often insist on the necessity of visibility as a tool to overcome oppression and ensure queer bodies are seen and heard (Ferfolja et al., 2020; Pieri, 2019). Queer visibility is often seen as a necessary step towards liberation. When queer people are visible, our mere presence challenges heteronormativity and attempts to rewrite spaces of exclusivity. However, queer visibility can also be dangerous, citing discrimination, harassment, and violence. Normative ideas of professionalism regulate knowledge production and subjectivities in higher education. These ideas flow through the experience of being as an outsider, or being in a place that one does not belong. The hegemonic logic of sexuality views heterosexuality as the unproblematic norm, relegating queerness as the deviant other. This marginalisation or silencing of queerness, operates as a restriction of belonging for queer staff and students. The invisibility of queer staff in higher education further disempowers queer students and silences queerness.

However, "visibility is not a fixed binary state of visible/invisible; rather, it always embeds and attaches with invisibility and hypervisibility simultaneously" (Trinh, 2022, p. 756). On the one hand, it can be empowering for queer people to be visible and to be able to share their experiences with others. I seek visibility in the world around me. On the other hand, queer visibility can expose one to vulnerabilities of discrimination, harassment, and violence. I conceal my identity from those around me, rendering the personal invisible in spaces deemed risky. The contradiction of sheltering identity to fit into a bubble of professional identity has implications that work both for and against individual and collective wellbeing.

Queering self-care

> Caring for myself is not self-indulgence, it is self-preservation, and that is an act of political warfare.
>
> Lorde (1988, p. 130)

For Lorde, speaking on conditions and from understandings of racism, sexism, homophobia, apartheid, and imperialism, self-care is a deeply political concept. Self-care becomes a technique of governance, a duty to care for oneself in the face of adversity (Lorde, 1984, 1988). In this, individuals who are unable to overcome structural inequities are deemed inevitable. Rather than viewing silence as inherently futile, I consider black, crip, and queer arguments that assert silence exists to allow new possibilities and practices in the university (Smilges, 2022). Recognising the fluidity of self-care, we disrupt the perception of self-care as objective or goal oriented. There are no linear means to an end, instead there is just surviving over and over again.

Neoliberal self-care focuses solely on the individual, obscuring the structural or socio-political means of injustice (Michaeli, 2017). Thinking about individual wellbeing feels fraught, while structural conditions continue to other precarious bodies. A queer ethic of self-care is not just about individual wellbeing, but also about social justice. In line with scholars before, I frame self-care as relational, in opposition to neoliberal individualist techniques of care (Michaeli, 2017). Queering self-care looks beyond binaries of healthy/unhealthy, or positive/negative ways of coping, offering radical and contextual possibilities of wellbeing (Michaeli, 2017). For Lorde (1988), self-care was not a participatory act of consumer capitalism or a mindfulness seminar. Self-care was about sustaining the ability to enact change; in itself, a radical act. This kind of radical self-care is not solely about happiness (though not to say queer joy is not important), it is about finding ways to exist in a world not yet queer. Muñoz (1999) indicates possibilities for queer joy that looks beyond failure, self-management, and standards set for others. Understanding the "limits of the here and now" (Muñoz, 2009, p. 169) that can be transversed and transgressed through disidentification as an act of world making, a survival strategy of the minority.

Activism and silence are often seen as two opposing forces. However, they can also be considered as complementary tools of queer wellbeing. Activism can work to create inclusive and supportive environments, forming spaces for queer bodies to exist. Silence can be a tool to protect from discrimination and harassment, a tool of wellbeing. Framing the current limitations of the institution, I look to how silence and activism are used as tools of self-care – understanding action and inaction as forms of queer self-care in a departure from individualistic notions of self-care to a queer, radical and collective self-care.

Queer silence, or is it?

You as an alive and functioning queer are a revolutionary.

Rand (2014, p. 1)

The language of silence has a long history in queer studies and activism as both a form of resistance and form of complicity (Smilges, 2022). Silence is often linked to voicelessness, however to be silent does not mean there is nothing to be said. Queer silence can be a form of resistance, or a challenge to normative structures through the refusal to participate within them. Silence is both done by and done to queer bodies. It is used as a strategy of preservation and protection, while simultaneously used as a tool to oppress and marginalise. Its use in academia is two-fold: while silence can function as a tool for normalising marginalisation and oppression, it also holds liberatory potentials as a tool of eliciting possibilities. Silence allows new possibilities of being and acting, disrupting existing or entrenched patterns of thought and practice (Hatzisavvidou, 2015).

Silence draws attention to the vulnerability and discomfort of human experience. In this, silence uses discomfort as a tool to productively challenge societal norms and evoke social change. The queer existence is political; our lives and rights are consistently debated in policy and practice. Utilising discomfort and questioning normative structures allows reflection and acknowledgement of how normative structures uphold and perpetuate oppression, such as heteronormativity.

However, the concept of silence itself is contradictory as our bodies themselves are never completely silent (Pieri, 2019). We exist in environments of constant soundscapes, movements, and actions. For queer people, this environment is steeped in heteronormativity through complex settings of norms and definitions of normalcy (Pieri, 2019). Even in conditions of total silence, our bodies are always speaking. If the concept of silence implies the absence of intention, there is no such thing as silence. I consider the purpose of silence is to make people listen, to consider novel approaches, and to understand both the self and beyond the self. Silence allows us a moment to rewrite the sound around us. It is an action through which we are able to participate in hegemonic constructions quietly.

Quiet revolutionaries

Silence also invites a reconsideration of what we consider to be activism, something many of us do on our own terms and in our own time. Activism is not restricted to the loud protests of individuals or groups who make known their desire for systemic change. Some may argue silence as counterproductive, but for members of marginalised groups who face everyday consequences of discrimination, silence is a productive form of self-care. Through the notion of self-care, I regard activism as both the action and inaction, the loud and the silent. Activists are all of us who are actively working to highlight the injustices around us, even and often quietly. When all is difficult, we locate stories through art, through community, and through silence. Our stories are not always told in words.

to speak up does not mean to be loud
to be different does not mean to be small
to care does not mean to sacrifice.

don't shrink yourself to fit the minds
      of those who refuse.

i don't want to lead a revolution
i just don't want to always think twice.

I have grown weary of the perceived responsibility I have to educate others. I do not wish to be an inherent advocate, nor to carefully consider the ways I communicate. We see silence used as a tool to convey messages of queer liveability, such as SILENCE = DEATH. However, in considering self-care as self-preservation, queer silence can be a strategic decision, a choice made often out of fear of discrimination or harassment (Smilges, 2022). While there is comfort in silence, there is simultaneously discomfort. Some consider silence as a stance of disempowerment; however, I regard silence as a process of self-preservation through the careful consideration of verbal and non-verbal communication. We perform through silence and passivity as a mode and method of communication.

Reimagining self-care as personal, political, and collective

Forms of community can offer support, information, friendship, and a sense of belonging vital for wellbeing (Formby, 2017). Establishing collectives from individual stories is vital in creating spaces of care, as it is "from shared critical dissatisfaction we arrive at collective potentiality" (Muñoz, 2009, p. 189). The notion of community reaffirms positive understandings of identity, through providing physical or metaphorical space to exist (Formby, 2017). Being able to see yourself reflected in those around you, through shared ideals and identities is important to understand that one is not alone, particularly within the silence. As both relationships and contexts are frequently in a state of flux, we require ongoing negotiation of space and belonging. The intention is not to escape from or smooth out any tangles, but rather to find ways of working within the tensions. In queer research, we speak as a means of opening possibilities and conceptualising desired words, encouraging a radical imagination of a world free from the constraints of binaries and normativity. By looking to the possibilities of a queer futurity and drawing upon experiences of the present we can begin to reimagine and conceptualise alternatives in higher education.

As individuals we may have proactive approaches to self-care; we may practice this in benefit of our wellbeing, or in spite of it. However, this does not necessarily mean we have the resources for managing stressors uniquely experienced by minority groups (Vaccaro & Mena, 2011). I develop ideas here not as a push for revolution, but for collective self-care to become a revolutionary possibility in the neoliberal university. Vaccaro and Mena (2011) argue the need for communities of care, or collective supports, where individuals experience attitudes, values, and structures of belonging. These spaces are particularly imperative as a resistance to concealing, supressing, and denying identity in traditional spaces and the impact this has on one's sense of self.

Self-care as a concept is remarkably flexible, referencing any activity or practice used by individuals to calm or preserve oneself, a concept that has come to be synonymous with 'me-time'. Often it is perceived as something engaged in by an individual, like taking time off work, getting a massage, or sitting on the couch watching tv with a facemask and a block of chocolate. Today, self-care is frequently reduced to the consumption of products through a one-sided transactional process. Our conceptions of self-care have fallen short from what was once intended as "an act of political warfare" (Lorde, 1988). What was intended as an invitation for collective survival has become another form of individualism. Self-care has never been an individual act, but inextricably linked to the wellbeing of others. I write here in response to mainstream conceptions of self-care – exercise, sleeping well, yoga, knitting, and so forth. While these are legitimate and valid methods of sustaining oneself, considerations of how one survives (and thrives) in one's day-to-day life cannot be mandated through a step-by-step self-help guide. We need to consider beyond the self-help guides and daily rituals of positive affirmation to reimagine radical communities of care and nurturing. We need to find ways to create, collaborate, and form communities of care that are sustainable, and advocate for the marginalised among us. We need to acknowledge collectively that while feelings are part of the struggle, it is the struggle itself that we ultimately need to enact change to, not ourselves.

The self in self-care enables the colonial and capitalist fallacy that we must look out only for ourselves. The problematic nature of the term lies in its structure: self. Self-care is an idea grounded in the neoliberal tradition of caring for ourselves, rather than understanding ourselves as inextricably linked to others. Self-care under capitalism is understood as a commodity that enables further productivity, seen as something to maximise productivity, growth, and other capitalist metrics of progress (Michaeli, 2017). In reality, self-care is a fundamental contradiction to capitalism as it becomes a reclamation of autonomy within institutional structures, an act of political resistance (Lorde, 1984, 1988). Considering ourselves as individuals in an already individualistic society is innately more limiting than helpful. Embracing that we are interdependent beings provides possibility to create worlds of care and relationships. Caring for the self and caring for society are connected, whereby care is most meaningful when it is reciprocal. Collective care cannot be captured by capitalism; it cannot be brought, sold, defined by its price, or an exclusionary practice (Lynch et al., 2021). Collective means for all. The importance here is not only on collective care, but also the shared collective accountability for care. We are responsible to and for others, ensuring that needs are met to create a culture of care.

We cannot teach without considering care. Students cannot fully engage in learning where there are barriers, when they are in distress, or when needs are not being acknowledged. By reframing pastoral care from the burden of neoliberal work cultures, we are able to reconsider creating proactive spaces that develop ongoing and sustainable cultures of care. Pedagogies of care are not new, but there are new crises that demand their inclusion in teaching and learning (Gravett et al., 2021). We can foster open and inclusive spaces by including care resources in teaching modules, addressing wellbeing regularly and openly with students, allowing space for open conversations, and weaving in opportunities to reflect. Space and time to reflect is important for those who are navigating environments not designed by or for them, such as neurodiverse, queer, migrant, Indigenous, and others. Creating communities of care in spaces of education asks for a reconsideration of how we can teach with justice, equity, diversity, and inclusion at the centre, beyond paying lip service to the institutional buzz words.

Innovative and creative approaches to practice self-care often sit in competition with the neoliberal forces and agenda of universities. We must slow down, share our ideas and our anxieties with others, and look to how we can create new spaces of inclusion. Give yourself space, time, and grace, not just in times of chaos; create environments that foster and empower self-care, while acknowledging the obligations to care for and with others; check in with the people around you – small gestures such as a quick message often mean more than we know to others; advocate for structural changes in to build spaces of belonging for those who are marginalised.

Conclusion

Nowadays, we look to self-care as a revolutionary solution to collective problems (it is not). We must rethink the utility of self-care in academia, and look to slow down, detract from oppressive systems, and consider new meanings of productivity in a profit-driven system. Returning to Lorde's words, self-care is not self-indulgence but, instead, an act of self-preservation. Working in a system that is not designed or built for us, care is a political act necessitating the inclusion of collective care within institutional structures. I move with a desire for a rethinking of the ways we care for ourselves and for each other, with a desire for collective forms of self-care to become a revolutionary possibility. As we move forward into the unknown, pay attention to the silence around you. What is (not) being said? Whose voices are (not) being heard? Which stories are (not) being told? Where is the sound (not) coming from?

References

Adams, P. (2020). Making the invisible visible: Poetic explorations of a cross-cultural researcher. In E. Fitzpatrick & K. Fitzpatrick (Eds.), *Poetry, method and education research: Doing critical, decolonising and political inquiry* (pp. 172–182). Routledge.

Breeze, M., & Taylor, Y. (2018). Futures and fractures in feminist and queer higher education. *Journal of Applied Social Theory*, 1(2), 1–11.

Butler, J. (2009). Performativity, precarity and sexual politics. *AIBR. Revista de Antropología Iberoamericana*, 4(3), i–xiii. https://doi.org/10.11156/aibr.040303e

Calvard, T., O'Toole, M., & Hardwick, H. (2020). Rainbow lanyards: Bisexuality, queering and the corporatisation of LGBT inclusion. *Work, Employment and Society*, 34(2), 356–368. https://doi.org/10.1177/0950017019865686

Costa, C. (2020). The politics of academic work: Professional identities and intellectual selves in neoliberal times. In M. Murphy, C. Burke, C. Costa, & R. Raaper (Eds.), *Social theory and the politics of higher education: Critical perspectives on institutional research* (pp. 87–96). Bloomsbury.

Ferfolja, T. (2018). Young LGBTQ teachers: Work and sexual citizenship in contradictory times. In P. Aggleton, R. Cover, D. Leahy, D. Marshall, & M. L. Rasmussen (Eds.), *Youth, sexuality and sexual citizenship* (pp. 203–216). Routledge.

Ferfolja, T., Asquith, N., Hanckel, B., & Brady, B. (2020). In/visibility on campus? Gender and sexuality diversity in tertiary institutions. *Higher Education*, 80(5), 933–947. https://doi.org/10.1007/s10734-020-00526-1

Formby, E. (2017). *Exploring LGBT spaces and communities: Contrasting identities, belongings and wellbeing*. Routledge.

Ghaziani, A. (2011). Post-gay collective identity construction. *Social Problems*, 58(1), 99–125. https://doi.org/10.1525/sp.2011.58.1.99

Gravett, K., Taylor, C. A., & Fairchild, N. (2021). Pedagogies of mattering: re-conceptualising relational pedagogies in higher education. *Teaching in Higher Education*, 1–16. https://doi.org/10.1080/13562517.2021.1989580

Hatzisavvidou, S. (2015). Disturbing binaries in political thought: Silence as political activism. *Social Movement Studies*, 14(5), 509–522. https://doi.org/10.1080/14742837.2015.1043989

Lorde, A. (1984). *Sister outsider: Essays and speeches*. Crossing Press.

Lorde, A. (1988). *A burst of light: And other essays*. Firebrand.

Lynch, K., Kalaitzake, M., & Crean, M. (2021). Care and affective relations: Social justice and sociology. *The Sociological Review*, 69(1), 53–71. https://doi.org/10.1177/0038026120952744

Michaeli, I. (2017). Self-care: An act of political warfare or a neoliberal trap? *Development*, *60*(1), 50–56. https://doi.org/10.1057/s41301-017-0131-8

Moore, J. (2018). Lived poetry: Stirner, anarchy, subjectivity and the art of living. In J. Purkis & J. Bowen (Eds.), *Changing anarchism: Anarchist theory and practice in a global age* (pp. 55–72). Manchester University Press.

Muñoz, J. E. (1999). *Disidentifications: Queers of colour and the performance of politics.* University of Minnesota Press.

Muñoz, J. E. (2009). *Cruising utopia: The then and there of queer futurity.* New York University Press.

Murray, Ó. M. (2018). Feel the fear and killjoy anyway: Being a challenging feminist presence in precarious academia. In Y. Taylor & K. Lahad (Eds.), *Feeling academic in the neoliberal university: Feminist flights, fights and failures* (pp. 163–189). Springer.

Oliver, C., & Morris, A. (2020). (dis-) Belonging bodies: Negotiating outsider-ness at academic conferences. *Gender, Place & Culture, 27*(6), 765–787. https://doi.org/10.1080/0966369X.2019.1609913

Pieri, M. (2019). The sound that you do not see. Notes on queer and disabled invisibility. *Sexuality & Culture, 23*(2), 558–570. https://doi.org/10.1007/s12119-018-9573-8

Prendergast, M. (2009). "Poem is what?" Poetic inquiry in qualitative social science research. *International Review of Qualitative Research, 1*(4), 541–568. https://doi.org/10.1525/irqr.2009.1.4.541

Rand, E. J. (2014). *Reclaiming queer: Activist & academic rhetorics of resistance.* University of Alabama Press.

Richardson, L. (2001). Getting personal: Writing-stories. *International Journal of Qualitative Studies in Education, 14*(1), 33–38. https://doi.org/10.1080/09518390010007647

Richardson, M. (1998). Poetics in the field and on the page. *Qualitative Inquiry, 4*(1), 451–462. https://doi.org/10.1177/107780049800400401

Smilges, J. L. (2022). *Queer silence: On disability and rhetorical absence.* University of Minnesota Press.

Trinh, E. (2022). Visibility. In K. K. Strunk & S. A. Shelton (Eds.), *Encyclopedia of queer studies in education* (pp. 756–757). Brill.

Vaccaro, A., & Mena, J. A. (2011). It's not burnout, it's more: Queer college activists of color and mental health. *Journal of Gay & Lesbian Mental Health, 15*(4), 339–367. https://doi.org/10.1080/19359705.2011.600656

Chapter 5

Diversity killjoy

The places in-between

Raine Melissa Riman

Introduction

The motivation to conceive and author this chapter stems from my personal narrative as a hybrid; a journey that mirrors the statement from *The Borneo Post*, a local newspaper in Sarawak. With one parent native and the other not, and raised in a household of mixed heritage, my upbringing among relatives of varied educational backgrounds from outside Sarawak, has driven me to choose the word 'place' as central to my identity. 'Place' has become a crucial aspect of the *self* as I navigate my journey. At the time of writing, my professional activities span various academic engagements which intersects with industry, and adds another dimension to my hybrid identity. This exploration is also shaped by the place-making of hybridity within today's media landscape, particularly Hollywood's current preoccupation with themes of diversity and representation, where hybrid identities play a central role in various forms of media, from fictional productions to transcultural documentary filmmaking and even food shows. However, when the complexities of being a hybrid are beyond production storyboarding and are a daily negotiation, this place-making of hybridity can be argued to be a trope for exoticism; a result of colonialism and nation making. It's essential to note that the concept of hybridity is not a recent subject of interrogation but rather a foundational concept in cultural studies and postcolonial studies, also currently prominent areas of focus in media and communications research. Scholars such as Ien Ang and Rey Chow are just a few examples of those who delve into and examine the nuances of identity within the context of the interplay between Asia and the West (Chin, 2021).

I have consistently struggled with my birthplace and its society, to which I hold a deep connection. Raised in a family where open dialogue and the encouragement to question one's surroundings were valued, I have come to realise that my relationship with this place is far from straightforward. It requires constant navigation to balance between conforming to one identity or other, or perhaps blending both. However, my sense of self is in a perpetual

DOI: 10.4324/9781003457510-6

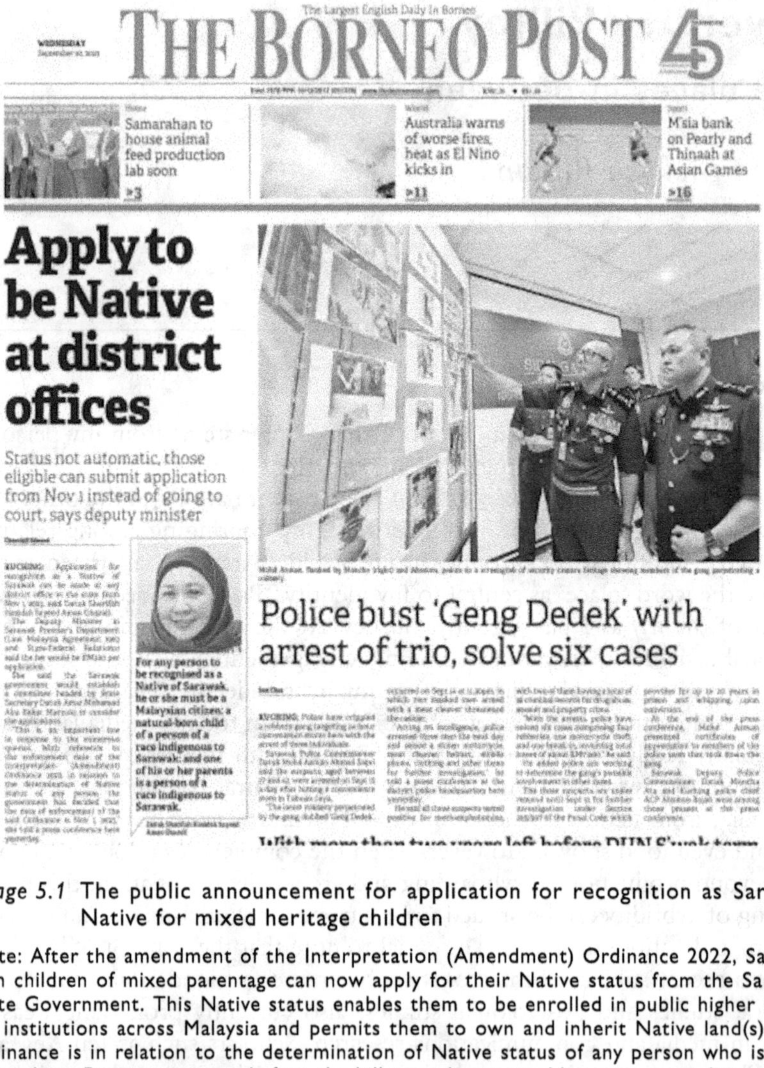

The Largest English Daily In Borneo

THE BORNEO POST

Samarahan to house animal feed production lab soon ›3

Australia warns of worse fires, heat as El Nino kicks in ›11

M'sia bank on Pearly and Thinaah at Asian Games ›16

Apply to be Native at district offices

Status not automatic, those eligible can submit application from Nov 1 instead of going to court, says deputy minister

For any person to be recognised as a Native of Sarawak, he or she must be a Malaysian citizen; a natural-born child of a person of a race indigenous to Sarawak; and one of his or her parents is a person of a race indigenous to Sarawak.

Police bust 'Geng Dedek' with arrest of trio, solve six cases

Image 5.1 The public announcement for application for recognition as Sarawak Native for mixed heritage children

Note: After the amendment of the Interpretation (Amendment) Ordinance 2022, Sarawakian children of mixed parentage can now apply for their Native status from the Sarawak State Government. This Native status enables them to be enrolled in public higher learning institutions across Malaysia and permits them to own and inherit Native land(s). This ordinance is in relation to the determination of Native status of any person who is born Sarawakian. Previous process before the bill amendment would require an applicant to go through a court hearing process. With this new amendment, one is still required to apply to the District Office – yet without going through the court procedures – with a fee of RM100 (approx. AUD30).

From "Apply to be Native at district offices" by E. Churchill, *The Borneo Post*, 2023.

struggle with the diverse identities that have shaped me as a part of various communities. Whether it's embracing my Malaysian or Sarawakian heritage, identifying as a researcher, navigating roles outside academia, or determining my place as a native or otherwise, this continuous negotiation of identity is a fundamental part of my life.

Autoethnography: Leaning into the *self*

> We depend on stories as much a e depend on the air we breathe … One of the main goals of autoethnography is to put meanings into motion, and the best way to do that is to tell stories.
>
> Bochner and Ellis (2016, p. 76)

Storytelling has always been a major part of my life. My childhood was filled with stories of myths, legends, poetry, history, and many more. My grandmother, an indigenous Iban who descended from a family tree of storytellers and spiritual healers, has always been that source of traditional knowledge for me and my siblings. Stories for us indigenous people are a source of power, inspiration, imagination, knowledge, traditions; the list is an exhaustive one. Through storytelling, through the lessons that were conveyed by the elders, is the only way to convey the position that I am in now. My favourite story of the Iban culture concerns death, wherein humans are creatures of the in-between – are in-betweeners. We do not just exist in this realm, but our spirits exist everywhere, interconnected within the different layers of realms connecting Earth and heaven. Here, a human being is not limited to a single identity but can be many things and exist in many ways. Existing as I am as a hybrid, coexisting in different cultures and lived experiences, this is perhaps the story that I most relate to. To understand the self, I have always depended on anthropology. Anthropology has always been that tool of comfort that I can use simultaneously to question further and critique to understand this place that I am physically bound to right now. However, anthropology isn't without its issues.

Having initially trained as a fieldwork researcher following my master's study, I have consistently wrestled with the practices of traditional anthropology here. Traditional anthropology tends to favour the preservation of conventional concepts and practices of the 'native' people, frequently of "exotic" nations. It remains sceptical about the idea of mobility and is inclined towards the older evolutionist perspectives on societies. As suggested by Dimitris Dalakoglou (2017), there exists a level of resistance, or rather avoidance, when it comes to challenging the established spatial, cultural, and epistemological boundaries of anthropology. Akhil Gupta and James Ferguson (1992, p. 7) refer to this as "place-culture isomorphism", suggesting that culture is intricately linked to a specific place, often confined within national borders. Foucault (2012 [1970]) notes that pushing the boundaries of this paradigm may disrupt the established order in the field of anthropology.

I began my journey into anthropology 13 years ago, right in my own backyard of Sarawak. This region, nestled in Malaysian Borneo, holds an important position in the history of classical anthropology, significantly influencing its theoretical frameworks. This context also adds to the discourse surrounding Sarawak itself – often depicted as a place suspended in time, perpetuated by its national identity and its own tourism campaigns as an exotic indigenous utopia, thereby presenting an anthropological conundrum. In response to this predefined narrative, I find myself straddling the positions of both insider and outsider, weaving a personal narrative rife with the tensions of navigating these often unexpected boundaries. Born partly "native" and partly "non-native", I embody a hybrid identity, as defined by the constitutions that have shaped the nation I am tied to by birth. When my body traverses from one place to another, I often envision moments where the *self* it embodies undergoes a process of stretching and expansion, adapting to fit a certain frame that it is expected to conform to.

This sensation reflects the film "Everything, Everywhere, All at Once", a collection of intricate and perplexing pieces that, as aptly described by Daniel Kwan in an interview, symbolise chaos and a nihilistic moment in existence where no single narrative coherently fits. Kwan's description succinctly encapsulates my polarising journey and experiences in navigating my sense of belonging within the intersection of international academia and the local industry; one that also reminds me of the many stories from my grandmother – of being human – of being not one, but many.

In this chapter, I explore my sense of place by employing autoethnography as a method to delve into the complexity of negotiating my hybrid self within a multicultural society. I focus on my conflict with the various tensions at play and a system that fails to acknowledge my indigeneity, one that I would have to legally apply for in order to be recognised within the discourse, because of my hybridity. This chapter also recounts my experiences of being presented as the token brown person during an international conference abroad and my recent involvement in a production.

Through this lived experience, through my anthropology training, I delve into this piece to demonstrate how academia has cultivated a space that empowers individuals like me to write, forging a place of care. "We write ourselves into existence", as Sara Ahmed (the 'feminist killjoy') articulated in a blog post dedicated to the late bell hooks. "We write together. And we write back against a world that, in one way or another, makes it hard for us to exist on our own terms" (Ahmed, 2022, para 14).

Complaint! Writing back against the world

As much as academia allows us to write back against the world, there also exists overwhelming pressure to narrate our stories within prescribed frameworks that may not always align with the compassionate sharing of our experiences. At various junctures of writing this chapter, I found myself seeking guidance from my PhD supervisor to ensure that my story would not come across as a mere outpouring of frustration or discontent. I was on an anxious journey to strike a balance, desiring to maintain a scholarly approach while authentically conveying the intricacies of my experiences. It was during that process that I serendipitously stumbled upon Sara Ahmed's (2021) thought provoking work, *Complaint!* Ahmed's (2021) exploration of her interview process when compiling *Complaint!* led her to a profound revelation: that the spoken words that constitute complaints serve as a form of testimony. Shoshana Felman and Dori Laub (1992, p. 3) define testimony as the process of "bearing witness to a trauma". Ahmed takes this concept further, asserting that complaints often become an integral part of the crisis surrounding the trauma itself. In light of this perspective, it feels appropriate for me to share my own experiences through a series of complaints. A particular passage from Ahmed's introduction (2021, p. 4), describing a scenario of one's experience with being silenced, resonated with me profoundly:

> she sits there silently. A question of silence: she can hear how she was not heard; she knows how and why she is passed over. She is just a secretary; she is the only woman seated at the table of men: she is not supposed to have ideas of her own; she is supposed to write down their ideas.

I found myself reenacting a version of that narrative at an academic conference last year. The resemblance felt uncanny, but this time the dominating power stemmed from racial space. I was expected to perform what I see as a curated identity of an 'authentic' indigeneity on a subject matter that had been the source of tension for many people with hybrid identity like me – native land rights. For me, matters on native land rights have always been either a dinner conversation with my elders or an academic discourse. Unlike my elders, I have never had any experience living on or even been in the legal position to own native land. To set the scene, I was in a lecture hall surrounded by audiences who had never known or met or interacted with an indigenous person before, at least that was what I was told. For them, I looked exactly like them, a Southeast Asian. I was then introduced as 'the native', at this point already feeling like a subject from the colonial period. This performance that was expected of me was an act of tokenism, orchestrated by an individual who hailed from the same place as I did – a hybrid themselves. What followed was an episode of silencing. I was constantly being talked over and silenced before I could reposition my identity to the audience. Moments later, I chose to continue the silence in an act of *saboteur*, against the notion of what a native person should be in that context; a noble savage.[1] Perhaps the question we should now ponder is not whether the subaltern can speak (Spivak, 2010), but rather, if the subaltern wishes to speak.

My encounters with this erasure of the complexities of my hybridity did not conclude with the conference; they permeated into all aspects of my work within the university, local institutions, and, recently, an international production job. The tension between my self-perception as a hybrid cosmopolitan self and the expectations placed upon me as a representative of indigeneity or nativity remains an ongoing theme, one that calls for a critical examination within both academic and societal spaces. On one hand, this place wants me to remain as the naive native, but on the other hand it rejects my nativity, because what I am now is against what a native should be; one that chooses to write back against the world, one that challenges the notion and definition of a native, one that does not want to pay the RM100 (USD21) native registration fee because it is simply her birthright.

A visceral tension

For many years, I have been overwhelmed with the burden of conforming to the stereotype of being perceived as a native, particularly when indigeneity is co-opted as a corporate strategy within the tourism industry. In this setting, we are consistently positioned as the exotic, frequently called upon to grace various events with choreographed performances of traditional indigenous dances and to showcase traditional livelihoods as the centrepiece of the tourism board's staged presentations. It was only about a month ago that my team and I orchestrated what we referred to as a 'social experiment' during a culture and art festival. This event may have been one of the first of its kind, drawing attention to the rich diversity of percussion cultures in Kuching City, bringing together communities with various heritage backgrounds, both native and non-native. This initiative quickly garnered attention on social media, serving as a reflection of the place we've become – a stage. What we accomplished with our festival stands as a testament to the evolving identity of our locale. It's a place where we take pride in showcasing our remarkable cultural heritage, where people of all races and heritage backgrounds come together to celebrate this cultural diversity. However, it's also a place where, despite this proud celebration of multiculturalism, diversity, and inclusivity, there exists a paradox. This paradox lies in the fact that these celebrations often feel like a construct driven by neoliberal interests, and simultaneously, they reject the products of multiculturalism, diversity, and inclusion – individuals like us, the hybrids who straddle multiple worlds.

Individuals like myself have been attempting to establish their place, a journey akin to those of Sara Ahmed (2023) and bell hooks (2009). It entails the pursuit of a sense of belonging, a genuine understanding, and the desire to feel truly at home. This struggle is not unique to any single person; it affects many academics within my circle. This experience aligns with the concept of 'repatriation', as discussed by Chin (2021). Here, repatriation involves academics returning to their home country after completing their education, training, and building their careers elsewhere (Chin, 2021, p. 131). Yet, in contrast to Chin's concept of repatriation, the negotiation of in-betweenness in my case is a result of what I describe as a visceral tension. Life, whether in the personal or professional sphere, revolves around the concept of hybridity. My academic experiences and training have never stemmed from a single source or place. They often involve a combination of various locations and work cultures both from Asia and the West, including research projects that require collaboration with experts and academics from different parts of the world. This dynamic contributes to an ongoing negotiation of in-betweens, identity, and a sense of place. The journey of negotiating between Asia and the West, of navigating the complexities of 'here, there, and elsewhere' as discussed by Trinh Minh-ha (2011), would, for me, largely take place within the realm of this place that I currently call home.

My early sense of identity was shaped by my upbringing within a family environment that encouraged critical thinking and questioning of the world, which stood in stark contrast to the prevailing nature of the public education system. As I embarked on my journey through public university, I found myself navigating a landscape rife with micro-aggressions. My status as the "Other" was underscored by distinctions of race, language, and religion that set me apart from the majority. This identity marked me as an outsider within an academic space that should ideally serve as a safe haven for all students. However, I couldn't help but confront the numerous instances of racial discrimination that unfolded within this supposedly inclusive and nurturing environment. My journey was further marked by ongoing tensions as I sought to establish myself in the local industry. Here, my academic background was consistently overlooked and erased, and I felt the weight of the prevailing ethos that prioritised entrepreneurship as the ultimate pursuit. This emphasis created additional spaces in which micro-aggressions flourished, fuelled by a deeply ingrained, misogynistic ideology of business ownership. In these spheres, the challenges I faced extended beyond those rooted in academia to encompass a broader set of prejudices and biases that hampered my progress within the local system. A failure to progress within the local system because my understanding and nuances of knowledge in this sense, my worldview, do not fit within this space anymore. That wish to live elsewhere, in another place, to pursue academic excellence where I could explore a different forms of experiences, to be a better version of myself, has also contributed to the visceral tension, of not being able to leave, of being confined to a place where hybridity is a blessing but also a curse.

Shame: The doing and undoing of the *Self*

As an academic of colour, there are moments when I confront the shame of not feeling 'brown enough' or 'yellow enough' to be an adequate representative of my hybrid cultural identity. I frequently find myself thrust into the position of being a spokesperson for the brown community. More recently, I've even been called upon to defend my heritage, which also includes aspects of 'yellow' identity. In a country where we all navigate multiple tensions and intricate intersections, my experiences sometimes serve me well, while at other times, they may backfire. This place I occupy has never been a straightforward one. It is also crucial to acknowledge that not everyone shares the privilege I do when it comes to unpacking the complexities of their identity. Recognising this privilege is a humbling realisation that helps keep me grounded, or at least that's my belief. The ongoing process of 'doing and undoing' the self represents a journey of self-discovery and reflects the intricate dance between personal identity and societal expectations.

Last year, I had the privilege of consulting on a production, commissioned by a prominent international media establishment. Throughout the production process, I observed how emotions and identity were being exploited to market a story. This story could have been ethically developed if it were narrated through the perspective of qualified local experts, rather than being constructed through the media's obsession with exoticism as an 'aesthetics of diversity' (Segalen, 2002). Throughout this production journey, I found myself constantly adapting my hybrid identity to meet the production's requirements. It wasn't until a Zoom conversation with my group of research peers that a friend pointed out how frequently I was 'doing and undoing' my identity; not from a negative perspective, but rather, it was a celebratory one. I however at that same moment, felt a sense of shame in representing; not representing hybridity, but representing one aspect or the other. My identity became a vulnerability. In search of understanding the shame and guilt I felt, I turned to a conversation between Tarana J. Burke and Brene Brown (2021) and I quote:

> but as a Black woman, I often felt like I had to contort myself to fit into the work and see myself in it...what is the Black experience with shame resilience? ...Because white supremacy has added another layer to the kind of shame we have to deal with, and the kind of resilience we have to build, and the kind of vulnerability that we are constantly subjected to whether we choose it or not. My lived experience told me that the entire idea and experience of vulnerability feels like a very dangerous place to play, an unsafe think to even consider or think about as a Black person in this country. As I read your work about vulnerability being the foundation of courage and the birthplace of love and joy and trust – these are the places that didn't fit. I was forced to contort myself and try to understand my reaction of, Oh, no. Vulnerability means something very different to me. That was a big learning for me – just naming vulnerability and talking about it and thinking about it.
>
> Tarana J. Burke (Burke & Brown, 2021)

While I don't have the space or time here to delve further into my sense of vulnerability, the conversation I quoted above has provided me with insights into the shame I grapple with. This shame stems from not feeling 'native enough', and admitting this vulnerability could be perilous. It would require unpacking and repacking my identity, which can be an arduous process. Sometimes, it seems easier to contort myself and fit into the dominant narrative and discourse. This by no means is meant to impose on the black experience or their trauma but that I find solidarity in this processing and perhaps this is a space where individuals like me can engage in further introspection.

The dining table as my third space

We are born and have our being in a place of memory. We chart our lives by everything we remember from the mundane moment to the majestic. We know ourselves through the art and act of remembering. Memories offer us a world where there is no death, where we are sustained by rituals of regard and recollection.

bell hooks (2009, p. 5)

The concept of a "third space" has been my refuge in this multifaceted environment, a sanctuary where I can fully embrace my academic self, my everyday self, to question and to reconcile with my hybrid self. Homi Bhabha introduced the idea of the "third space" to describe a hybrid cultural identity that emerges from the intricate interweaving of elements from different cultures. In his work (Bhabha, 2012 [1994]), he delves into hybridity as a liminal space in-between where the "cutting edge of transition and negotiations" takes place.

For me, this third space reveals itself through the presence of food. Places like restaurants and cafes become settings for negotiating identities. I've always been captivated by how food constructs our identity, and how our identity, in turn, influences our food choices. Food, to me, tells stories that transcend geopolitical borders and racial constructs, highlighting the intricate intertwining of culture and roots. It's in these culinary spaces that we uncover stories, memories, and nostalgia that connect us beyond physical or cultural boundaries, emphasising the deep connection of our diverse heritages. Moreover, food serves as a vessel for memory and a portal to my encounter with my hybrid self.

Quoting Stephen Satterfield in Morrison & Satterfield (2021), in the Be the Bridge podcast,

this type of work, in which food is the basis, really allows us the opportunity to ground ourselves, find ourselves, take pride in our ancestry and in our history. This goes for everyone. And in finding that space for ourself in the world, hopefully, develop the empathy and capacity to make that space for others, you know? In that kind of shared human experience, that is rooted in tradition, and legacy, and ancestry we all are part of. That is a collective human story.

This collective human story brings me back to the family dining table with dishes that represent the hybrid identity of my family. That dining table stands as an egalitarian space, free from the constraints of hegemony, where both cultures are celebrated. The idea of gathering around the family dining table, reminiscent of my grandmother's dining table, is a story of reclamation and the power of connecting with my hybrid identity. It's about resisting the conventional conception of multiculturalism and the type of diversity that often excludes, inadvertently erases, distorts, and obscures the everyday lived experiences of people who exist within layers of complexity, beyond the definitions of constitutions. The dining table is the space where I embrace my native identity and my Chinese identity simultaneously. The same dining table was a space of temporality and shelter for those in need. My grandmother's dining table was a third space, not just for me but also for others, a place devoid of prejudice. It was also at the same dining table that we celebrated both our native and non-native aspects through food and fellowship. It is at this very table that others found the comforting feeling of home.

However, it is a shame that this very dining table that I envisioned to be my third space, where I can freely consume cultures of duality, now exists in tension, in a space of temporality. My grandparents' house, nestled on a land with a native land title, right in the heart of the city, stands ownerless. My late maternal grandmother, the sole native Sarawakian of my family, married my Chinese grandfather and produced a line of non-native descendants who, by law – at the time of writing – are unable to inherit the native land. The dining table, once a symbol of inclusivity and cultural celebration, now reflects the complexities of identity, heritage, and the legal tension that disrupt the harmony of such spaces.

This is my story of reclamation: I replicate the experience of my grandmother's dining table at my own dining table in my apartment. Here, I position my blue Mac, the faithful tool I use to pen the stories of my interrogation and the narratives of reclamation that delve into the complexities of my hybrid identity. My dining table has transformed into my own version of that cherished space, where I navigate the intricate terrain of my existence, contemplate my academic pursuits, and explore the nuances of my identity. It's a place where the legacy of my family's cultural celebration and the power of

Image 5.2 The blue Mac on my dining table

Note: This marble dining table, once located at my parents' home, holds cherished memories of tea and snacks shared with my siblings, grandmother, and parents. It's always been my favourite piece in our living room and is a quintessential *Peranakan* household fixture. The term Peranakan typically refers to individuals descended from intermarriages between locals and foreigners in Southeast Asia. While each country in the region has its unique interpretation of Peranakan, the essence remains rooted in people of mixed-heritage backgrounds.[2]

embracing my diverse heritage continue to thrive, even in a world marked by tension and transition. This transformation takes place not on a plate but on a screen, where the stories of my past and present, of tension and care, converge to shape the narrative of my journey.

Conclusion: This place is a paradox

In her preface titled "To Know Where I Am Going" for *Belonging: The Culture of Place*, bell hooks (2009) pays homage to a lyric by Tracy Chapman. Although the question's etymological roots may seem simple, answering it from a specific standpoint can be complex. In hooks' *Belonging: The Culture of Place*, she spoke of finding herself, finding her place, finding where she belongs, and that her return to her home was the self-care that she needed. While at this moment in time, this home that I am in, is my place in-between.

The reality I find myself in, in this place, is one that often challenges the commonly celebrated notion of diversity. It's a tension, a conflicting reality that we often fail to address. We hang on to the idea that our version of diversity is our greatest gift to the world while we fail to recognise our own diversity, the hybrids that exist and are operating within this mundane place. Instead diversity is transformed into a spectacle driven by capitalist interests, designed to appease the 'naive natives'. Exploring and expressing these complex emotions, to put the pen to paper has been a challenging endeavour, sometimes painful.

It's a process that has at times moved me to tears, forcing me to confront my shame and vulnerability, and ultimately to admit that this place – the place I've known to be home – may no longer serve my life's purpose. I am also reminded of a recent conversation with an award-winning filmmaker, Dr. Robin O'Sullivan (personal communication, 2023), who aptly said, "This is not the right place for you. You can't grow here". These words echo in my mind, reminding me that sometimes our paths must diverge from the familiar in order to truly thrive.

This essay has been a journey of introspection and self-discovery, exploring my intersections of identity, culture, and place. It's an ode to the complex nature of our lives as academics, equipped with the tools that enable us to navigate the complex terrain of our existence and awareness, critically. It's also a tribute to this place, a place that I hold a deep love for because of my roots, but also the same place that has at times shamed me for simply being who I am; our relationship with the places we call home is often a deep layered one, filled with both affliction and conflict. And so I end this chapter with the belief that it is my call to be the 'diversity killjoy', to confront the paradoxes of diversity, and to find the path that aligns with our true selves and aspirations.

Notes

1 See Rowland's critique on the return of the noble savage for more detailed discussion.
2 See Koh (2013).

References

Ahmed, S. (2021). *Complaint!* Duke University Press.

Ahmed, S. (2022, September 20). Feminism as lifework: A dedication to bell hooks. feministkilljoys. https://feministkilljoys.com/2022/09/20/feminism-as-lifework-a-dedication-to-bell-hooks/

Ahmed, S. (2023). *The feminist killjoy handbook: The radical potential of getting in the way* (1st edition). Seal Press, Hachette Book Group.

Ang, I. (2012). *On not speaking Chinese: Living between Asia and the West.* Taylor & Francis.

Bhabha, H. K. (2012 [1994]). *The location of culture* (2nd edition). Taylor & Francis.

Bochner, A. P., & Ellis, C. (2016). *Evocative autoethnography: Writing lives and telling stories.* Routledge.

Burke, T., & Brown, B. (Eds.). (2021). *You are your best thing: Vulnerability, shame resilience, and the black experience* (unabridged). Penguin Random House.

Chin, B. (2021). Exploring cultural identity through coffee. In N. Lemon, *Creating a place for self-care and wellbeing in higher education* (1st edition, pp. 131–143). Routledge. https://doi.org/10.4324/9781003144397-12

Chow, R. (1991). *Woman and Chinese modernity: The politics of reading between West and East.* University of Minnesota Press.

Dalakoglou, D. (2017). *The road: An ethnography of (im)mobility, space, and cross-border infrastructures in the Balkans.* Manchester University Press.

Felman, S., & Laub, D. (1992). *Testimony: Crises of witnessing in literature, psychoanalysis, and history.* Routledge.

Foucault, M. (2012 [1970]). *The order of things* (2nd edition). Taylor & Francis.

Gupta, A., & Ferguson, J. (1992). Beyond "culture": Space, identity, and the politics of difference. *Cultural Anthropology, 7*(1), 6–23. https://doi.org/10.1525/can.1992.7.1.02a00020

hooks, b. (2009). *Belonging: A culture of place.* Routledge.

Koh, J. (2013, August 26). *Peranakan (Straits Chinese) community* [Singapore Government Agency website]. Singapore Infopedia. https://www.nlb.gov.sg/main/article-detail?cmsuuid=1138ea9d-9dbe-4f09-9fef-ba2c7105eb91#:~:text=Peranakan%20in%20Indonesian%20and%20Malay,Arab%20Peranakans%20and%20Java%20Peranakans

Minh-ha, Trinh T. (2011). *Elsewhere, within here: Immigration, refugeeism and the boundary event.* Routledge.

Morrison, L., & Satterfield, S. (2021) *Be the bridge*, podcast (228). https://bethebridge.com/episode-28-stephen-satterfield/

Rowland, M. (2004). Return of the "Noble Savage": Misrepresenting the past, present and future. *Australian Aboriginal Studies*, Issue 2, 2. https://www.researchgate.net/profile/Michael_Rowland5/publication/279180967_Return_of_the_'noble_savage'_Misrepresenting_the_past_present_and_future/links/5592067b08ae47a34910c815.pdf

Segalen, V. (2002). *Essay on exoticism: An aesthetics of diversity* (Y. R. Schlick, Trans.). Duke University Press. https://doi.org/10.2307/j.ctv125jg90

Spivak, G. C. (2010). "Can the subaltern speak?" revised edition, from the "History" chapter of Critique of Postcolonial Reason. In R. C. Morris (Ed.), *Can the subaltern speak? Reflections on the history of an idea* (pp. 21–78). Columbia University Press. http://www.jstor.org/stable/10.7312/morr14384.5

Repositioning learning and teaching for self and others

Chapter 6

Confronting failure as self-care

Critical honesty as a springboard for positive change in teaching and learning

Christopher Little

Introduction

Despite all best intentions, and despite working to what we might understand as best practice as teachers, sometimes a moment in teaching simply does not go well. Sometimes, as hard as we try, it just does not work. This will be a familiar feeling for many educators across all education sectors. Yet, how often do we admit this to our students there in the moment?

This chapter takes an incident from my teaching where, despite preparing what seemed to be a positive, student-focused seminar in terms of planning and teaching style, the seminar just did not engage or enthuse the students. Rather than enduring this failure until the class ended and then carrying this around with me for days, weeks, months, or years, I decided to talk to my students about it, mid-seminar, in the hopes that we could confront the aspects of my teaching and their learning that were not aligning and co-create a more positive set of outcomes with the time we had left in the seminar. This was a revelatory experience for me and my learners, transforming my whole perspective on teaching. The lessons from this experience have stayed with me since and remain a core part of my teaching practice today.

This chapter will explore the concept of critical honesty in more depth. To encourage a full reflection on this incident and these concepts, Manouchehri's (2002) 5-stage reflective model will be used to structure and extend the discussions here, addressing the following stages:

1 Describing
2 Explaining
3 Theorising
4 Confronting
5 Restructuring

This model encourages not only a retelling of the tale but also encourages practitioners to confront challenging aspects of their thoughts, feelings, and reactions, as well as encouraging considerations of how to ensure future practice is improved. This established model of reflective practice has allowed

DOI: 10.4324/9781003457510-8

Image 6.1 Antique broken Japanese beige bowl repaired with gold kintsugi technique (Montalti, 2020)

me to iteratively develop the narrative presented here and encouraged said confrontation and a contextualisation against relevant educational research.

Kintsugi is the ancient art of repairing broken items, typically ceramics, highlighting cracks and joins with gold, silver, or platinum, to embrace and value imperfections and the process of repair – "It is even more beautiful and precious once broken and repaired" (Santini, 2019). This chapter will explore piecing a failing session back together with students, resulting in a better educational experience and a pivotal moment in my career.

The chapter will embrace pedagogic confrontation as an opportunity for self-care. It will work towards a teaching philosophy of critical honesty and of embracing the uncomfortable moments in teaching while there is still time to course-correct them. In doing so, we can be free from carrying the emotional burden of poor seminars and lectures around with us, and focus on a kinder, co-created pedagogy that serves us as educators, and our students, better.

Description – what happened?

I delivered a 2-hour seminar about critical use of literature, literature reviews and academic voice to a group of Masters Social Work students as part of the regular weekly timetable of taught content. I designed this seminar in collaboration with other colleagues on the course, ensuring that it was constructively aligned to the unit and course learning outcomes (Biggs & Tang, 2020), and built on previous lectures and seminars – using contextual knowledge, to help students to see the links between topics. To give students a low-stakes practice run, formative assessments mirrored those of their summative ones. I also used core reading from the programme and related professional body practice documents to make the seminar more authentic to their careers as social workers.

The seminar I planned had opportunities for individual and group work and an active learning strategy which has often been found to lead to positive outcomes for students (Hendrickson, 2021; Pratt-Adams, Richter, & Warnes, 2020). My teaching resources were designed to be as inclusive and disability-friendly as possible, proactively taking into consideration guidance from the British Dyslexia Association on creating dyslexia and neuro-diversity-friendly teaching resources. This approach was also carried out in conjunction with additional individual reasonable adjustments requested by those students with disclosed disabilities through the university's formal systems for supporting individual students with disabilities.

The seminar was about academic voice at the Masters level and the challenges and opportunities afforded by literature reviews within dissertations at Level 7. The student group contained students from different disciplinary backgrounds and countries of origin so I ensured that learning materials and teaching strategies explicitly addressed academic conventions for not only our programme, but the wider university and the UK Higher Education (HE) sector.

I felt I had done everything to ensure it went well. Despite still feeling nervous about teaching after more than a decade as a teacher and academic, I am a confident-seeming educator and had won some internal teaching awards at my institution for my practice. I believed I had constructed a seminar that considered my experiences of teaching to that point, as well as what was considered more widely to be effective practice. The seminar was tailored to the specific group and played to my strengths as an educator.

Explanation – so, why wasn't it working?

Around 30–35 minutes in, however, I was acutely aware that I was labouring to keep this well-designed seminar going – it simply was not working for the students. When I became aware of this, I observed my students – they were working but there was no energy in the room; when I asked open questions, responses were not forthcoming; group work was quiet and forced. I circulated while students were working in groups and checked everyone was ok with the seminar, they politely told me that it was fine.

I had designed what I felt was a great seminar. In that moment, however, when confronted by it failing but being told "it was fine" (even though the students and I knew it was not), I defensively decided that the students were the problem. It simply could not have been me (a seemingly confident, experienced, award-winning teacher) or my conscientious design process. This is not something that I would usually like to admit to myself – that I blamed my learners – but this book is giving us all space to think about our practice differently, and sometimes that means confronting hard truths. My educational research and scholarship have often focused on educational initiatives which proactively support and empower typically disadvantaged student groups like international students or students with disabilities. I do not subscribe to deficit student models of higher education. These beliefs are important to me, and a core part of my teacher identity. However, at that moment, ashamedly, I felt affronted and allowed the seminar to continue for another 20 minutes whilst internally blaming the students for the it failing. We then broke to allow them a comfort break and to allow me time to think and reflect.

During this time, with the students absent, I looked at the seminar again, took stock of how I was feeling, and looked at the work the students had left out on the tables. Things were getting done, but not to the level they or I would have hoped – student work was complete but superficial and not getting to the depth of the subject matter as I had designed. Finally, while the seminar was not a hostile space, it was not a pleasant learning environment. I could not understand why it was not working and why my learners were unhappy.

So, at that moment, I decided to admit things were not going well and ask them why. This is something that I was hugely nervous about, but I did not want to do another hour of this and I was sure they did not either. When the students returned, I opened by saying "This is not working is it? Like, at all?" Over the next 10 minutes we explored the reasons why it was not working for them, or for me, and worked together to explore what they wanted and how they wanted to learn, co-creating a new structure which allowed for productive teaching and learning. HE students are often surveyed at the end of units or end of courses, however here students appreciated being asked for their input while it had time to be effectively actioned for their learning.

In discussing how I had planned the seminar with them, it became clear that in my adherence to the belief that active learning with busy classrooms full of the energy of teaching and learning leads to better learning, I had left little space for them, for *their energy*. In their reflections on the lecture as a mode of education, Jones (2007, p. 404) notes that "effective education at heart must proceed from engagement" in a way which gives space for both disciplinary content and the preferences, needs, and motivations of learners. This is a belief I have long held and been successful with. However, I needed to ask myself whether I had planned for student engagement or student activity, or both. I had hoped both, but these students were not able to engage with the teaching and learning activities I had planned. In my current role as a Senior Lecturer in Academic Development working with new university educators, I often see educators mistaking activity for engagement and, more importantly, learning – I had fallen into that same trap here.

The students, the majority of whom were mature students with previous degrees, explained that most of them had been successful in their previous education by learning in calmer, more didactic ways. My way of teaching was also a little out of alignment with how the rest of their teaching staff taught them in the programme. Importantly, this was a professionally accredited course that many were undertaking in addition to paid work, and many expressed that they felt they did not have the mental energy to do everything they were already doing and then to learn a new way of learning. While my belief in active, authentic, and constructively aligned learning remained, and remains, I needed to acknowledge their learning preferences and understand that, by trying to make my teaching work for them, I had not tailored it *to them*.

This group simply wanted a more instructional, lecture-based way of learning. They wanted me to lecture material to them, leaving space for question-and-answer sections. They were not looking to sit passively, but to actively engage with a more instructional style by taking notes and engaging in questions. This instructional style is not something I enjoy, but it can be effective and engaging. As Crawford notes: "the audience may be sitting without talking (an oversimplification of 'passive') but is fully and actively engaged in synthesising the flow of the lecture" (2016, p. 2).

That is what we then did. I delivered each slide as a lecture, removing some group tasks and creating moments of silent thinking time before asking them for any questions. The second part of the seminar was wonderful. Students were re-energised, they were more attentive, took more notes, asked and answered more questions when being lectured than they had before and smiled more. Simply put, for these students, I was now a better teacher – a weight had been lifted from me.

Theorising – what research and literature led me here?

The signature pedagogies which inform my work are Mezirow's (2003) theory of transformative learning and Knowles's andragogy (1984) – these theories align with and inspire my teaching styles and preferences. I feel we have a moral obligation to base our practice in higher education around educational research into teaching and learning which was conducted with adults. A combination of Knowles' and Mezirow's work points me in the direction of adult learning which is working towards an end goal of autonomous and independent learners. As such, my practice has recently been influenced by the works of Kevin Gannon, in his work 'A Radical Hope' (2016), and David Gooblar's

'Missing Course' (2019). Gooblar and Gannon discuss a pedagogy of compassionate practice and radical hope, centred upon creating respectful and adult-based learning with a key focus on inclusive and equitable practice, and this is something I try to instil in my teaching.

Despite having taught in both Further and Higher Education for over 10 years, I 'fell' into a teaching career, rather than necessarily planning my career towards this end point. As such, I have wrestled with my nerves and anxieties as a teacher. In this instance, my leap of faith in admitting my failure to students was rewarded, with my experience echoing what others have found. Cook-Sather (2020) talks about the potential for these co-creation conversations to "unfold in the brave spaces of pedagogical partnership" (2020, p. 894), potentially leading to more equitable teaching practices and mutual empowerment. Similarly, Mangione and Norton (2023) discuss "the importance of modelling vulnerability to our students by letting down our barriers and allowing students to have more control and ownership over the learning that happens during the teaching process" (p. 375). They go further, suggesting that this honesty and vulnerability should be thought of as one the "defining characteristics of a pedagogy of excellence" (p. 376).

McDougal's (2021) excellent discussion of vulnerability for both students and academics highlights the inherent risks in being vulnerable as an academic, but also the courage bound within it and the high potential for professional and emotional rewards. This is very much what I felt at that moment of asking my students what was going wrong – I was naturally worried about they would say about me and my teaching, but I was also immensely proud of myself for having the courage to do this in the moment, for wanting to make things better to the extent that I would take that risk – a practice I would now highly recommend to fellow educators. Regardless of their feedback in that moment, I would have felt pride. However, true to McDougal's position, the emotional rewards of my critical honesty were great – the seminar got better, students learned more, and I knew they and I would be happier for this act of self-care.

The work of Dr Liz Morrish, *Pressure Vessels* (2019) and *Pressure Vessels II* (Morrish and Priaulx, 2020), has resonated with me since I was fortunate enough to see a keynote by her discussing the escalation of poor mental health in Higher Education staff. Morrish highlights, for example, that between 2009 and 2015, counselling referrals for university staff rose by 77 per cent (2019). Morrish's work is crucial and powerful and since becoming aware of it, I have been mindful in my teaching practice, and in my work supporting new and experienced teachers, to foreground pedagogies which are hopeful and compassionate for both students *and staff*. We exist in an imperfect Higher Education sector where many colleagues are under increasing pressures, growing class numbers, and escalating workloads. I am also aware that these challenges, as with many others, are amplified for colleagues who are not white, middle-class males like me (Heffernan, 2022). However, in my practice, in the space which I can influence, acts such as this moment of critical honesty, enacting co-creation and a relational pedagogy (Murphy & Brown, 2012) stand as one way in which I try to proactively protect my mental health.

Confronting

As noted previously, when the seminar was failing, I defensively felt that it could not have been me or my planning that was the reason. In that moment, I blamed the students. The students were not bringing enough energy, the students were not trying hard enough – it was *their* fault, not mine. Admitting my blaming of the students to myself was extremely challenging at the time and a real threat to my own student-centred, socially just teaching philosophy. Confessing that moment here is equally nerve-wracking, but I wanted critical honesty to be a real thread through this chapter.

Of course, it was not them. Strangely though, it was also not entirely me. The pedagogical decisions made were based on years of experience and an awareness of educational research and sector-recommended good practice. This moment of teaching simply did not work for these learners, and although it was tailored to their programme, it was not tailored to them as individuals. However, on this last point, it is often hard in the demanding environment of HE to tailor everything to everyone every time, so we must also be kinder to ourselves in these moments of critical honesty to acknowledge that we work in an imperfect system.

This seminar should have worked, and with another group it may well have. With this group, it did not. The discussion with the learners about it not working was what allowed me to leave any guilt or negativity about that behind. The critical honesty of the learners was crucial in me being able to move from mistakenly defensively reasoning that the problem was them, through to mistakenly apportioning a significant amount of 'blame' to myself, to a realisation that sometimes the best thing we can do with our learners, who know themselves as learners better than anyone, is to simply give them the space to take some ownership of their learning and guide us as educators.

I was perhaps guilty of also trying too hard, of throwing too much at the learners – something I am sure many educators can identify with. I love teaching and sometimes that can lead to an overzealous approach. As I touched on above, I have often been told that I seem highly confident when I teach, but in truth, I still get nervous about teaching. Clance and Imes's conceptualisation of imposter syndrome as "I'm in this position because my abilities have been overestimated" (1978, p. 241) is a feeling with which I can certainly identify. Wilkinson's recent (2020) autoethnographic study of their imposter syndrome revealed three dominant themes: a high level of nervousness; a difficulty in managing disengaged students; and worrying about appearance. These themes also resonate with me. Colleagues have often described me as an energetic teacher, bouncing around classrooms, and filling taught sessions with student group work and activities. This all leads to a highly energetic teaching practice that gives the image of confidence, but in fact provides good spaces for me to hide within. These activities, and my accompanying energy also impact my nervousness about managing disengaged students. My classes simply would not provide space, or time, for them to disengage – but did they truly always provide spaces for them to meaningfully, with contemplation and space, to learn? I do not think I can always say my teaching practice has done this. Here, the seminar in question provides a perfect example of space being filled with activity. Of course, this was done with the intention of creating a positive learning environment, but it also will have been steered by my self-esteem to provide few opportunities for my own overestimated abilities to be questioned, to use Clance and Imes's phraseology.

Being honest about this element of my teacher identity, in this moment, has been beneficial to me as a teacher since. It has encouraged me to occasionally fight my instincts to 'fill' classes, and it has resulted in a more enjoyable teaching experience. I was undoubtedly using such active learning strategies as they have been proven to be effective, as mentioned before. I suspect I was also doing this to take the attention off me and to help me hide my nervousness during teaching. This moment proved a real instance of confrontational, but positive, change in myself. It led to me seeking out additional opportunities to develop my confidence as a teacher. This was a catalyst for my educational research, encouraging me to find out if my teaching was effective.

Restructuring

The conversation with my students during the seminar was a watershed moment for my self-belief that gave me a huge boost in confidence for several reasons. Firstly, the moment of relief I felt on discussing with my learners as to why things were not working was a pivotal moment in my battle with imposter syndrome and my self-confidence. It revealed that while this particular seminar was not working for them, my teaching had been received how I always wanted it to be – students said they could see all the effort I was putting into the seminar, and could see why I had designed it in the way that I had, and that this one simply had not worked. Hearing this from students first-hand was hugely beneficial to my image of myself as a teacher. I had perhaps feared a confrontation in the adversarial sense of the word, but what I experienced was more of a moment of co-creation.

Second, I had muted my imposter syndrome, if only momentarily, to have the confidence to put myself in a position of vulnerability with my learners. Although I have always found the idea of power hierarchies within classrooms uncomfortable, we nevertheless must admit that they are there. Consequently, admitting something is not working within these traditional power dynamics, no matter how democratically you approach your teaching, is brave. When I asked them why it was not working, there was always the possibility that they would be far less kind with their words than they were, or they could have remained disengaged and silent – both responses would have been catastrophic to my confidence. I remain, to this day, proud that I took that step, and the students rewarded this act of courage with kindness.

Finally, as I have hinted at throughout this chapter, I felt immediately lighter, removed from the weight of delivering another hour of uncomfortable and ineffective teaching. By acknowledging and challenging the issue of misaligned teaching strategies, I was also free of the weight of this failure beyond the end of the timetabled seminar, where it would have undoubtedly fed any thoughts of self-criticism or imposter syndrome. In the opening section of this chapter, I refer to being free from dragging this weight with me and that is how it felt. I knew that after the discussion was over, and I got back to teaching how the students wanted to be taught, I would be able to take the positives with me.

Conclusions and recommendations

In my experience, when a class is going poorly, and we become aware of this, we as educators rarely make, or find, the time to address the situation *in situ*. In confronting a failing seminar, I was able to co-create a more positive outcome for learners and consequently to care for myself better. Throughout my career, I have enjoyed discussion-based teaching and learning focused on student group work. I have, however, never enjoyed delivering instructional lectures from the front of the classroom or lecture theatre in the didactic tradition, yet I *loved* the rest of that seminar and, consequently, was a better educator at that moment.

For colleagues reading this chapter who are looking for a way forward in transforming their own critical honesty with students, enacting Mangione and Norton's (2023, pp. 383–384) five principles of daring to be vulnerable are an excellent place to start:

1 Learning to be courageous in trying new teaching methods.
2 Learning to trust student and colleagues and displaying our own being as trustworthy to others.
3 Learning to be authentic in our teaching.
4 Learning to be more aware of ourselves and others.
5 Learning to be reflective rather than reactive.

When I reflect upon the incident discussed in this chapter, I can see how my practice aligned with these principles of courage, trust, authenticity, awareness, and reflexivity. Their shift away from concepts of frailty towards *daring to be vulnerable* gives me great hope in how teaching in HE may change moving forward – working not only towards a more equitable experience for students, but also for academics.

I have since redoubled my efforts to gather as much information about students before and during teaching, working to check in with students more frequently in informal ways throughout sessions and units of study. As educators, we undoubtedly have preferences in our ways of teaching, but I have now relaxed my hesitance around didactic lecturing, seeing it as another valuable tool in a good educator's toolkit. This experience taught me that you can put as much effort as you like into a particular teaching and learning strategy, but if it fundamentally does not align with your students, it will only go so far. This awareness and willingness to change and adapt has undoubtedly saved me from countless other stalling seminars and lectures since. This is another recommendation for colleagues looking for opportunities to practice self-care – if your session feels off, ask your students, ultimately they are the experts in how their learning is going.

The lessons learned here have also served me well in other aspects of my career. Academic publishing, for example, can often be a challenging environment and we can sometimes be guilty of taking critiques of our work, from anonymous reviewers, as personal attacks. Consequently, we often disengage from receiving the lessons within this feedback. My experience in the seminar taught me to understand my audience more, to engage with feedback on my performance as openly as possible, and to be kinder to myself, and others. This has been invaluable in my publication record and, in my current role supporting other colleagues, in helping them to build their academic publication records too.

This incident echoes elsewhere in my life, both professional and personal, teaching me that critical honesty, while not always comfortable, is often valuable if done with fairness and kindness. As you can hopefully feel through these pages, this moment became a clear act of self-care. In that moment, I confronted a situation that was a negative experience for the learners and me, and in doing so prevented the situation from doing further damage to them and myself after the seminar ended. This moment clarifies for me that when reflective practice is student-centred, considerate of our preferences and experiences as educators, and, crucially, kind in those moments, there are few better acts of self-care available to us as educators.

References

Biggs, J., & Tang, C. (2020). Constructive alignment: An outcomes-based approach to teaching anatomy. In L. K. Chan & W. Pawlina (Eds.), *Teaching anatomy: A practical guide* (pp. 23–30). Springer.

Clance, P. R., & Imes, S. A. (1978). The imposter phenomenon in high achieving women: Dynamics and therapeutic intervention. *Psychotherapy: Theory, Research & Practice, 15*(3), 241–247.

Cook-Sather, A. (2020). Respecting voices: How the co-creation of teaching and learning can support academic staff, underrepresented students, and equitable practices. *Higher Education, 79*(5), 885–901.

Crawford, R. (2016). The traditional lecture: A case of Academic Chuunibyou? *Compass: Journal of Learning and Teaching, 9*(13). doi: 10.21100/compass.v9i13.319

Gannon, K. M. (2016). *Radical hope: A teaching manifesto*. West Virginia University Press.

Gooblar, D. (2019). *The missing course: Everything they never taught you about college teaching*. Harvard University Press.

Heffernan, T. (2022). Sexism, racism, prejudice, and bias: A literature review and synthesis of research surrounding student evaluations of courses and teaching. *Assessment & Evaluation in Higher Education, 47*(1), 144–154.

Hendrickson, P. (2021). Effect of active learning techniques on student excitement, interest, and self-efficacy. *Journal of Political Science Education, 17*(2), 311–325.

Jones, S. E. (2007). Reflections on the lecture: Outmoded medium or instrument of inspiration? *Journal of Further and Higher Education, 31*(4), 397–406.

Knowles, M. S. (1984). *Andragogy in action: Applying modern principles of adult learning*. Jossey-Bass.

Mangione, D., & Norton, L. (2023). Problematising the notion of 'the excellent teacher': Daring to be vulnerable in higher education. *Teaching in Higher Education, 28*(2), 373–388.

Manouchehri, A. (2002). Developing teaching knowledge through peer discourse. *Teaching and Teacher Education, 18*(6), 715–737.

McDougall, J. (2021). 'Excruciating' and 'exquisite': The paradox of vulnerability for students and academics in enabling education. *Access: Critical Explorations of Equity in Higher Education, 8*(1), 97–109.

Mezirow, J. (2003). Transformative learning as discourse. *Journal of Transformative Education, 1*(1), 56–63.

Montalti, M. (2020, October 16). *Antique broken Japanese beige bowl repaired with gold kintsugi technique stock photo*. iStock. https://www.istockphoto.com/photo/antique-broken-japanese-beige-bowl-repaired-with-gold-kintsugi-technique-gm1280370448-378700388

Morrish, L. (2019). *Pressure vessels: The epidemic of poor mental health among higher education staff*. Oxford: Higher Education Policy Institute.

Morrish, L., & Priaulx, N. (2020). *Pressure vessels II: An update on mental health among higher education staff in the UK*. Oxford: Higher Education Policy Institute.

Murphy, M., & Brown, T. (2012). Learning as relational: Intersubjectivity and pedagogy in higher education. *International Journal of Lifelong Education, 31*(5), 643–654.

Pratt-Adams, S., Richter, U., & Warnes, M. (2020). *Innovations in active learning in higher education*. University of Sussex Library.

Santini, C. (2019). *Kintsugi: Finding strength in imperfection*. Andrews McMeel Publishing.

Wilkinson, C. (2020). Imposter syndrome and the accidental academic: An autoethnographic account. *International Journal for Academic Development, 25*(4), 363–374.

Chapter 7

Finding wonder and awe together in higher education

Linda Noble[1] and Malgorzata Powietrzynska

We are all equal in awe

We have arrived at a pivotal point in our collective history. Famine, epidemics, conflict, and migration undermine the sustainability of communities around the globe (cf. Daher et al., 2021). Challenges of extreme weather, floods, and drought endanger the ecosystem and the biosystems of plant and animal life (Nel et al., 2014). On an individual level, substance abuse and mental disease negatively impact self-care and threaten the harmony of human existence (Rehm & Shield, 2019). Our quality of life depends upon weaving our individual values into the awe-inspiring, colourful, textured fabric of our shared humanity. Dacher Keltner's (2023c) recent research has shown that awe can inspire an increased connectedness with others. Awe may be framed as "the feeling we get in the presence of something vast that transcends your current understanding of the world" (Keltner, 2023c, p. 7). When we wonder and engage in open-ended inquiry, we feel awe and can focus on what we find meaningful in life beyond the strivings of the self. Experiences of awe may lead us to take actions that can benefit the common good. In education, time pressure and traditional approaches to teaching | learning can stifle opportunities to experience awe. Our collective wellbeing requires being open with curiosity and wonder to take skillful actions together that can benefit our connection, interconnection, and coexistence.

As teacher educators, in the context of socio-economic-environmental distress, and as co-authors of this chapter, we must continue to explore different asset-based approaches (Flint & Jaggers, 2021) that our teacher candidates can adopt to nurture their students' sense of self-efficacy towards creating a better future. Asset-based pedagogies view students' diversity, including culture, language, disability, socio-economic status, immigration status, and sexuality, as characteristics that add value and strength to classrooms and communities. For example, Zaretta Hammond's (2015) Culturally Responsive Teaching offers a framework that includes Awareness and Learning Partnership which supports self-inquiry, knowing and owning one's cultural lens and can help students cultivate a positive mindset and sense of self-efficacy. Similarly, Gloria

DOI: 10.4324/9781003457510-9

Image 7.1 Awe by Chiara Leopardi

Ladson-Billings' (1995) Culturally Relevant Pedagogy model proposes developing students' cultural competence to assist them in the development of positive ethnic and social identities, while supporting critical consciousness. Ladson-Billings (1995) suggests that inequalities are a logical result of a racialised society in which discussions of race and racism are being muted, ignoring the tensions that exist between and among multicultural clusters. Stemming from Ladson-Billings's work, Gholdy Muhammad's (2023) Historically Responsive Literacy framework is built on what she labels as learning pursuits that include criticality, a cognitive skill that has the potential for a humanising approach to problem-solving and understanding power, inequality, equity, and oppression. Bettina Love's (2019) Abolitionist Teaching is centred upon intersectional racial justice in and beyond the classroom through civics education, community coalition building, and critical theory. Love (2019) argues that we want to do more than survive and she suggests that we commit *spirit murder* when we dehumanise. For Love (2019), *freedom dreaming* is the beginning of abolitionist teaching. She says,

> Freedom dreaming is imagining worlds that are just, representing people's full humanity, centering people left on the edges, thriving in solidarity with folx from different identities who have struggled together for justice, and knowing that dreams are just around the corner with the might of people power.
>
> Love (2019, p. 103)

To quote Keltner (2023c), "Our default mind blinds us to the fundamental truth, that our social, natural, physical, and cultural worlds are made up of interlocking systems" (p. 248). As authors of this chapter, we are informed by such writings of Hammond, Ladson-Billings, Muhammad, Love, Keltner and others who, rather than seeing our separateness, view us as interrelated and dependent. We seek transformation that has the potential to humanise education and therefore we elevate practices of self-care in our contemplative pedagogy (Powietrzynska et al., 2021). Acts of self-care such as meditation and mindfulness provide insights that can empower us and our students to respond to crises in meaningful and creative ways. In the next section, we reflect upon our journey to nurture connection in an effort to humanise higher education through engagement in contemplative practices that can evoke awe and at the same time, mediate our self-care and the wellbeing of our diverse student body as frequently documented in their self-reflections.

Journeying together towards awe

For the past 7 years, our (Linda and Malgorzata's) mutual academic work has involved co-teaching graduate-level teacher education courses, co-researching, co-writing, and co-presenting (Powietrzynska & Noble, 2021). Working in tandem, which may not be typical for higher education in general and for the contingent (adjunct) workforce in particular, is in itself a form of self | other care. As noted elsewhere (Noble & Powietrzynska, 2021), this team approach supports our self-awareness (as we call each other in), self-management (as we model for each other), and social relationships (CASEL[2] competencies). In our relationship, as Mark Nepo (2020) would suggest, we lean in softly listening to each other with a willingness to be changed by what we hear. Importantly, we also elevate the significance of self-care in our teaching practice by making it a part of our course content through incorporating relevant literature featuring extensive research originating in university labs such as the Center for Healthy Minds at the University of Wisconsin–Madison which is directed by the world renowned neuroscientist Richard Davidson. In addition, we make adjustments to our pedagogy. For example, consistent with approaches to grading for equity (Feldman, 2018), we create spaces during class periods for students to collaborate on assignments. This practice is recognised and appreciated by our students for its impact to not only minimise the out-of-the class workload but also to capitalise upon the social constructivist nature of teaching and learning (Vygotsky et al., 1994). Included in our pedagogy is explicit modelling of and engagement in short social-emotional learning (SEL) practices in which students may turn inward in support of their wellbeing. When sourcing practices, we came across and have been sharing with our students a "Being kinder to yourself" video (Greater Good Science Center, 2020) in which an army psychiatrist who works with the active duty population models a self-compassion break (Greater Good in Education, 2023e). As a part of the Science of Happiness series, this brief practice is one of many research-tested strategies featured on the Greater Good in Education (GGIE) website. In this video in particular the concept of self-care is supported by research conducted by Kristin Neff and Chris Germer (2013), the authors of a training programme called Mindful Self-Compassion. We often hear from our students how appreciative they are for being able to give themselves permission to prioritise their wellbeing in this simple act of self-care.

We were fortunate to be invited to join an international team of educators from Egypt, India, Canada, and the US as writing fellows with the GGIE. In this role, we were able to experience a transformation from curators and consumers to creators of SEL practices. As part of our work around awe our team created several practices using a template furnished by the GGIE leadership. The template is meant to provide educators with a road map on how to prepare for and engage in the practice as well as the research behind it including evidence that it works and why it matters. Through this work and the evolution of our philosophical framework and pedagogy our perception of the purpose of education has shifted. Our current vision to humanise education aligns directly with the GGIE vision in service of kinder, happier, more equitable schools, towards building a thriving, resilient, and compassionate society. GGIE's mission is to present education professionals with practical, scientific insights that help them bring the science of a meaningful life into their lives, schools, and classrooms. It draws on disciplines such as SEL, character strengths, and mindfulness. As GGIE writing fellows, one of our first challenges was to read Dacher Keltner's 2023 seminal book, *Awe: The New Science of Everyday Wonder and How It Can Transform Your Life*, and based on the concept of awe create a collection of research-based practices. What we found interesting and unique was the approach that GGIE has taken in creating the practices that align with the GGIE mission and vision. Our work is collaborative rather than competitive, our timelines are efficient and flexible, feedback is both rich and critical, our sharing is invitational in being authentic and vulnerable, and tenderness is the bridge to our interconnection. Overall, our experience is evidence that even in such a prominent institution as the University of California, Berkley where GGIE originates, it is possible to create *conscious spaces* (Alexakos, 2021) that support wellbeing. Being part of this nurturing process has given us hope for joy and criticality (Muhammad, 2023) in higher education as a pathway back to our humanity, and an appreciation of our interbeing (Nhất Hạnh, 2017).

Learning to weave with the awesome fabric of our shared humanity

Dacher Keltner and Jonathan Haidt's (2003) research on the science of awe suggests that awe can foster student | educator wellbeing at the psychological and neurological level. Keltner (2023c) suggests that awe deactivates the Default Mode Network (representational processes related to memory cells) which can have the effect of reducing activation in the self-focus region of the brain. He claims that this is the manner in which the complex emotion of awe can calm down the voice of the self to foster empathy and prosocial relationships (Keltner, 2023c). By helping to shift us away from a reductionist disposition, awe can cultivate a mindset of our being embedded in a more complex network of connection, belonging, and inclusion. This element of diversity, equity, and inclusion is a core value in Hammond's, Love's, and Muhammad's work. Barbara Fredrickson (2003) offers a physiological understanding of this process to be the activation of the vagus nerve which she concurs promotes calm (as in self-compassion) and social engagements. We note that when together with our students we enact practices that can mediate a sense of wonder in teaching | learning; awe is present and frequently promotes kind tendencies, as our perceptions are less polarised. In our classroom, when we are more open to wonder and finding common ground, we take opportunities for cogenerative dialogues (Tobin, 2014). When mindfully listening and speaking about thorny issues (Alexakos et al., 2016) we aspire to shift from sensing that we are separate selves towards having a stronger connection to our community and our shared humanity. In these moments, the conflicts of our times are perceived as part of a greater whole. Keltner (2023c) suggests that transformative feelings of awe can be found in experiences with the eight wonders of life that include moral beauty, collective effervescence, nature, music, visual design, spirituality and religion, life and death as well as epiphany. In the following sections, we wish to share a few highlights from our work that may help in raising awareness of non-judgmental curiosity, wonder, and the power of awe to benefit wellbeing in higher education.

Awe in nature

"What is awe?" Awe begins in encounters with the eight wonders of life. The experience of awe unfolds in a space of its own, one that feels good and differs from feelings of fear, horror, and beauty. Our everyday lives offer so many occasions for awe.

Keltner (2023c, p. 26)

Research studies suggest that awe is deeply connected to experiences in nature (Piff et al., 2015). Conversely, being disconnected from the natural environment can result in awe-deprivation. Indeed, increasingly in a globalised world, technology such as social media has lured us away from the natural environment.

The very first GGIE practice that we co-designed, *Look Up Vibe* or *LUV Moment* (Greater Good in Education, 2023d), was an invitation to take a pause, slow down, and simply look up at the sky to experience the interconnected nature of life. Practising LUV moments can lead one to becoming more aware of life unfolding (Keltner, 2023a). In an academic context, it can serve as grounding and orientation towards an academic pursuit (Anderson et al., 2020). The objective is to slow down by taking a momentary pause to notice the environment. This practice affords an opportunity to notice and pay focused attention to shifting patterns and sounds. These ritualistic encounters bring mindful awareness to being a part of a force larger than the self (Bai et al., 2017). In our graduate level classes, reflections recorded with the use of tools such as a Mood Meter, Padlet, or a digital chat waterfall, provide impactful testimonies about the transformation of this grounding experience. Notably, the experience of goosebumps or shivers (the physiological manifestation of awe) are often reported.

Awe in visual design

Our aesthetic capacities for creation and appreciation have allowed us to see the geometries of the natural and social worlds and navigate those worlds with greater intelligence. Across history, awe-inspiring visual art has allowed us to find hints of what we make together of the ever-changing mysteries of life … Visual art has shocked and awed people into new ways of seeing the world.

Keltner (2023c, p. 190)

Finding Wonder through Art in Community (Greater Good in Education, 2023a) is another GGIE practice that we designed which focused on taking a neighbourhood walk to capture an image of a visual design that inspires awe. We modelled this practice on a photovoice methodology (Foster-Fishman et al., 2005). In this approach photographs and their associated narratives are used to identify and represent issues of importance to members of a particular community. The practice invites the use of principles which Keltner (2023c) suggests can elicit awe: repetition, light/dark contrast, parts signalling the presence of a holistic process, and hints of vastness. Seeking glimmers of awe in our everyday lives and in our higher education classrooms can be empowering. We use this principle when, at the beginning of each semester, we introduce ourselves individually by identifying with visual artefacts. We reflect upon the emotions and sensations we feel in relation to our artefact by way of presenting ourselves to each other. We find that sharing our artefacts frequently elicits explicit articulations about a shared sense of our interconnectedness. Through this task we experience a sense of authentic presence mediated by engaging with visual design. Research tells us that awe-inspiring visual art experiences can contribute to increased happiness and health (Jackson, 2003) that can lead to building a culture of sharing and collaboration in the classroom and beyond.

Awe in music

In musical awe we hear the voices and feel the sounds of our culture. We recognize, we understand, our individual identity within something larger, a collective identity. A place, and a people. We find what is often seemingly far away – home. In this we find immense happiness. This can be true in hearing music that has deep cultural roots, and in music we might not immediately understand.

Keltner (2023c, p. 162)

Our work on the GGIE practice *In Harmony with Sound* (Greater Good in Education, 2023b) afforded us in its design an exploration of music as a powerful elicitor of awe (Keltner, 2023b). An enactment of this practice involves experimenting with listening to and creating rhythmic sounds and body movements (hands, feet, fingers, and mouth) that can evoke collective effervescence (Cohen, 2021). A sense of feeling energetically connected to others can increase commitment to shared goals academic or otherwise by infusing them with a sense of purpose, and meaning (Anderson et at., 2020). We seek ways to bring music into our classroom for opportunities to cultivate empathy (Rabinowitch et al., 2013) and nurture cooperative engagement (Li et al., 2011) that can enrich our teaching | learning experience. During brain breaks, transitions, and/or free-writes when we have experimented with listening to rhythmic sounds we have found that listening to music with students frequently contributes to a more empathetic and cooperative classroom (Kokal et al., 2011). Music has the power of bridging. In one class session, we introduce a video-based activity that involves engagement with what we refer to as an unlikely musical collaboration. In it, a British rock group, Coldplay, together with an exiled Iranian actor Golshifteh Farahani perform an Iranian protest song *Baraye* translated to English as "because of" (*The Guardian*, 2022). The musical performance illustrates a sense of oneness and interbeing embodied by the performers as they articulate universal values of social justice and freedom. After 5 minutes of mindful listening, the weight of the pregnant pause holds us together in silence, with a palpable sense of awe nearby. Indeed, music has been found to be a source of awe among people from distinct cultural backgrounds (Cowen & Keltner, 2017) which in many ways is mirrored by the eclectic cohorts with whom we work in our inner city higher education spaces.

Awe in the life cycle

Being part of this scientific story of awe has taught me that the evolution of our species built into our brains and bodies an emotion, our species-defining passion, that enables us to wonder together about the great questions of living: What is life? Why am I alive? Why do we all die? What is the purpose of it all? Our experience of awe hints at faint answers to these perennial questions and moves us to wander towards the mysteries and wonders of life.

Keltner (2023c, p. 250)

In higher education, stress and anxiety are on the rise leading to feelings of disconnection and self-focus. It is important to re-member the complexity, diversity, and interconnectedness of life. In our classroom, through our emphasis on collaboration, in heterogeneous groups students are encouraged to shift their attention away from their small selves and towards their connection to others and to life itself. Taking time to contemplate a broader view of life can be an awe-inducing experience. *Life is a Gift* (Greater Good in Education, 2023c) is a GGIE practice we designed in which watching a video about the human life cycle can provide an opening to experience awe and gain a greater sense of perspective. Part of the practice involves using a contemplative tool, a heuristic (Powietrzynska & Noble, 2021), to engage in reflection upon the life cycle towards raising awareness of the construct. A small yet important component of the activity is to highlight that in a critical inquiry into the life cycle, the concept of family structure may vary. The purpose of this is to be explicit in diverse representations. Researchers found that experiences of awe may decrease existential isolation (Edwards et al., 2023), which is often linked to depression, suicidal ideation, lower in-group identification, and lower self-esteem (Helm et al., 2020). Transformation of the self brought about by awe is a powerful antidote to the isolation and loneliness that is epidemic today. By cultivating open-mindedness and humility, awe may ultimately support greater diversity, equity, inclusion, and belonging in classrooms, in schools, and beyond.

Invitation to slow down and look up for self-care

A LUV Moment

As you look up you may notice the sun is holding her warm blanket to gently wrap around your body.
Perhaps you might join in the conversation with the bird family who are chatting about their last flight perched above your head.
You may decide to stay a while and lay down a smile for another friend to rest upon, cushioned under the fold of her wings.
Or perhaps notice darkness distracted by fleeting shadows on their way to find light.
However mother nature beckons you, look up to drink in the patterns she pours for you to savour from her overflowing cup.
Listen attentively to her mysteries, her ever evolving wonders of life.
Now allow nature to take your hand on this journey that is the work your life has called you to.
Allow the self to be transformed, trusting the universe knows and sees all.
Look up often and enjoy LUV moments.

Notes

1 Corresponding author: Linda Noble, LMN1@nyu.edu.
2 Collaborative for Academic, Social and Emotional Learning.

References

Alexakos, K. (2021). Conscious spaces and self. In K. Tobin & K. Alexakos (Eds.), *Transforming learning and teaching* (pp. 362–381). Brill. https://doi.org/10.1163/9789004507609_018

Alexakos, K., Pride, L. D., Amat, A., Tsetsakos, P., Lee, K. J., Paylor-Smith, C., Zapata, C., Wright, S., & Smith, T. (2016). Mindfulness and discussing "thorny" issues in the classroom. *Cultural Studies of Science Education, 11*, 741–769. https://doi.org/10.1007/s11422-015-9718-0

Anderson, C. L., Dixson, D. D., Monroy, M., & Keltner, D. (2020). Are awe-prone people more curious? The relationship between dispositional awe, curiosity, and academic outcomes. *Journal of Personality, 88*(4), 762–779. https://doi.org/10.1111/jopy.12524

Bai, Y., Maruskin, L. A., Chen, S., Gordon, A. M., Stellar, J. E., McNeil, G. D., Peng, K., & Keltner, D. (2017). Awe, the diminished self, and collective engagement: Universals and cultural variations in the small self. *Journal of Personality and Social Psychology, 113*(2), 185–209. https://doi.org/10.1037/pspa0000087

Cohen, Z. (2021, August 30). What is collective effervescence? Why we need it and how to put it in our syllabus. *The Core Collaborative.* https://thecorecollaborative.com/what-is-collective-effervescence/

Cowen, A. S., & Keltner, D. (2017). Self-report captures 27 distinct categories of emotion bridged by continuous gradients. *Proceedings of the National Academy of Sciences of the United States of America, 114*(38), E7900–E7909. https://doi.org/10.1073/pnas.1702247114

Daher, B., Hamie, S., Pappas, K., Nahidul Karim, M., Thomas, T. (2021). Toward resilient water-energy-food systems under shocks: Understanding the impact of migration, pandemics, and natural disasters. *Sustainability, 13*(16), 9402. https://doi.org/10.3390/su13169402

Edwards, M. E., Helm, P. J., Pratscher, S., Bettencourt, B. A., & Arndt, J. (2023). The impact of awe on existential isolation: Evidence for contrasting pathways. *Personality and Social Psychology Bulletin.* https://doi.org/10.1177/01461672221144597

Feldman, J. (2018). *Grading for equity: What it is, why it matters, and how it can transform schools and classrooms.* Corwin.

Flint, A. S., & Jaggers, W. (2021). You matter here: The impact of asset-based pedagogies on learning. *Theory into Practice, 60*(3), 254–264. https://doi.org/10.1080/00405841.2021.1911483

Fredrickson, B. L. (2003). The value of positive emotions: The emerging science of positive psychology is coming to understand why it's good to feel good. *American Scientist, 91*, 330–335. DOI: 10.1511/2003.26.330

Foster-Fishman, P., Nowell, B., Deacon, Z., Nievar, M. A., & McCann, P. (2005). Using methods that matter: The impact of reflection, dialogue, and voice. *American Journal of Community Psychology, 36*, 275–291. https://doi.org/10.1007/s10464-005-8626-y

Greater Good in Education (2023a). *Finding wonder through art in community.* https://ggie.berkeley.edu/practice/finding-wonder-through-art-in-community/

Greater Good in Education (2023b). *In harmony with sound.* https://ggie.berkeley.edu/practice/in-harmony-with-sound/#tab__1

Greater Good in Education (2023c). *Life is a gift.* https://ggie.berkeley.edu/practice/life-is-a-gift/

Greater Good in Education (2023d). *Look up vibe. (LUV Moment).* https://ggie. berkeley.edu/practice/look-up-vibe-luv-moment/

Greater Good in Education (2023e). *Self-compassion break for adults.* https://ggie. berkeley.edu/practice/self-compassion-break-for-adults/#tab__1

Greater Good Science Center (2020, January 23). *Being kinder to yourself* [Video]. YouTube. https://youtu.be/AyQdeYjXUhE?si=IR8beG06pcwyAqRl

Hammond, Z. L. (2015). *Culturally responsive teaching and the brain.* Corwin Press.

Helm, P. J., Medrano, M., Allen, J. J. B., & Greenberg, J. (2020). Existential isolation, loneliness, depression, and suicide ideation among young adults. *Journal of Social and Clinical Psychology, 39,* 641–674.

Jackson, L. E. (2003). The relationship of urban design to human health and condition. *Landscape and Urban Planning, 64*(4), 191–200. https://doi.org/10.1016/ S0169-2046(02)00230-X

Keltner, D. (Host). (2023a, January 19). Why we should look up at the sky [Audio podcast]. *The Greater Good Magazine.* https://greatergood.berkeley.edu/podcasts/ item/why_we_should_look_up_at_the_sky_the_science_of_happiness

Keltner, D. (2023b, January 25). *How musical awe embraces us in community. Porchlight.* https://www.porchlightbooks.com/blog/changethis/2023/awe

Keltner, D. (2023c). *Awe: The new science of everyday wonder and how it can transform your life.* Penguin Press.

Keltner, D., & Haidt, J. (2003). Approaching awe, a moral, spiritual, and aesthetic emotion. *Cognition & Emotion, 17*(2), 297–314. https://doi.org/10.1080/ 02699930302297

Kokal, I., Engel, A., Kirschner, S., Keysers, C. (2011). Synchronized drumming enhances activity in the caudate and facilitates prosocial commitment – if the rhythm comes easily. *PLOS ONE, 6*(11), e27272. https://doi.org/10.1371/journal. pone.0027272

Ladson-Billings, G. (1995). Toward a theory of Culturally Relevant Pedagogy. *American Educational Research Journal, 32*(3), 465–491. https://doi.org/10.2307/1163320

Li, Y., Lynch, A.D., Kalvin, C., Liu, J., & Lerner, R. M. (2011). Peer relationships as a context for the development of school engagement during early adolescence. *International Journal of Behavioral Development, 35*(4), 329–342. https://doi. org/10.1177/0165025411402578

Love, B. (2019). *We want to do more than survive: Abolitionist teaching and the pursuit of educational freedom.* Beacon Press.

Muhammad, G. (2023). *Unearthing joy: A guide to culturally and historically responsive curriculum and instruction.* Scholastic Professional.

Neff, K. D., & Germer, C. K. (2013). A pilot study and randomized controlled trial of the mindful self-compassion program. *Journal of Clinical Psychology, 69*(1), 28–44. https://doi.org/10.1002/jclp.21923

Nel, J. L., Le Maitre, D. C., Nel, D. C., Reyers, B., Archibald, S., van Wilgen, B. W., Forsyth, G. G., Theron, A. K., O'Farrell, P. J., Kahinda, J. M., Engelbrecht, F. A., Kapangaziwiri, E., van Niekerk, L., & Barwell, L. (2014). Natural hazards in a changing world: A case for ecosystem-based management. *PLOS ONE, 9*(5), e95942. https://doi.org/10.1371/journal.pone.0095942

Nepo, M. (2020). *The book of awakening: Having the life you want by being present to the life you have.* Red Wheel.

Nhất Hạnh, T. (2017). *The art of living: Peace and freedom in the here and now.* HarperCollins Publishers.

Noble, L., & Powietrzynska, M. (2021). Bushwhacking a path forward: Contemplative pedagogy for well-being in education. In N. Lemon (Ed.), *Creating a place for self-care and wellbeing in higher education: Finding meaning across academia* (pp. 147–158). Routledge.

Piff, P. K., Dietze, P., Feinberg, M., Stancato, D. M., & Keltner, D. (2015). Awe, the small self, and prosocial behavior. *Journal of Personality and Social Psychology, 108*(6), 883–899. https://doi.org/10.1037/pspi0000018

Powietrzynska, M., & Noble, L. (2021). Illuminating relational nature of teaching | learning using heuristic methodology. In K. Alexakos & K. Tobin (Eds.), *Transforming learning and teaching: Heuristics for educative and responsible practices* (pp. 189–206). Brill. https://doi.org/10.1163/9789004507609_010

Powietrzynska, M., Noble, L., O'Loughlin-Boncamper, S., & Azeez, A. (2021). Holding space for uncertainty and vulnerability: reclaiming humanity in teacher education through contemplative | equity pedagogy. *Cultural Studies of Science Education, 16,* 951–964. https://doi.org/10.1007/s11422-021-10035-x

Rabinowitch, T.-C., Cross, I., & Burnard, P. (2013). Long-term musical group interaction has a positive influence on empathy in children. *Psychology of Music, 41*(4), 484–498. https://doi.org/10.1177/0305735612440609

Rehm, J., & Shield, K. D. (2019). Global burden of disease and the impact of mental and addictive disorders. *Current Psychiatry Reports, 21*(10). https://doi.org/10.1007/s11920-019-0997-0

The Guardian (2022, October 31). 'We send our support': Coldplay perform Iranian protest song Baraye in Buenos Aires [Video]. YouTube. https://www.youtube.com/watch?v=aJb3uc1D1D8

Tobin, K. (2014). Twenty questions about cogenerative dialogues. In K. Tobin & A. Shady (Eds.), *Transforming urban education.* SensePublishers. https://doi.org/10.1007/978-94-6209-563-2_11

Vygotsky, L. S., & van der Veer, R., & Valsiner, J. (Eds.). (1994). *The Vygotsky reader.* (T. Prout, trans.). Basil Blackwell.

Chapter 8

Beware the awareness gap

A novel support framework for design education

Shaun Britton

Introduction

In the animation field, *character* typically refers to a fictional agent in a linear or interactive narrative. *Character design* then, refers to the development of said agents: here described as the drawn or sculpted iterative development of a person/animal/thing acting in stories and other designed experiences (NFG-Man, 2006; O'Neill, 2015).

I teach character design at university, having developed the first iteration of this delivery over 20 years ago. Currently, I teach into some of the classes, and manage a team of staff who complete delivery of these experiential, participatory art-experiences (Meyer & Wood, 2019). Typical students in these classes are enrolled in animation and game-design degrees.

We ask students in the unit to design across stages: from divergent ideas to convergent character design. Like other forms of iterative design (Nottingham, 2019, Chapter 2), students work contextually in each stage to solve a design problem – in this case: how do you make an engaging character? They gather appropriate visual research materials, and improve their abilities, along the way adhering to regular deadlines. Their final delivery is a detailed, digital design document housing their rough and more considered outcomes.

While students are passionate about their field, and exemplars in that space are colourful and affecting objects and experiences, the journey for students – from amateur admirers to professional practitioners – can be challenging. The gap between these states can be vast for some students, and teachers may struggle to support their disparate journeys. Students can like what they see in finished, professional art and animation – which can represent a lifetime of an artist's skill development – but be disappointed in their own outcomes which they see as falling short of that excellence. This is an *awareness gap*, where students can struggle to emulate what exemplars they see, without an understanding of the design prowess required.

It is important to show students how they start their journey with us; also, to show them what abilities they'll need thereafter to become experts. In a typical year, this is challenging. Post COVID-19 lockdowns, with students and

DOI: 10.4324/9781003457510-10

staff recovering from isolation and dealing with uncertainty, those challenges are exacerbated.

From typical in-person design instruction, through online delivery via software during isolation, we now deliver on-campus again, with a greater understanding of the effectiveness of different modes of delivery (Britton, 2022). With this knowledge, and because of pandemic-related stressors (Allen, 2020; Roccella, 2022), I saw the opportunity to develop a novel support-system to tackle these challenges, the visual component of which is intended to fill a gap in current design research.

This system is my *Depict, Collect, Select (DCS)* framework, which I use to support healthy learning and teaching for staff and students in my classes; it is a focus on their wellbeing and their empowerment to self-care. In this chapter, I outline the form and function of the DCS, present a look at its use on campus, and expound its industry and academic underpinning.

Iterative design classes: Character-art generation

Typical students in these 12-week, introductory design classes are in their first year of university, and some have never drawn a character or studied design. The axiom – everybody can be taught to draw – consequently underpins delivery. Teachers are from academia and/or the design industry and work as casual or permanent university staff; the foundational unit of classes sits within Bachelor-level Animation and Games degrees.

Our digital animation classrooms each house 24 students, who have access to desk space for traditional paper sketching/sculpture, a computer for design tasks, and a Wacom Cintiq screen (www.wacom.com) for digital sketching and animation. Therein, students move through an iterative design process, working through rough design concepts to one finished character, supported along the way with their collection of visual references and relevant information. We guide them to work with their own themes and characters in class, encouraging them to own their work and their journey. Characters are not animated here, instead drawn and sculpted, though simplicity of shape and form (Thesen, 2020) is encouraged for potential movement. For their final submission, students present a digital folio showing a gamut of design from rough thumbnail sketches to final graphics.

With this heterogeneity of students and need for imaginative outcomes, it is important to carefully structure learning and teaching but foster an inspirational, playful environment within those constraints. This dichotomy between creative exploration and focus reflects the positioning of this art form within the design industry, where outcomes can look frivolous and fun but are products that need to make money for clients. To emphasise this, we show commercially successful, fanciful exemplars in class, including designer toys, video games and animated shorts and features.

Specific industry processes and academic principles are embedded in the DCS framework. The former ensures that classes are industry relevant, and we use best-practice to shape design outcomes. The latter provides clear structure, to facilitate effective and manageable student/teacher collaboration, with healthy participation.

The Depict Collect Select (DCS) framework

The DCS framework is a combination of digital reference material, and a supporting pedagogy with that reference in focus. There are three DCS components:

1 A visual model (Image 8.1(a)): used to clarify process.
2 Task forms: used to personalise progress.
3 Supporting teaching delivery: used to support users of 1 and 2.

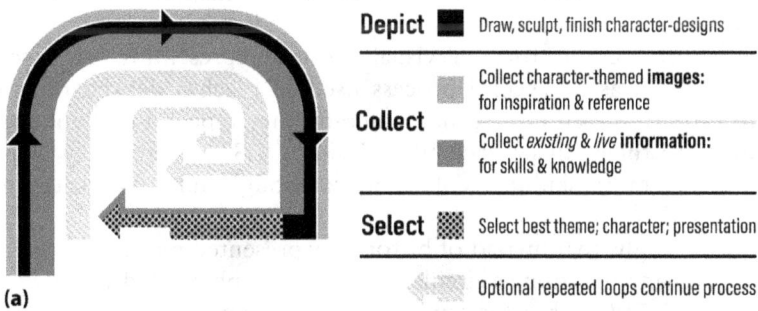

Depict ■ Draw, sculpt, finish character-designs

Collect
Collect character-themed **images:** for inspiration & reference

Collect *existing* & *live* **information:** for skills & knowledge

Select ▓ Select best theme; character; presentation

░ Optional repeated loops continue process

(a)

(b)

Image 8.1 The Depict, Collect, Select (DCS) visual model with description and design examples. (a) A single-task loop (and indication of suggested internal addition of two loops to continue design process). (b) Example of depiction that a three-task loop would represent

The visual model (1) depicts an interconnected set of activities needed to complete class exercises, providing a standard for users; students use the task forms (2) to customise their activities, these serving as their contextual repository of essential information; we employ the supportive delivery (3), using pedagogical and psychological concepts, and deliver these with a novel in-person use of online communication technology.

First DCS component: Visual model

In class, I use this pictorial interpretation of our design process for a first reference point, as most of our students are familiar with visual communication (Barnes, 2011); specifically, infographics, used to "help illustrate relationships between concepts and procedures, communicate processes, present the content of a lesson, and summarize important information" (Kuba & Jeong, 2023, p. 28).

There is a long history of visual models representing iterative design, described as a "cyclical process used to reach a desired outcome" (Sharp, 2019, p. 44). Our students iterate: they repeat a cycle of activity and improve their skillset each time. Using DCS parlance, they progressively depict more skilfully; collect more thoughtfully; and select more appropriately.

Unsurprisingly, that myriad of historically presented models share similar visuals, showing iteration as circular or looped graphics (Bydrec, 2021; Design Council, 2003), but for our needs there is a gap in knowledge there. Existing models typically simplify those cycles as solid graphic blocks with no internal detail. I extended this research by designing a model that details what happens in those stages – there are interconnected activities in there – which I feel better describes iteration in our classes (and iterative design generally).

This first component in the DCS framework, the DCS visual model, is shown in Image 8.1. The darker, singular graphic loop can be used to represent one collective design task (a) or repeated as a chain of tasks (the addition here of shaded loops within the first) to represent sequential development. An example of possible creative outcomes from this latter sum of three loops is shown in Image 8.1(b).

One DCS loop shows the eponymous collection of activities – depict, collect, select – undertaken during one design task. Repeated three times (adding internal loops), the graphic can represent, in this case, one class project of three tasks (Image 8.1(b)). For the latter, through each stage, the speed and detail of depiction, type of collection, and parameters of selection change, with students encouraged to think creatively and work contextually throughout. The three-loop model here represents an inward journey, from outer divergent to convergent (Dekker, 2020) character finalisation at its centre. One loop includes the co-dependent depict and collect activities, then a select activity undertaken before completion. Depict and collect form an organic arch, suggesting that this process is continual; select moves from a corner, straight back to task completion or a next loop, suggesting that this process slows for a moment as design outcomes are examined/considered/edited in the process.

I have carefully chosen each of the three words in the DCS acronym (with the *ict/ect* assonance as a mnemonic device) to describe the activities used in design iteration. In our classes, students draw, but they also physically sculpt and graphically finish characters, so the term draw, for example, would not adequately describe what happens here; they depict, or physically represent characters in different ways. Students draw pictures to describe character shape, sculpt a character to describe form, and finish characters with different media. They can use traditional techniques (pen/paper) or digital techniques (design software); they can traditionally (but not digitally) sculpt their characters (Spencer & Taylor, 2011).

In one loop, depiction is shown as a black line, moving between two types of collection: *images* and *information*. Students collect character-themed imagery for inspiration and for visual reference, graphically presented on the outside of each black line as constant support for effective depiction. Students also learn from gathering information, represented in the model by the line to the inside of the black line. Note the white line separating images but not information from depiction. This feature represents best-practice for image and information collection as it relates to depiction-support: images should be referred to but not copied; information is meant to infuse and shape depiction.

Students collect two types of information along the way: *skills* and *knowledge*. Skills include drawing practice and colour selection; knowledge includes concepts like gestalt theory (Behrens, 1998) and perspective (Montague, 2013). *Existing information* includes established skills and knowledge from academia and industry. *Live information* includes the dynamic, teacher feedback guiding student progress, and any information gathered from the observation of our surroundings: people, built and natural environments, et cetera.

While the depict and collect activities are interchangeable (i.e.: students have their own preference for what they do first, and often move between them), the third activity happens after these, before the next loop. Select is the process whereby students consider then pick the most appropriate designs to work with for a next stage. This choice is ideally with support from a teacher, based on the latter's understanding of what is required for subsequent loops. In the model, collect live information continues into select to show this desirable, supportive collaboration. The funnel-like shape for the select activity shows that some designs may be discarded at task-end; the halftone pattern represents both individual outcomes (with fewer characters in each loop) and a sieve used for sorting.

Overall, the DCS visual model graphically presents the importance of the interrelated activities contextually undertaken in a task: informed, iterative character *depiction*, the invariable *collection* of images and information as perennial support contiguous to this, and the role of informed *selection* at the culmination of a stage before the end of a process or the beginning of the next. Of prime importance here, is that effective design does not happen in a vacuum. From this model, for apprehensive participants, there is a clear outline of process, and a constant reminder that connection and support is advantageous and available.

Second DCS component: Task forms

With the visual model as reference for process, we can then help students personalise their progress by encouraging them to fill out one DCS task form per activity. This form is a simple text matrix (like a Microsoft Excel table) presented as an interactive PDF. Within the form, in interactive fields, students are expected to fill in details relating to the collective depiction, collection, and selection components of an activity. They contextualise their journey by describing their type of depiction, purpose of collection, and criteria for selection. As noted, early design iteration is rapid and wide-ranging (one task), subsequent development is more focussed consideration (next task) and so on.

Details in the form include: a student's outline of the speed, detail, and number of depictions (fast, more considered, many drawings?); type of collected information (reference photographs, information about perspective drawing?); and criteria for selection (most popular, most accurate, most colourful character?). This information helps a student identify what they need to advance, and how they personalise their progress. This archive is also intended to lessen the number of repeated questions to staff, as students hold their own information about class goals and personal project nuances. The task forms become more than general repositories in a focussed design stage when students work with their own themes beyond general iteration. Focussed themes could include, for example, designs of robots, bugs, or cats. Their collection support could then respectively include mechanical diagrams, animal imagery, or feline art they can learn from.

The DCS visual model is an infographic used for clarity and connection; the task forms are used as affirmation and exploration of those principles for a student's personal progress. If the model can be used as logistical support, the task forms are the start of emotional support (Bradley, 2010) where students can plan for subsequent creativity: they have a chance to enjoy themselves (drawing, sculpting, researching their favourite movies/games) when basic requirements are met.

Third DCS component: Delivery

I support the presentation and use of the DCS model and task forms with a specific teaching approach, employing fundamental pedagogical principles, psychological concepts, and technology for customisable but manageable delivery.

Fundamental pedagogy

It is important to ensure that we employ fundamental pedagogical principles in class to support students (and not assume that extensive industry experience translates to effective teaching (Naval, 2019)). We *chunk* learning material (Volz et al., 2019, p. 27) to allow students to focus on discrete packets, rather than too much information at once, exemplified in the grouping of class activity into stages. We *scaffold* support (p. 93) so students have targeted help when needed, then given independence once concepts are learned and design exploration is required. We *progressively disclose* information (p 85), which helps students keep their focus on present deliverables.

In the DCS model, these principles are reflected in the distinct visual arrangement of depict, collect, then select tasks (chunking), and its flexibility to add loops together as representation of progressive activity (scaffolding of tasks and progression disclosure of new ones).

Psychological concepts

Our familiarity with current psychology research about Self-Determination Theory (SDT) informs specific delivery of the DCS framework. SDT

> posits that the satisfaction of basic psychological needs for autonomy (i.e., volitional behaviour in accordance with one's values), competence (i.e., to experience mastery and feel effective), and relatedness with others (i.e., a sense of belonging and connectedness with others) are crucial to personal growth and wellbeing.
>
> Elphinstone et al. (2021, p. 1)

With this in mind, using the DCS toolkit, we encourage students to, respectively: have choice within their projects (as they personalise their progress), experience satisfaction with their work in scaffolded stages (by highlighting achievement during their process), and help us build physical and online community throughout their studies.

Use of technology (and timetable)

In addition to those principles, we engage with Discord (www.discord.com) – an online instant-messenger application – in physical classrooms for delivery. Used in the creative industry as a group communication tool, participants can send text and images to inform and inspire peers. While its operation as an industry staple would suggest its inclusion in class as appropriate, it is the novel use of its online features in a real-world setting that makes it beneficial within this framework.

We are now back in physical classrooms, after a period of online delivery during COVID-19 isolation. While unit expectations (activities; assessment) can translate well across modes, teacher delivery differs here. For example, we can give in-person, on-campus feedback (as verbal or drawn instruction) in the middle of activity as teachers move about a classroom. This traditional over-the-shoulder technique means most students receive timely information about the quality of their work in progress, but that feedback is limited to one individual (and a neighbour or two).

Online, during isolation, it was difficult to see students working, so we typically gave feedback at the end of a task, as students finished then presented onscreen or uploaded work for comment. Feedback came later in their process and students may have needed to backtrack to a more appropriate path, but we could share that feedback more readily to other students using distribution software.

Now back on campus, we use Discord, with a staggered set-up of class times and the help of multiple staff (and on occasion students) to provide constant student support, while managing staff wellbeing. We can offer constant summative feedback and distribute this widely.

We use the software like this: students can upload their depiction and collection to Discord at their individual computers in physical classrooms; teachers sit at the front of the class and provide feedback on those uploaded images, displayed on a projector for all to see. From here, if the student is comfortable with the request, we turn visual feedback into before-and-after animated gifs (Miltner & Highfield, 2017) then reupload that material to Discord for all the classes to see. We do the same for verbal or typed feedback about the quality of their image collections and advise on their selection needs as well.

While we expect all students to sign up to Discord and be present online, we give them choice for this student feedback – they can: lurk on Discord and not share their work; upload and receive private feedback in direct messages with teachers; upload and take part in public feedback. Whatever the choice, students see the plethora of growing feedback from their own and other classes in the design unit. Most students share publicly, a small number of students lurk digitally, and a smaller number still choose to receive physical feedback at their desks.

This flexibility can still be efficient and even enjoyable for staff, who can benefit from this type of delivery as well: we can produce drawn or typed feedback and leverage its impact (in front of the class to 20-something students, and over Discord to hundreds); as practitioners we can produce art live, engaging students in the showing and ourselves in the making (Case, 2022). This means we limit our need to repeat ourselves for individuals (lowering stressful staff workloads), students respect our ability to professionally produce what they aspire to, and we can create (something pracademics may miss doing (Mynott & Zimmatore, 2022)).

If staff have finished class feedback, we can move onto queued feedback from other classes, sitting in Discord. With careful attention, some exceptional students can also provide feedback to their peers (beyond the usual support they give each other), as long as other students have a choice about who they collect feedback from (by direct-messaging specific individuals/groups within the software using the @teacher, @student features). It is essential that those reviewers be positive and compassionate to students and align with teacher delivery. With a staggering of class times through a given week, with teachers working within their own class times, students can receive feedback across multiple days outside of their assigned class as they complete homework activity.

Two final notes here about this novel use of technology. One: our in-person use of online technology, by multiple staff, aims to alleviate the potentially negative effects of mediated communication (Conway & Britton, 2023; Forbes & Gedera, 2019) where a lack of purely online social cues could lead to miscommunication. Staff can guide the online community to positive connection, and use software features for rarely needed, more dramatic control (*kick off* and *mute* participants, for example). Two: beyond supporting the mental health of participants, this approach favours good physical health too. On our return to classes after pandemic isolation, understandably apprehensive participants were worried about physical distancing in physical locations. The ability to offer remote feedback in a physical space is still an advantage in these uncertain times.

Discussion

We use the DCS model, forms, and delivery to promote wellbeing and self-care in my character design classes. As students try to bridge their awareness gaps, we try to: lower their anxiety of uncertainty (by clearing up process – SDT Competence); encourage them to engage in self-care and enjoy their tasks (by giving them ownership of their progress – SDT Autonomy); and focus on the wellbeing of students and staff using a novel mix of pedagogy, psychology, and technology. Personally, use of the model and the forms take some load off my delivery (as a back-up method of information presentation), and the setup of online sharing means that staff can help each other monitor progress and provide feedback across spaces. Overall, this support allows me to manage and teach into the unit more effectively, and to focus more on my wellbeing and self-care.

The design and features of the DCS model include detail about the interconnected activities within each task, information typically lacking from the visual interpretations of iterative process in contemporary design research. Perhaps concerns about the importance of simplified depiction kept designers from adding in detail, but in our case, I believe we have an informative (but appropriately simplified) tool that meets our needs.

The design of the task forms is intended to foster autonomy in students, so they have choice about the designs they produce and the decisions they make. They can gather information from disparate sources and shape their progress with this repository of relevant personal data, for a chance to enjoy subsequent creativity.

Our delivery includes: the use of pedagogical principles (sometimes lacking in a tertiary environment taught by industry experts); psychological concepts (which current research tells us is useful for wellbeing); and the novel use of technology (guiding and maximising the efforts of staff and students).

Limitations to this research includes the abstract nature of the visual model, and the need for DCS teachers to have strong, varied skillsets. Additionally, we are in the initial stages of DCS use, at this point in writing at the end of the first semester of its utilisation. I will need to collect data about DCS use in class, to provide more than general information about the intention of its setup and its degree of effectiveness for delivery and support.

Of the abstract nature of the DCS visuals: some individuals may struggle with making semantic connections between graphics and the activities they represent. For these students, we deliver in different ways (verbally or with further demonstration) but this can lessen the efficiency that the DCS could provide.

Of the delicate balance needed for effective and supportive delivery: this can be challenging and does require the strict management of participants, technology, and logistics. Dedicated staff need to confidently depict in front of a physical and online community, simultaneously identifying what needs improving and fashioning the best feedback. We currently have capable, talented staff; unfamiliar staff may struggle with these unique requirements.

For the research that would add to our understanding of the DCS framework: data are needed to test its current effectiveness and future refinements. For example, of interest are the factors that determine the type of participation students are comfortable with; additionally, whether animating elements in the visual model would improve its effectiveness. A look at the interconnectedness and complexity of the DCS framework, in part or whole, is also warranted.

Anecdotally, what is pleasantly surprising about the use of the DCS in class so far has been the willingness of first year students to share their work, receive and offer feedback, and embrace the use of the model and task forms. The framework does seem to show potential, and I look forward to exploring its effectiveness with quantitative and qualitative analysis.

DCS framework: Strategy for design educators

While I use the DCS framework to support character design delivery, it is suitable for use across iterative-design education outside of that speciality. Some suggestions here, for use of the DCS, in part or in full, for support in your classroom or practice.

Use the DCS model:

- To learn about and/or clearly present the interconnected activities needed for effective iterative design development.

Use task forms:

- To organise overarching project-related information.
- To contextualise information during more advanced stages of a project, where individual refinements to output are helpful.

Use the specific delivery technique:

- To help structure and time the presentation of learning material.
- To support the wellbeing of staff/students and encourage them to self-care.
- To offer consistent support and feedback to students, at the same time making the process sustainable (and even enjoyable) for staff.

Consider some DCS features:

- Pracademics can practice; staff have visual and text-based backup; their feedback can be leveraged; their workload is more manageable.
- Students can help themselves and each other; they choose their level of engagement; they use all or parts of the DCS framework to better navigate their awareness gap.

Conclusion

With the COVID-19 pandemic disrupting traditional learning spaces, something needed to be done differently to engage overwhelmed participants during their challenging design studies upon their return to physical classrooms. With this in mind, and lessons learned from our previous, reactive online delivery, I developed and use my Depict Collect Select (DCS) framework in my character design classes – a system also appropriate for use across general iterative design education. It consists of three components: a visual model, standardising process for participants; task forms, personalising learning; and specific delivery, selectively employing pedagogy, psychology, and technology as further support.

The artefacts and instruction are intended to help students and staff bridge the awareness gap – the perceived and real difference between a student's current abilities and what they need to professionally practice. Exemplars in animation and games are affecting, but the rigorous process to gather skills to make them is demanding; students can struggle to see their path from here to there, and staff can struggle to support them.

The first component in the DCS system is a visual model, which presents the design process as a set of three activities needed for success: depiction of designs, collection of images and information, and the subsequent selection of designs for a next stage or outcome. The model includes elements from existing visual models but adds to the study of design research by filling a gap there: now including information about the interconnectedness of activity within those previously opaque representations.

The second artefact, task forms, are used to personalise student journeys; they can add overarching or specific information pertinent to a student's project. This is a repository of information useful for their progress; a second hub of information as companion to the model acting as a visual guide to process.

The third component is a specific teaching delivery, supporting the use of the first two artefacts. With this: information is clearly and thoughtfully presented in a timely manner; the wellbeing and care of participants is of prime importance; and staff can offer constant summative feedback to students and look after themselves in the process.

A recently developed framework, the logical next steps are to gather data from participants about its use, so its effectiveness can be measured, informed refinements suggested, and its use beyond its current limited application tested.

References

Allen, K. (2020). Belonging in an age of technology. In C. McMahon (Ed.), *Psychological insights for understanding Covid-19 and media and technology* (pp. 72–85). Routledge.

Barnes, S. B. (2011). *An introduction to visual communication: From cave art to Second Life*. Peter Lang.

Behrens, R. R. (1998). Art, design and gestalt theory. *Leonardo (Oxford)*, 31(4), 299–303. https://doi.org/10.2307/1576669

Bradley, S. (2010). Designing for a hierarchy of needs. *Smashing Magazine*. https://www.smashingmagazine.com/2010/04/designing-for-a-hierarchy-of-needs/

Britton, S. (2022). Interactive immanence. *Visual Communication Quarterly*, 29(2), 136–144. https://doi.org/10.1080/15551393.2022.2059665

Bydrec (2021). *A comprehensive comparison between the agile, scrum, and waterfall methodology*. Bydrec. https://blog.bydrec.com/a-comprehensive-comparison-between-the-agile-scrum-and-waterfall-methodology

Case, C. (2022). *The handbook of art therapy*. Routledge.

Conway, S., & Britton, S. (2023). Let's argue! Designing satire in digital games. *Design Issues*, 39(2), 41–56. https://doi.org/10.1162/desi_a_00716

Dekker, T. den (2020). *Design thinking*. Noordhoff Uitgevers.

Design Council (2003). The double diamond. Design Council. https://www.design-council.org.uk/our-resources/the-double-diamond/

Elphinstone, B., Egan, P., & Whitehead, R. (2021). Greater autonomous motivation for study and basic psychological need satisfaction by being presently aware and 'letting go': An exploration of mindful attention and nonattachment. *Motivation and Emotion, 45*(1), 1–12. https://doi.org/10.1007/s11031-020-09836-4

Forbes, D., & Gedera, D. (2019) From confounded to common ground: Misunderstandings between tertiary teachers and students in online discussions. *Australasian Journal of Educational Technology, 35*(4). https://doi.org/10.14742/ajet.3595

Kuba, R., & Jeong, A. (2023). Demystifying visual design: A sequential analysis of design processes in infographic visual composition. *Journal of Visual Literacy, 42*(1), 26–47. https://doi.org/10.1080/1051144X.2023.2168394

Meyer, M., & Wood, L. (2019). Rethinking the roles of the art educator as participatory artist, researcher and teacher (P)ART: A South African perspective. *International Journal of Education through Art, 15*(3), 265–280. https://doi.org/10.1386/eta_00002_1

Miltner, K. M., & Highfield, T. (2017). Never gonna GIF you up: Analyzing the cultural significance of the animated GIF. *Social Media + Society, 3*(3), 205630511772522. https://doi.org/10.1177/2056305117725223

Montague, J. (2013). *Basic perspective drawing: A visual approach.* Wiley.

Mynott, J. P., & Zimmatore, M. (2022). Pracademic productive friction: Boundary crossing and pressure points. *Journal of Professional Capital and Community, 7*(1), 45–56. https://doi.org/10.1108/JPCC-11-2020-0093

Naval, E. (2019). *The curse of knowledge.* University Center for Assessment, Teaching and Technology. https://ucatt.arizona.edu/news/curse-knowledge

NFGMan (2006). *Character design for mobile devices: Mobile games, sprites and pixel art.* Rotovision.

Nottingham, A. (2019). *The graphic design process: How to be successful in design school.* Bloomsbury Visual Arts. https://doi.org/10.5040/9781350050815

O'Neill, R. (2015). *Digital character development: Theory and practice.* A. K. Peters.

Roccella, M. (2022). *The impact of the COVID-19 emergency on the quality of life of the general population.* MDPI – Multidisciplinary Digital Publishing Institute.

Sharp, J. (2019). *Iterate: Ten lessons in design and failure.* MIT Press.

Spencer, S., & Taylor, R. (2011). Sculpting, from traditional to digital. In S. Spencer & R. Taylor (Eds.), *ZBrush character creation* (Chapter one). Wiley.

Thesen, T. P. (2020). Reviewing and updating the 12 principles of animation. *Animation: An Interdisciplinary Journal, 15*(3), 276–296.

Volz, A., Higdon, J., & Lidwell, W. (2019). *The elements of education for teachers: 50 research-based principles every educator should know.* Routledge.

Chapter 9

Doing things differently through the lenses of Gestalt philosophy and practice-based learning

A hopeful outlook on the benefits of co-creating with students to support wellbeing for the Higher Education community

Julia Ouzia[1] and Estrella Sendra

Introduction

This dialogical chapter, co-authored by a psychologist and trainee Gestalt practitioner, and a cultural industries researcher with a common interest in critical and creative pedagogy (Ouzia, 2022; Sendra, 2020), emerges from an optimistic perspective that transformation of Higher Education (HE) towards a sustainably thriving and hopeful community is possible. It departs from the shared curiosity of exploring what this may look like. Inspired by bell hooks' "pedagogy of hope" (2003) and Gestalt philosophy (Perls et al., 1951/1994), our aim is to introduce a *Gestalt-informed hopeful pedagogy*, and to present a compelling case for the importance of such hopeful pedagogy for the wellbeing of the entire HE community. Despite the increasing interest in hope and education (e.g., Freire, 1992/2014; hooks, 2003; Zembylas, 2022), academic discussions based on empirical research and practical experience remain scarce. Similarly, although Gestalt philosophy has informed a wealth of literature on organisational development, only few have commented on its applicability to pedagogic practice (e.g., Bourgault du Coudray, 2020). Given Gestalt philosophy's emphasis on raising awareness through relational contact in the pursuit of change (ibid), exploring the links between its theoretical assumptions and pedagogic practice seems a worthwhile endeavour. Throughout this chapter, we will focus on a specific practice-led third-year undergraduate module, titled 'Events and Festivals: From Conception to Realization' (E&F), as a way of illustrating the intersections of hooks' pedagogy of hope and Gestalt philosophy in our educational practice. The result is a seven-element model encompassing (1) community care; (2) embodied lived experience, (3) creative, and experiential learning; (4) active listening; (5) horizontal collaboration; (6) contextual consideration/engaging with the wider society; and (7) hope.

DOI: 10.4324/9781003457510-11

Our analysis questions the ways in which hopeful horizontal co-creation between students and educators and practice-led learning can contribute to wellbeing in HE. Creative learning and assessment methods, as applied in E&F, convert the classroom into a hopeful and creative situated learning environment that favours reflection on the transformative, active role we all have in the world around us. We will start by offering an overview of E&F and the outcome of its co-creation, the CMCI Winter Festival, 'The Festival' hereafter. This student-led creative project was precisely the event where we, Estrella and Julia, met, and it inspired this interdisciplinary co-authored chapter. We will then introduce the two key theoretical frameworks put in dialogue in this chapter to examine this practice-led module; hope and Gestalt philosophy.[2]

We hope that, by sharing this pedagogic practice, we can make both a theoretical contribution as well as encourage a methodological intervention. In co-authoring this chapter, we have collaboratively embarked on the journey of questioning what the goal of HE is, what the expected skills to be learned both by students and us as educators are, and whether we are missing skills that can foster wellbeing. This chapter and the framework introduced within are, in essence, an overview of some of the answers we have found to these questions and the process we have gone through to make sense of them. Ultimately, we invite educators to be creative and experimental through the adoption of a Gestalt-informed hopeful pedagogy; to rethink their pedagogy collaboratively with students whilst paying attention to the wider context they operate within.

Co-curating the third-year undergraduate module 'Events and Festivals: From Conception to Realization'

E&F is a module which, as its name suggests, has been informed by hopeful *excitement* from its conception to its realisation. We highlight the word excitement because this has rarely been the subject of academic enquiry in relation to HE (hooks, 1994). Excitement is, however, a crucial element of engaged pedagogy, an embodiment of the love entailed in pedagogic practice. It is also a defining feature of festivals. In the academic year 2022/23, further factors contributed to fostering excitement among class members – students and educators (Sendra, 2020); the module would be delivered for the first time with the first cohort of the BA Culture, Media and Creative Industries in King's College London (KCL). Thus, the excitement was intrinsically linked to a promise (and hope) of upcoming celebrations.

These students had been significantly impacted by the global COVID-19 pandemic; there had been almost nonexistent opportunities for social encounters and community building, other than those mediated by screens. E&F was the first practice-led module where students were faced with the challenge of co-curating and co-producing a three-day festival within a set timeframe of only 10 weeks. This was arguably a daunting task that could only be realised through hope. Modelling such excitement and hope was a given responsibility for Estrella as the convenor, whose excitement was supported by her recent appointment as a lecturer. The module was designed, or rather co-curated, as a production plan composed of weekly phases, informed by theory, research and practice, and structured through a series of practical formative assessments. As explained in the syllabus, the module brings students together to work in collaborative teams in the planning, development, and execution of The Festival. It aims to encourage collaborative public-facing project realisa-tion, reflection on professional practice and creative skills, and consideration of the steps involved in planning and executing a series of festival events. In 2022/23, it was assessed through a two-part creative portfolio, a 2,000-word group festival report, documenting the process and outcomes of the delivery of an event as part of The Festival, and a 2,000-word individual self-reflective commentary.[3]

The success of this experiment, leading to the celebration of a very well at-tended first edition of The Festival, with the theme 'Embracing Youth', was rooted in, and indeed made possible because of, collaboration and care. Whilst I, Estrella, had the privilege to design this module from scratch, informed by my own research and working practice, I am indebted to the then BA programme director, Kate Macmillan, for her administrative support and for securing the funding for the event, arranged by Flo Cowan, the then Business Support Manager. Thanks also goes to Johanna Kieniewicz, Head of Educa-tion and Research Collaborations in The Culture Team at KCL for agreeing to partner up with us to realise the festival events in the Inigo Rooms, at Som-erset House, London.

All these individuals expressed and demonstrated full trust in Estrella's abil-ity to lead a module that posed obvious challenges due to its logistics and the large student cohort of almost 150 students. What followed was an end-less chain of collaboration and support. The teaching team was composed of two lecturers, Estrella and Natalie Wreyford; three seminar tutors, including Estrella, Natalie and David Francis; two external guest speakers, the film cu-rator, impact producer and author, Nadia Denton, and Kate Ward, a Lead Management Consultant and Counterculture Partner; as well as internal guest speakers, namely Vinicious de Carvalho, Vice Dean of the Faculty of Social Science and Public Policy; Alison Duthie, Director of Programming in The Culture Team and various colleagues of hers, who advised students in the pre-production phase, namely Jocelyn Cheek, Matt Fryer, Saly Pembroke, and Amy Murat. They all acted as Advisory Board members of the event, facilitat-ing, advising, and making resources and tools available for students to be able to apply and perform their creativity.

These multiple voices and experiences fostered a safe and supportive learn-ing environment where students felt comfortable taking risks and putting their creativity into practice. Contact was not limited to the classroom, but ex-tended outside of it, across the campus, in public and private spaces inhabited by class members, or online, through close teamwork. Students proactively appointed further contributors that would enrich their events by providing more resources or exciting activities, while enhancing the social impact and transformative dimension of their events. Colleagues in the department spread the word, contributing to audience building. It was a community effort, driven by the promise and hope for a successful outcome.

The opening ceremony, celebrated a couple of days prior to the festival, was illustrative of the degree of collaboration, and the support and admiration from fellow students and tutors impressed by the achievement of the CMCI students. Despite a train strike and the snowy weather, the Great Hall at KCL was crowded with students, family, friends, and CMCI colleagues as well as staff members across the faculty. Some of the charities which had partnered with events sent representatives who gave short speeches. The environment was one of absolute joy and pride, of the confirmation of what was possible, and with it, articulation and performance of ideas about the world. This was precisely the way in which success was celebrated in the opening words by Estrella. Students had made history in curating The Festival, "their story challenging Euro-patriarchal biases of knowledge, carefully and collectively curating their own stories of the world".[4] It included this opening ceremony, and 14 different events across three days featuring a series of interactive identity-based multidisciplinary exhibitions and activities, on themes including sustainability, gender, queer cultures, migration, and body-positivity.

Image 9.1 Students at The Festival, in the event called 'Under the Reminiscing Tree'
Photo source: Emma Lupianez (2022).

The Festival itself was no different in its collaborative ethos. The tireless and problem-solving skilled Matt Fryer, Head of Business and Operations in The Culture Team, had made himself available for the festival set-up, quickly improvising transformations of the space into an exciting festival venue. Students further collaborated with one another. They efficiently coordinated and produced The Festival, but also supported each other's work, either as artists, co-producers, interior designers, donors of objects for display, or audience members. CMCI colleagues also attended and actively participated in the events.

The image above is an excellent illustration of the hopeful environment at The Festival, and of the 'festivalisation' of this university space into a culturally engaging place to dream of possible futures, 'under the Reminiscing Tree'. This featured the work of two artists: DJ Ruairidh Johnston and arts student Olivia Delacour. Johnston had cabled plants and connected them to a sound system via a laptop, producing music and showing different soundwaves, depending on the way in which the plants were touched. The space was decorated and illuminated in an intimate way, with a sculpture of a tree built specifically for the festival by an arts student from the University of the Arts London, Olivia Delacour. A video on continuous display revealed the process of making the tree. There was also a table with stationery and cans. Participants were invited to reflect deeply on their relationship with climate change and the environment and to write messages or dreams for the future, customising and decorating the cans, which were then left under or on the reminiscing tree. It was during the following event that we, the authors, met each other. The curators of 'A Conversation about Mental Health' had made a short film with students speaking about their mental health, drawing on issues such as the pandemic and the expectations made upon a diverse body of university students. Julia delivered a short presentation about Gestalt philosophy, and within the joyful, festive environment, a safe space emerged where all were welcome to think about our mental health. We soon realised the strong link between what was being presented and what was being performed; that is, between Gestalt philosophy and The Festival – a performance of practice-led learning, and of the hope that it is possible to generate happiness and wellbeing in the classroom (hooks, 2003).

Conceptualising hope in Higher Education

We have spoken about hope, but what is it? Hope is a basic human need. As one of the leading scholars on critical pedagogy puts it, in his emblematic proposal of *Pedagogy of Hope* (Freire, 1992/2014), derived from his earlier groundbreaking work, "we need critical hope the way a fish needs unpolluted water" (p. 2). Paulo Freire makes it clear that this cannot just be a theoretical value or idea: "[H]ope, as an ontological need, demands an anchoring in practice" (ibid). Further, hope is an indispensable ingredient of dreams.

It is needed for any social struggle, as a motivation and belief in a possible transformation.

Twenty years ago, radical educator bell hooks published *Teaching Community: A Pedagogy of Hope* (2003), emphasising the importance of hope in education, and optimistic that there are ways towards justice, and that this can be achieved, at least to some extent, through applied and situated knowledge. As Michalinos Zembylas puts it, "to speak of hope, it is to speak about the capacity or drive of humans for a better future against all odds" (2022, p. 28). When brought to education, hope creates fruitful spaces of resistance, of rejection of the status quo, and of constructing alternative futures rehearsed in the present (ibid). And yet, offering a hopeful outlook to young people has been considered as a major challenge of teaching (Boyd, 2020). It requires the educator to engage in activism, to be hopeful about students' potential to play a role in the struggle for social justice (ibid). Hope can thus be seen as a catalyst for activism, in that "knowledge can and should be used to amplify human freedom and promote social justice, not simply to create profits or future careers" (Giroux, 2007, p. 40). The range of themes curated and performed in The Festival are illustrative of the possibilities of expression and performance of desires for social change that can emerge from the context of a classroom, when put into practice through creative learning and assessment methods. Through their co-curated events, class members were hopeful that another world was possible, more sustainable, more inclusive, embracing youth in an intersectional and plural world. The embracement of hope does not come without risks. A hopeful pedagogy is thus one shaped by courage (Giroux, 2007) and acknowledgement of vulnerability (hooks, 1994), of the high chances of making mistakes, of normalising the appearance of these and of adopting a problem-solving approach that differs from what Freire referred to as the "banking education system", where students are passive learners and recipients of the knowledge deposited by tutors (1970/2018, p. 72). A problem-solving approach to education often requires action, that is, practice-led learning. It departs from an understanding of students as reflexive "transformers of the world" (Freire 1970/2018, pp. 27-29). Practice-led learning is a creative form of pedagogy that understands "education as the practice of freedom", a perspective theorised and performed by Freire (1970/2018) which has inspired radical and critical educators, such as hooks.

Gestalt philosophy and hooks' pedagogy of hope

We now aim to outline the ways in which the pedagogical approach employed in the E&F module can be viewed through the lens of Gestalt philosophy and hooks' pedagogy of hope. Gestalt philosophy informs a humanistic psychotherapeutic modality developed by Frederick ("Fritz") and Lore ("Laura") Perls and Paul Goodman in the first half of the twentieth century, also referred to as Gestalt Therapy (GT).[5] GT was comprehensively introduced in a seminal text authored by Perls et al. (1951/1994) as a wholistic approach working in the here-and-now with what is *figural* for a client, i.e. what is most concerning in the present moment, whilst also being mindful of their ground, that is, their history, and the wider circumstances of their life. Notably, GT relies heavily on experiential learning where a client explores their current context with the support of their therapist to facilitate their awareness of the many mechanisms which may influence it (Zinker, 1977). This is part of the basis from which an argument can be made that Gestalt philosophy and education can and, in fact, do intersect (Bourgault du Coudray, 2020) and, indeed, corresponds to Perls et al.'s initial intent to support not only therapists, but also to provide a framework for educators, medical professionals, and the general public to rely on (1951/1994). To fully determine the intersection of Gestalt philosophy and critical pedagogy, it is worth considering the pillars Gestalt therapy rests on (Bourgault du Coudray, 2020): dialogic relating, phenomenological method, field theory, and experimentation[6].

1) Dialogic relating

GT is markedly influenced by the thinking of philosopher Martin Buber (1958/1970) who distinguished between *I–It* and *I–Thou* relating. Notably, these two forms of relating are both essential for human survival and wellbeing; they highlight the difference between *doing and achieving* in a relationship (I–It) versus *being* in a relationship (I–Thou; Mann, 2021). In therapeutic practice, client and therapist may rely on I–It relating when drawing up a therapeutic contract, whilst in moments of connection and/or resonance, the ground is laid for I–Thou relating. Correspondingly, GT aims to achieve this moment of true meeting through embodied presence, inclusion, and confirmation.

This pillar resonates with the dialogic and collaborative dimension of critical pedagogy and of the E&F module. Dialogic relating requires coming together, an act that "strengthens community" (hooks, 2003, p. 36). The shift from problem-perception to excitement only happens through true meeting of team-members. This requires the willingness and ability to read "the emotional climate" (ibid, p. 133) of class members, and initiating conversation through care and love.

Dialogic relating also involves an acknowledgement of each individual and their potential contributions, the hope that we all have something to bring to a collective project. As hooks notes, "as a classroom community, our capacity to generate excitement is deeply affected by our interest in one another, in hearing one another's voices, in recognizing one another's presence" (1994, p. 8). As the screened documentary film shows (https://youtu.be/dsy0aLrWGho?si=DKLBDD1p1KqoYJap), The Festival was characterised by excitement, highly relying on the recognition of achievement. The student who acted as the festival producer explicitly referred to this in their opening speech: "This is an exciting moment for all of us". There was a sense of accomplishment recognised by staff members throughout the ceremony. Marion Thain, Executive Dean of the Faculty of Arts and Humanities, claimed enthusiastically: "This is an extraordinarily incredible moment". In a similar tone, Kate Macmillan expressed pride: "I am so proud of students in this CMCI cohort – amazing". Suggesting that in a time of large cohort sizes and high workloads, the possibility of I–Thou relating in HE may seem idealistic and utopian. In keeping with Gestalt philosophy, we invite the reader to notice their embodied reaction to our words. Here we argue that Buber's ideas are scalable if considered a general philosophical approach to education. We suggest that embracing hope in HE is a brave act that can foster a horizontal, safe learning environment. This is based on trusting, respectful, caring and acknowledged interdependence which leads to a kind of satisfaction that differs from the personal, self-centered one intrinsic in a capitalist neoliberal system. Instead, the satisfaction deriving from hope relates to the awareness of the role that students – like every person – have in the creative transformation of the world. This individual awareness derives from a situated collective experience of co-creation and dialogue, which fosters a sense of wellbeing which is also of a collective dimension, since it derives from a shared action within a context of horizontalism – another concept found in GT, promoting equal importance of all experiences and ideas.

Horizontalism fosters empowerment and, correspondingly, when students were asked to share tips with future producers of The Festival, they were encouraging students to enjoy the agency attributed to them, with phrases like: "Go big! Dream big!" or "Try whatever ideas you have. Even the crazy ones!". This invitation was illustrative of the transformation in the perception of creative learning experiences. As hooks notes, sometimes, due to "the fixation on degrees rather than education", there is an initial "resistance to forms of learning that are not based on rote memory or predictable assignments" (2003, p. 130). HE and the very often precarious and unpredictable job market have fostered a disruptive environment of competition in the classroom (ibid). Horizontalism, we argue, is essential for a thriving HE community. It is our role as educators to elicit this experience in our students. In doing so, we of course need to hold that power dynamics are an inherent part of academia, where the assessor meets the assessed and, in many countries, the paid staff meets the paying student. It is up to us to demonstrate to students that these power dynamics do not influence how we meet them in dialogue. Only if students feel met, understood, and respected will they take ownership of their work and succeed.

2) Phenomenological method

The phenomenological method relies on the thinking of Edmund Husserl and was applied to therapeutic practice by Ernesto Spinelli (2005). At the heart of the phenomenological approach is the therapist's effort to get as close to the client's experience as possible. The reader may note that commitment to dialogue and the phenomenological method are intrinsically linked and, indeed, Gestalt philosophy proposes a wholistic perspective with the individual at its core (Perls et al., 1951/1994). Phenomenological interventions support the here-and-now focus of GT by emphasising what is evident in the present.

The link between phenomenology and pedagogy is probably strongest when, as educators, we assess our students. Indeed, the commonly championed assessment for learning approach (Sambell et al., 2013) promotes the agency of the learner to make sense of their own learning in authentic tasks. In E&F, students are required to provide the initial evaluation of their work through a group festival report. This is complemented by an individual self-reflexive commentary. Educators need to outline how well this has been achieved. In doing so, we bracket our own interpretation of the material to a certain extent, describe our understanding of what the student has provided, and allow every argument to hold equal value, if it is convincingly presented. Especially in authentic or creative assessments (e.g., podcasts, blog posts, video essays, etc.), what is being assessed is not only the accuracy of the material included, but also the experience of engaging with it. This is in itself a relational experience between educator and student, in that the student provides an experience for the educator to respond to. During The Festival, educators embodied the space through active participation and engagement with the event documentation and evaluation submitted by students. Each event feedback took shape of a review which then was included in a The Festival Catalogue,[7] a resource for future cohorts.

3) Field theory

Field theory is a social psychological theory originally proposed by Kurt Lewin (1943). Broadly speaking, the theory posits that a person's behaviour is influenced by their environment. Contemporary thinking around a field theoretical approach in GT has expanded on this notion to encourage practitioners to consider that everything impacts everything else and is potentially relevant (Parlett, 1991).

The relevance of field theory to educational practice is arguably one of the most figural elements of our time. Current efforts to decolonise curricula and promote disability inclusion are direct responses to what is happening in the wider field. We have become increasingly aware of the areas in which education has, to date, perpetuated systems of power and privilege and it took a global pandemic, an all-encompassing disruption in the field, to accelerate this work. Importantly, the field in which our students and we as educators operate is dynamic, highlighting the importance of creating systems that can cope with change sustainably. As such, education through a field-theoretical lens pays attention to what is happening in wider society at any given moment in time.

In a module such as E&F, the wider field can, at times, conflict with the reality of a tight deadline, which can lead to moments of friction among team members. The module addresses this in a week entitled 'Event Planning: How to Plan for When Things Go Wrong', designed and facilitated by Natalie, where students are invited to consider all possible scenarios. Here realism was quickly transformed into a hopeful safe space conveying key skill in festival production. After being given a few minutes to imagine the worst possible scenarios tutors adopted a rather performative tone: "Guys, I heard your event went so wrong. What happened?" This triggered laughter among many students. However, the seriousness of this fun learning experience was quickly noticed when they were invited to be constructive and creatively come up with solutions: "What did you do about it? What could you have done to avoid it?" This led to the production of a risk assessment and preventative problem-solving plan. Class members realised the transferrable skills in student feedback: "multi-tasking, problem solving, time management, leadership skills". Based on this practical experience, students featuring in the film conveyed an optimistic message to future festival producers: "Don't stress yourself. It will go well at the end!"; "Believe in the project"; or "Don't forget to have fun while you do it!

4) Experimentation

Whilst the literature commonly references three pillars, an experimental attitude is arguably foundational to GT as well as our chapter. As outlined above, the purpose of an experiment is to raise awareness for the client. Probably the most famous experiments in GT are the empty chair and the two-chair experiments, inspired by the work of psychodramatist Jacob Moreno. In short, the experiments allow the client to engage with a person (or a part of themselves) through dialogue and/or embodiment, supporting the client to explore how they relate to what is figural for them. In practice, experiments can be as small as suggesting a change in a hand movement or tone of voice, and as large as reenactments of situations as seen in mono- or psychodramas.

The Festival, like the module, was an experiment. The only guarantees that it would happen were, first and foremost, hope and planning. This led to several expressions of surprise among student feedback, such as: "We weren't sure if this was gonna work out until it actually did happen". However, its success was not an undeserved miracle. Students were vocal about the labour put in this festival: "We really put our blood, tears and sweat into this".

Towards integration: Conceptualising a Gestalt-informed hopeful pedagogy

The overlap between hooks' pedagogy of hope and Gestalt philosophy is striking. Both advocate for a relational, experiential, horizontal, and field-theoretical approach to learning about oneself and others. Notably, hope is considered an essential resource in GT (Joyce & Sills, 2018). In education, "when teachers work to affirm the emotional wellbeing of students, we are doing the work of love" (hooks, 2003, p. 133). Furthermore, both lines of thinking make the fundamental assumption that humans are inherently good and thrive in an environment which supports them in their uniqueness.

Writing this chapter has left both of us hopeful that by rethinking pedagogy, by doing things differently, we can achieve wellbeing in higher education and beyond. The question we asked ourselves here continuously is fundamental in nature: what *is* HE? Based on the literature we discussed and integrated here, we would propose the argument that HE is a place of meeting in service of

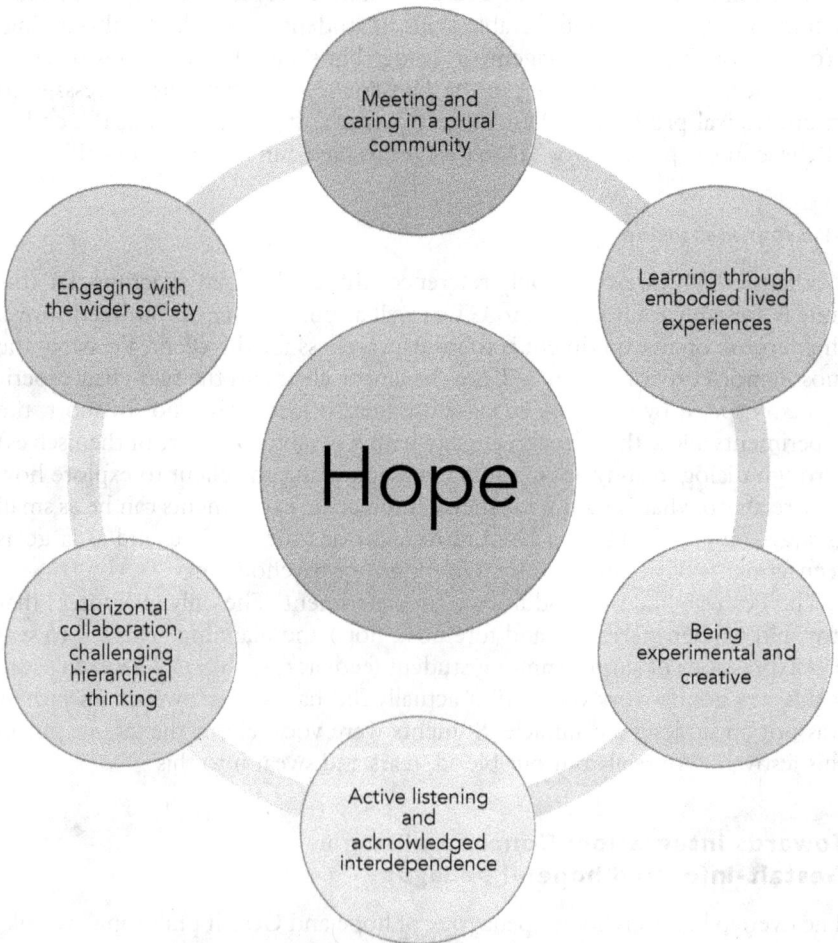

Image 9.2 Gestalt-informed hopeful pedagogy

society – whether we generate new knowledge, educate future professionals, or challenge established views of thinking, everything we do operates within the wider context of society, and any framework conceptualising our work must account for this. As such, our proposal for a Gestalt-informed hopeful pedagogy rests on the following principles which interlink, as illustrated in Image 9.2:

1 **Meeting and caring in a plural community** that operates at the intersection of our similarities and difference.
2 **Learning through embodied lived experiences** in a way that allows us to feel the impact of what we are learning.
3 **Being experimental and creative** in a way that promotes the creative and experimental expression of individuals.
4 **Active listening and acknowledged interdependence** in order to foster a safe and inclusive environment where students are aware of their individual agency.
5 **Horizontal collaboration, challenging hierarchical thinking** to allow students to make sense of their own learning.
6 **Engaging with the wider society** – only in doing so can we be of service to it, and to each other.
7 And finally, at the centre of it all, **hope**.

Notes

1 Corresponding author, julia.ouzia@kcl.ac.uk.
2 A short film about the 2023 festival made by Estrella can be accessed online via YouTube (8 December 2023): https://youtu.be/dsy0aLrWGho?si=DKLBDD1p1KqoYJap.
3 This assessment method has then been changed to a three-part creative assessment: a group creative project (the event itself – 50%), a group festival report (20%), and an individual commentary (30%). This is in order to recognise their effort and the learning value of practice, but it is also a decision in response to student voice about the amount of work put into the event itself and the feeling that this was not really assessed.
4 The full festival catalogue, which is an edited ensemble of the group reports submitted by students, can be accessed here: https://emckclac-my.sharepoint.com/:b:/g/personal/k2256255_kcl_ac_uk/EUobmFFfx9FJkudeu6AzN-EBhcH1Z7axH5c4lWIvA9o6VA?e=RCuu7a
5 In this chapter, we distinguish between Gestalt *Therapy*, which is a psychotherapeutic treatment modality, and Gestalt *philosophy*, which encompasses its underlying principles. For ease, we abbreviate Gestalt Therapy (GT) to differentiate therapeutic examples from applied philosophical thinking.
6 Note that, in some writing, experimentation is not considered to be a pillar of Gestalt philosophy. For the purpose of this work, we *do* consider it as such and will elaborate on this further below.
7 The catalogue is available at https://emckclac-my.sharepoint.com/:b:/g/personal/k2256255_kcl_ac_uk/EUobmFFfx9FJkudeu6AzN-EBhcH1Z7axH5c4lWIvA9o6VA?e=RCuu7a

References

Bourgault du Coudray, C. (2020). Theory and praxis in experiential education: Some insights from Gestalt Therapy'. *Journal of Experiential Education*, *43*(2), 156–170.

Boyd, D. (2020). The Beloved Community and Utopia: Hope in the face of struggle as envisioned by Martin Luther King, Jr. and Paulo Freire. In J. D. Kirylo (Ed.), *Reinventing Pedagogy of the Oppressed: Contemporary critical perspectives*. Bloomsbury Publishing.

Buber, M. (1958/1970). *I and thou*. Bison Books.

Freire, P. (1970/2018). *Pedagogy of the oppressed*. Bloomsbury Academic.

Freire, P. (1992/2014). *Pedagogy of hope: Reliving Pedagogy of the Oppressed*. Bloomsbury Publishing.

Giroux, H. A. (2007). Utopian thinking in dangerous times: Critical pedagogy and the project of educated hope. In M. Cote, R. J. F. Day, & G. de Peuter (Eds.), *Utopian pedagogy: Radical experiments against neoliberal globalization* (pp. 25–42). Toronto University Press.

hooks, b. (2003). *Teaching community: A pedagogy of hope*. Routledge.

hooks, b. (1994) *Teaching to transgress: Education as the practice of freedom*. Routledge.

Joyce, P., & Sills, C. (2018) *Skills in Gestalt counselling and psychotherapy*. Sage.

Lewin, K. (1943) Defining the 'field at a given time'. *Psychological Review*, *50*(3), 292–310. https://doi.org/10.1037/h0062738

Mann, D. (2021). *Gestalt Therapy: 100 key points and techniques*. Routledge.

Ouzia, J. (2022). Gestalt philosophy: What's in it for higher education (students)? Workshop presented at the Department of CMCI Winter Festival in London, United Kingdom, December 2022.

Parlett, M. (1991). Reflections on field theory. *The British Gestalt Journal*, *1*, 68–91.

Perls, F.S., Hefferline, R., & Goodman, P. (1951/1994). *Gestalt Therapy: Excitement and growth in the human personality*. The Gestalt Journal Press.

Sambell, K., McDowell, L., & Montgomery, C. (2013). *Assessment for learning in higher education*. Routledge.

Sendra, E. (2020). Video essays: Curating and transforming film education through artistic research. *International Journal of Film and Media Arts*, *5*(2), 65–81.

Spinelli, E. (2005). *The interpreted world: An introduction to phenomenological psychology*. Sage.

Zembylas, M. (2022). Affective and biopolitical dimensions of hope: From critical hope to anti-colonial hope in pedagogy. *Journal of Curriculum and Pedagogy*, *19*(1), 28–48. doi: 10.1080/15505170.2020.1832004

Zinker, J. (1977). *Creative process in Gestalt Therapy*. Random House.

Chapter 10

It's about Place

Inside Indigenising the curriculum

Megan McPherson and Tiriki Onus

Introduction

This Country has a long memory, and we are honoured to follow in the footsteps of the thousands of generations of artists. Megan is a settler artist, researcher, and educator. Tiriki is a Yorta Yorta and Dja Dja Wurrung artist, researcher, and maker. Both are guests to Naarm (Melbourne), to this Country of the Boonwurrung and Wurundjeri Woiwurrung peoples of the Kulin Nation. Tiriki acknowledges Country and explains,

> This is not my country. Although, this is country to which my family have been coming for thousands of generations. We are incredibly blessed to be able to make our art and tell our stories here on the lands of the Boonwurrung and the Wurundjeri Woiwurrung peoples of the Kulin Nation. Here we are, in this place, where artists have sung their songs, danced their dances, made their art and poured their story into this landscape since the beginning of all things.
>
> We are incredibly grateful for the generosity, the love, the care and the diplomacy which has been shown to us by those who speak for this Place. The owners who have bestowed upon us the gifts of their knowledge, and through collaborative processes which seek to amplify and celebrate the authority of our First Peoples and our dialogues with Country and place, have gifted to us much; we hope that we can do justice to the responsibility given to us.

In placing this Acknowledgement of Country at the beginning of this chapter, Tiriki has enacted a protocol of Indigenous diplomacy. Positioning themselves, through the authority of Elders, Tiriki and Megan work with responsibility and relationality. Megan is a collaborator and ally with an agenda of reparative and caring action in working with Indigenous Knowledges of Place.

DOI: 10.4324/9781003457510-12

Introductions are a vital part of diplomacy in Aboriginal and Torres Strait Islander communities as they establish the protocols of relationships. In Yorta Yorta scholar Kathryn Coff's words,

> Credentials are not what is most important to me. I would always begin a relationship by wanting to know what your name is, where in Country you're connected to and where your ancestors are from. It's a 'learning' for people to talk in a different way. I can feel energies change around the room when we talk like that because we start to see each other as humans rather than colleagues. People are craving to be seen like that.
>
> Coff and Lampert (2019, p. 24)

Place, positioning, context. We teach at a university on the unceded lands of the Boonwurrung and Wurundjeri Woiwurrung of the Kulin Nation, very close to the sites of the first internment camp for First Peoples in the Port Phillip Bay colony. In this university, as in almost all other universities in settler colonies, previous research practices have denigrated and humiliated First Peoples. We cannot change our histories. In just these few sentences, colonisation is writ large.

In the Indigenising curriculum, we choose thrivance (Jolivétte, 2021) and powerful stories of strength and determination that continue to inform, influence, and amply First Peoples' actions and practices. We do this work by Indigenising curriculum co-creation with creative and cultural knowledge and practices under the authority of Elders and Traditional Owners. We understand how to navigate the system, but we do so under their guidance and direction.

Indigenising curriculum with creative and cultural knowledge and practices challenges the teaching of the canonical pedagogies of Australian art education. Indigenising curriculum responds to the stories and making from Place, from long time ago and now, and shared histories of destructive settler colonisation, and the strengths of First Peoples. It is this space where the Wilin[1] academic suite of breadth and core subjects from the University of Melbourne positions itself. It responds to the call from Community and scholarship for more Indigenised curriculum, for First Peoples' knowledges to enter the academy in the "right" ways, and for many ways learning to occur.

In the push to Indigenise the curriculum in the contemporary university, art education needs to come to terms with how it intends to position itself, recognising and acknowledging the impact of settler colonisation within long and continuing First Peoples' histories. We need to reckon with history and contemporary affects and effects of the settler colonial disruption and displacement of First People with accountability. As Australia continues discussions with First Nations Communities, truth telling and the action of listening become embodied responses drawing on well established processes of healing and wellbeing for First Nations Communities. To do this centring with creative and cultural practices, places these accountable restorative, self-care, and healing learning and teaching practices within the bodies and wellbeing of learners and educators.

In this chapter, we discuss the development of a subject grounded in Indigenous Knowledges and Indigenous Knowledges amplified through the actions of experiencing creative and cultural practices led by First Nations' researchers, artists, and academics. This subject is compulsory for all Victorian College of the Arts (VCA) students in the creative and performing arts at the Faculty of Fine Arts and Music, University of Melbourne. This is a University "Discovery"[2] subject and holds induction activities to university learning for all first-year students within its learning outcomes.

Image 10.1 The Wilin Fire, Naarm 2023

Smoking ceremony with wattle, eucalyptus, and cherry ballart. Every year, first year students are Welcomed on to the campus and are invited to join a Smoking Ceremony. This fire creates a cleansing smoke preparing students for the experience of working with Indigenous Knowledges and entering Place.

Photo: Tiriki Onus.

Place, positioning, context

In Naarm (Melbourne), the river cuts through the city business district with re-tail and offices to the north and the arts precinct on the south side. Southbank houses the state and national arts organisations, concert halls, and galleries; it's also the home of the Southbank campus of the University of Melbourne's Faculty of Fine Arts and Music. Many of our students and staff cross the river every day multiple times, never realising the significance of the international diplomacies of crossing boundaries within the Kulin Nations.[3] As tourists stop to take photographs on the bridge of the city skylines, and Melbournians walk quickly past on their way, the significance of the river seems imperceivable.

The river is a place of flux, where diplomacies and responsibilities have been enacted for multiple millennia with generations of First Peoples, living, travel-ling through, and on the river. Before invasion, there was a waterfall to cross by foot where the Queen Street Bridge now stands. After invasion, the Bound-ary Road in North Melbourne was where displaced First Nations Peoples had to be across by nightfall daily or to be in danger of punitive colonial punish-ment. The Kulin Nation had to make way for sheep grazing, on now named Royal Park, a significant site for the Wurundjeri. The fires of these homelands could be seen from the top of the hill by the Yalukit Willam clan of the Boon-wurrung, where Government House now stands (Eildsen, 2014). It is here, just down from the Yalukit Willam clan home, where thousands of generations of artists, musicians, and dancers have continuously practised, that first-year VCA students now join university life with the Stories of Place subject.

The Stories of Place subject was developed in response to the university Discovery subject initiative. Discovery subjects aim to develop disciplinary excitement, skills for success, engagement expectations, and connection and belonging (University of Melbourne, 2022). They are embedded in the dis-cipline knowledges, with Stories of Place being the only subject grounded in Indigenous Knowledges and Place, which are both university research strategic aims (University of Melbourne, 2022). In this chapter, we centre Indigenous Knowledges of Place. Place is not about the soil and stones, but deeply relational knowledge of ourselves and the artists who have gone before us in this Coun-try. Furthermore, we focus on Place to contextualise learning about, and with, Indigenous Knowledges in reparative and careful ways. Indigenous Knowledges position Place with responsibility and care, rather than ownership or discovery. In the context of university learning, this Place-based approach becomes a way for students to situate themselves in relationship to the stories of Country and to examine the ways in which they learn to become a practitioner here.

To come with purpose

When almost 300 hundred first year students come onto campus, they are coming on to Country in the middle of an urban environment. Students' previous education and knowledge of First Nations histories may be nominal.

The first day of the university teaching year is grounded in diplomacy; students and staff are Welcomed to Country and smoked through invitation by Elders. Students are challenged to come on to Country with a purpose. They are given the responsibility to look after Country's waters and land, the old and the young, and themselves. We expand this challenge to their university commencement. We ask them to consider their purpose for coming to the VCA and how they want to be here in this Place, campus, and stories.

Students, becoming artists, are held in a relationship with Place, Country, and story by being immersed in a four-hour workshop, with First Nations artist-researchers invited to share story and practice. The subject takes over most of the week-one learning and teaching activities of the VCA. It is this shared interdisciplinary space that is the hallmark of the subject. It is relational, relationship building, and contextual. Students are further invited to respond to the experience in a yarning circle,[4] a placemaking soundscape experience or other creative and cultural practices, shared through storytelling. Over the first week the Discovery experience is 10 hours of learning, with another six hours of tutorials over the semester. The learning activities replace other subjects in this first week to give a truly collective interdisciplinary entry to the university learning experience.

Tiriki describes the action that the subject generates,

> in bringing those diverse and exciting artists for each of our students in all of the disciplines of the Victorian College of the Arts, they will see the relevance and diversity. They'll see that Aboriginal art is not just about dot painting. Aboriginal theatre is not just performed by Aboriginal people, but there are histories of intersection and celebration that have always been here, and we can pick up on that. When we see the relevance for our own art form and our practice, then it's much, much easier for us to feel like we've got a place in that narrative as well.
>
> Onus (2022)

Navigating between worlds

Grounding Stories of Place in Indigenous Knowledges, and cultural and creative practices, brings worlds into proximity with one another and adds context and positioning overtly to the pedagogies of the university studio. This positioning and context add complexity to an already complex situation. The university studio is described as: "learning through creative practice is learning to live with and in complexity and contradiction" (Orr & Shreeve, 2018, p. 233). In the university studio curriculum, what artistic practice is, what it is to develop a practice, and how this practice is recognised are significant (McPherson, 2018). The building of an identity as an artist is based in a particular practice's conventions, rules, and order (Shreeve, 2009). Values are transferred in the university studio (Budge, 2014). This knowledge may be affected by regionality, place, and location (Orr, 2011). In the process of teaching and learning to be an artist, there is also a validation of the teacher's understanding of what it means to be an artist, the relationship of themselves as practitioners, and conceptions of the art arenas and how the university fits into these (Orr, 2011). Students consent to embody and to stylise themselves to the rules of being a student in a university studio. When students are challenged with coming to Place "with a purpose", they reflect on their context, relationality, and the relevance of Place and story with their practice.

In the disciplines of art and music, terms such as artistic research or re-search-creation are used to describe the academic research of what we do in the academy. Research-creation is defined as "the ways that dialogic, socially orientated, and research-based practices are remade within the university-as-site" (Loveless, 2019, p. 2). This notion of remaking practice goes to the heart of artistic education practice in the university studio. University studio pedagogies can and may ask students to respond to complex situations where making, unmaking, and remaking happen, all at once to the self and to practice (McPherson, 2018). Students expect to be inducted into the university studio idea of what a practice is. What university studio pedagogies may forget is that there are many ways of artistic practice in multiple arts worlds (van Maanen, 2009). To enter a university studio where you are challenged to reflect on what your purpose is to shine a light on the ideas of practice and what they mean collectively, as well as individually.

> Research-creation, at its best, has the capacity to impact our social and material conditions, not by offering more facts differently figured, but by finding ways, through aesthetic encounters and events, to persuade us to care and do care *differently*.
>
> Loveless (2019, p. 106, original emphasis)

To come with purpose, and to experience Indigenous Knowledges taught by Indigenous artist-researchers is an approach to care about practice and Place, our context, and to consider what we care for in this site.

Care differently

To do care differently is to understand that Indigenous concepts of relationality are the key to this action. Shawn Wilson argues, "Rather than viewing ourselves as being in relationship with other people or things, we are the relationships that we hold and are part of" (Wilson, 2008, p. 80). This relationality is an important aspect of all education pedagogies (Smith, Tuck, & Wang, 2018, p. 9). In the university studio, relationality is present and legible in the ways students and teachers work together, how they work in Place, and how they work with care, differently. How we hold this space and Place, is the way we change the rules and order of prescribed or conventional ways of thinking and doing in the university studio. We challenge discipline ways of always doing the same and start to see the potential of working with care differently. We hold this space by Indigenising the curriculum with the diplomacies of Place, understanding the need for Indigenous Knowledges in the academy, and students' development of their practice through holding this relational positioning throughout their time in the university studio.

Notions of academic care as self-care, pedagogical care, and the responsibilities of accountability are questions and prompts that are asked throughout the subject. How this relates to Place gives insight into Indigenous ways of being, doing, and knowing (Martin & Mirraboopa, 2003). Care and wellbeing are inherent aspects in building communities and caring for communities. To contextualise Place is a re-becoming (Bang et al., 2014), and it is an act of care (Bang et al., 2014). Place and Land are very old pedagogies and centre culture (Styres, 2011) and those creative and relational practices that maintain cultures.

Urban Place for Stories of Place works "as sites of potential transformings – forming a nexus between epistemologies and ontologies of land and Indigenous futurity" (Bang et al., 2014, p. 39); it is the recognition and acknowledgement of Place. It's not just a Western art school, but a Place where creative and cultural practice continues. Place is context; it is stories; it is deep histories over time; and it is shared histories within the colonial systems. In grounding in Place and sharing stories of Place, the aim is for students to become aware of this information, and how they can hold, and share, these stories in reparative ways. Learning these stories is embedded in Place, and how to be in this Place becomes an active part of students' shared futures.

What does this centring of Place mean for students and staff, both Indigenous and non-Indigenous in the university community? Place holds long and shared histories; histories that start to become visible in the shared stories. By sharing stories, the workshop leaders are highlighting the strengths and thrivances in continuing practices. Andrew Jollivétte defines thrivance: "Thrivance in this sense means that Indigenous Knowledge systems, practices, and sociocultural engagements are placed at the center of decolonization efforts in Indian country" (Jolivétte, 2021, p. 468). For Tiriki, the realisation for students and staff that they are missing out on this wealth of Indigenous Knowledges is a counterpoint that is continuously highlighted. Engaging students and staff to look at the gaps in their knowledge, and to question the structures of colonisation that exist still today, for some, challenges their preconceived ideas of becoming artists in this Place.

Smith et al. prompt reflection and research when they state the critical questions for the "call to "Indigenize"—" *Who is making this call? Who is controlling the way that call is articulated? What Indigenous capacity is being developed and how is that being sustained over the long term?*" (Smith, Tuck, & Yang, 2018, p. 8). Smith argues, "A decolonizing agenda has to help Indigenous peoples to create and revitalize our own frameworks, language, theories, methodologies, and practices that work for us" (Smith, Tuck, & Yang, 2018, p. 7). It is in this environment, in this university community, that we use these critical questions to consider and reflect on how Indigenous Knowledges are situated in the academy, and how we as a community do the work with Indigenising and decolonising agendas with care. It is the guidance of this critical questioning that will inform the future of the subject and the Indigenous educational research approaches that we enact to strengthen, and evidence transformation and change.

Strategies to make, unmake, and remake a subject in Place

To simplify the complexity of the university studio pedagogies we give you a series of prompts in two approaches: Care labour and Allyship labour. This is not a binary, but rather an interrelated, situated, and embodied ecosystem of Place, diplomacies, and care. Care needs action, it needs to be embodied into making, and into transforming and becoming artists. The art school studio is a prime place for this labour. In the university studio, we work with stories all the time; we make and create our own stories in this Place, in context. In Stories of Place, we ask students to make, to become artists in Place with the knowledge that students and educators continue practices of making with diplomacies, under the authority of Elders, and creating spaces of and for Indigenous and shared futures.

Care labour

• **Collaboration and consultation**

The Wilin Centre for Indigenous Arts and Cultural Development has a long-standing collaboration with Senior Elders from the local area, developed since its inception in 2001. The leadership of this subject is First Nations, with First Nations and settler allies supporting day-to-day activities of a large cohort university subject. The subject underwent a period of academic development with discipline course leaders. The workshop activities are First Peoples led, with the Welcome to Country and Smoking ceremony a highlight of diplomatic action and storytelling to set the week of activities off. Students attend activities in interdisciplinary groups, which is an intervention which has long been called for in the university studio curriculum by both students and educators. This subject is needed to make this interdisciplinary social space a reality.

Allyship labour

• **Making activities**

Throughout the university studio, students are individually and collectively making. In Stories of Place, we ask students to make and create under the direction and authority of First Nations' artists, and to create spaces where they can challenge themselves to consider their positioning and their relationship to Place.

• **Making friends**

In each activity, students will introduce themselves in different ways, sometimes just by sharing their name and their discipline areas, sometimes sharing their story of to "come with a purpose". Instead of online quizzes usually offered in the Joining Melbourne Modules of university induction, we ask students to interact and discuss through these online modules.

• **Making connections to Place**

The understanding of a continuous relationship with Place and Country encourages reflection on what is the purpose of being on Country, in the university studio community, and the wider community.

• **Making allyship action**

In the yarning circles, students are asked to consider what allyship is in this university space. It is, for some students and educators, a first step on this path of caring action, for others it continues along their pathway. What does this subject mean for the university studio? For some studios willing to take up this prompt, it means students are given further insight into the Place in which they work. Allyship, as a university studio pedagogy, brings care into focus; through doing care, students and educators can consider what this care is doing? And through this reflection they can consider what it means to care differently in the university studio.

Always was, always will be, Aboriginal Land

In the university art school, how Indigenous Knowledges and creative and cultural practices are acknowledged, used, and given space are examples of how the art school positions itself within contemporary society. At the VCA, we do this within a compulsory subject, Stories of Place. It is a university induction subject with an agenda of acknowledging the long and shared histories of Place, of practice, and care. Practice and care are two of the themes at the forefront in the subject. We learn and teach within a Place that has known thousands of generations of collaborative cultural practice. How we do this directly responds to an ongoing call by Elders and Knowledge holders. This is the "purpose" with which we come.

And again, we restate Uncle William Bates call, "Always was, always will be, Aboriginal Land" (McBride, 2023).

Notes

1 Wilin Centre for Indigenous Arts and Cultural Development. Wilin is a Boonwur-rung language group word meaning fire.
2 The word "discovery" and its colonisation references are problematic in this con-text. We have shortened it to "Disco" when speaking about the subject at the VCA.
3 The Five Kulin Nations include Boonwurrung, Dja Dja Wurrung, Taungurung, Wathaurung, and Woiwurrung.
4 The yarning circle is an Indigenous cultural practice, where everyone has the chance to listen, and share with each other in a safe, non-judgemental space.

References

Bang, M., Curley, L., Kessel, A., Marin, A., Suzukovich III, E. S., & Strack, G. (2014). Muskrat theories, tobacco in the streets, and living Chicago as Indigenous land. *Environmental Education Research*, *20*(1), 37–55.

Budge, K. (2014). *Creative practice, value, and the teaching of art and design in higher education* (Doctoral dissertation, University of Melbourne, Graduate School of Education).

Coff, K., & Lampert, J. (2019, April). Mentoring as two-way learning: An Australian First Nations/non-Indigenous collaboration. In *Frontiers in education* (Vol. 4, p. 24). Frontiers Media SA.

Eildsen, M. (2014). *Yalukit Willam, the River people of Port Phillip*. Retrieved from https://issuu.com/copponline/docs/yalukitwilliam_12_december?fr=sMTZhMzE2NzE4MTY

Jolivétte, A. (2021). American Indian leadership: On Indigenous geographies of gen-der and thrivance. In M. Walter et al. (Eds.), *The Oxford handbook of Indigenous sociology* (online edn). Oxford Academic.

Loveless, N. (2019). *How to make art at the end of the world: A manifesto for research-creation*. Duke University Press.

Martin, K., & Mirraboopa, B. (2003). Ways of knowing, being and doing: A theo-retical framework and methods for indigenous and indigenist re-search. *Journal of Australian studies*, *27*(76), 203–214.

McBride, L. (2023). Always was, always will be, Aboriginal land. Australian Museum website. Retrieved from https://australian.museum/learn/first-nations/always-will-be-aboriginal-land/#:~:text=%E2%80%9CAlways%20Was%2C%20Always%20Will%20Be,Country%20has%20never%20been%20ceded

McPherson, M. J. (2018). *Subjectivity, agency and affect in the undergraduate univer-sity art studio crit* (Doctoral dissertation, Monash University).

Onus, T. (2022). *Stories of Place at the Victorian College of the Arts* (Faculty of Fine Arts and Music YouTube). Retrieved from https://www.youtube.com/watch?v=m8aGK6Dzlcc

Orr, S. (2011). "Being an artist you kind of, I mean, you get used to excellence": Iden-tity, values and fine art assessment practices. *International Journal of Art & Design Education*, *30*(1), 37–44.

Orr, S., & Shreeve, A. (2018). *Art and design pedagogy in higher education*. Routledge.

University of Melbourne (2022). *Advancing Students and Education Strategy: 2023–2030*. University of Melbourne. Retrieved from https://about.unimelb.edu.au/__data/assets/pdf_file/0031/384367/Advancing-Students-and-Education-Strategy.pdf

Shreeve, A. (2009). "I'd rather be seen as a practitioner, come in to teach my subject": Identity work in part-time art and design tutors. *Journal of Art and Design Education, 28*(2), 151–159. https://doi.org/10.1111/j.1476-8070.2009.01602.x

Smith, L. T., Tuck, E., & Yang, K. W. (2018) Introduction. In L. T. Smith, E. Tuck, & K. W. Yang (Eds.), *Indigenous and decolonizing studies in education: Mapping the long view.* Routledge.

Styres, S. D. (2011). Land as first teacher: A philosophical journeying. *Reflective Practice, 12*(6), 717–731.

Wilson, S. (2008). *Research is ceremony. Indigenous research methods.* Fernwood.

Van Maanen, H. (2009). *How to study art worlds; on the societal functioning of aesthetic values* (Kindle). Amsterdam University Press.

Connection, interconnection, and companions

Chapter 11

Reflecting on university heterotopias and the need for spaces of hope and possibility in higher education

Sarah Barradell,[1] Tracy Fortune, and Jeanette Fyffe

Opening reflection

We (the authors) met a little over 10 years ago through the Graduate Certificate in Curriculum, Teaching and Learning at our institution. Two of us had just finished, and one of us had just started. Our university had a vibrant centralised teaching and learning unit; a place to come and be inspired about deeply philosophical and practical questions about the idea of the university, about teaching and learning, with established educational researchers. Top teaching and learning scholars regularly visited our institution to challenge our thinking – these events allowed the time to think, discuss ideas, be innovative, and shake things up. The emphasis was definitely less on efficiencies and more on student learning and the academic and student experience – thriving and being enlivened. Our fellow academic classmates rose to the challenge of the provocations mindfully put to us. For all of us, the sense of possibility to imagine and innovate was real – there was little obsession with what cost or measurable outcomes this intellectual capacity building provided. Embargoed time and opportunity to think was of value in its own right. We questioned our values, explored what it meant to be taught, to teach, to learn, to grow. We traversed philosophy, ontology, axiology. We developed our ideas about educational research, and within a year of the last of us completing that programme we were attending writing retreats, submitting joint conference abstracts, and frequently speaking at our institution teaching and learning seminars. We were awarded institutional and, some of us, national teaching awards, and we went forth in our daily academic roles encouraged that ideas mattered; that thinking, reflecting, and questioning and, most importantly, the time to do those things was a given – that we could be scholars and inspire scholarship in others.

Reflecting on this narrative, collective memories from just over a decade ago, it seems like another time. "Did that really happen? What a luxury that was and what madness do we occupy now?" While we enjoy job security, and have become savvy in eking out time to think, to plan, to imagine, it comes at the expense of our

[1]Corresponding author

DOI: 10.4324/9781003457510-14

personal time more than ever before. We have moved institutions for opportunity with the hopes of recapturing those feelings, and have said goodbye to valued colleagues, a good number of whom shared their disillusionment with the academy as a reason for their departure. They began to question what called them in the first place as they watched their roles change and resources shrink; most importantly, the time to do the things that matter. The need for one's considered academic judgement, the opportunity to deploy it in meaningful encounters with students seems no longer possible unless there is a crafty way to account for that time under the cloak of a performance-sanctioned activity. Survival in the academy, finding joy in the academy, can seem to be all about one's willingness to buy into the games that need to be played.

Introduction

Our opening tells a tale of two universities. The university of the recent past, not even three decades ago, was once mostly for the public good. Teaching and research efforts focused on this objective; an objective established within the university's walls. Entry to the academic community was linked to the completion of further study and scholarship. This university was characterised by collegiality, autonomy, and academic freedom (Blackmore, 2020; Kinman, 2014). It offered nourishment to its academics, allowing them to learn and develop into their roles. Forward to the contemporary university; an entrepreneurial university where metrics and performance indicators reign. Business pervades higher education, with commercialisation and marketisation now driving consumer-oriented teaching and research (Lynch, 2010). Working conditions have shifted too; there is an intense focus on hustle culture, certain tasks are assigned workload but many others are not, even workspaces lack permanency with open plan offices and hot desking becoming the norm. This university existed pre-pandemic, but it has been amplified by decisions made by university management and governments in response to COVID-19.

Entrepreneurial universities have been described as '*careless*'; about their role, what knowledge is valued, what matters and the types of workplaces they provide (Lynch, 2010; Blackmore, 2020). It is in response to this carelessness that we sought (and created) a refuge from the pressures, tensions, even crises within academia to help us to care for ourselves, and the universities we might dream about. Over the course of 2018, we were part of a mentoring project intended to help doctoral students develop their academic identities. The project aimed to help the doctoral students to understand the academic contexts they were (aspiring to be) part of and to understand themselves a little more too. We consider the space that emerged among and between us to be what Foucault (1967) referred to as a *heterotopia* – an unsettling yet transformative space, where difference and tension is acknowledged yet offers hope not restraint.

The space of reflection, possibility, and hope

Our project intentionally set out to trigger deep discussion about what scholarly teaching was and what surviving in an environment that might not allow the time for this looked like. As the project unfolded, the space being created started to come into view. It felt like a safe space to explore contradictory feelings, associated with both ontological and practical elements of being and becoming an academic. We were more than facilitators in these conversations. This was our journey too. At the end of our journey, the space created could be seen as a haven for different ways of being. It was a space of play and joy too, where we shared our optimism about the university, a space where our passion about our disciplines, our research, and the values we held about encouraging real *thought* in teaching could find expression (Fortune et al., 2023). It was a space to engage in activities that harnessed our minds, passions, and imaginations.

As mentors we each came to the project with personal objectives: to give back and to pay forward, to counter the isolation that might be experienced in academia, to see the university in a different way, to provoke deep thinking, and to work closely with respected colleagues. Going into the project, we did not discuss how we would mentor or would occupy this space, but the mentoring process we unwittingly enacted and the environment we created was a form of care for ourselves and each other. A heterotopia.

Heterotopias

Although the word heterotopia has origins in medicine (to describe body tissue that develops in atypical places) (Johnson, 2006), Foucault is credited as popularising it as a way of thinking about a range of other or different (counter) spaces in society that simultaneously reflect and contest what is around them. Foucault provides historical examples of heterotopias, including asylums, prisons, brothels, gardens, and even boats: "heterotopia par excellence … a floating piece of space, … the greatest reserve of the imagination. In civilizations without boats, dreams dry up, espionage takes the place of adventure, and the police take the place of pirates" (1967, n.p.). Heterotopias are spaces that mirror and relate to existing spaces in ways that tend to disrupt and provoke the parallel space.

Heterotopic reflections

The image we are drawn to for this chapter is abstract and depicts the reflected world created inside a kaleidoscope. A kaleidoscope is typically constructed by placing two mirrors in a harmonious relationship with each other such that the reflections between each combine to create an almost magical space of possibility. The idea of reflection animates our contribution to this collection. We draw on reflection in two key ways: as deep thought and consideration, and as the throwing back of light or mirroring from a surface.

This chapter began with contrasting reflections on academic beginnings. They are reflections taken at different moments in time and at different career stages; reflections that plumb the memories and feelings of encounter with the university. The other notion of reflection that animated our thinking about this work is via heterotopias; as spaces of reflection, not just in the sense of deep thinking but in the idea of being seen and mirrored. The mirroring is validation. A kaleidoscope shows the power of amplified mirroring and the newness that can result. Physics describes reflection as the change in direction of a wavefront at the interface between two different media. There is also a law of reflection, which tells us that the angle of incidence is equal to the angle of

Image 11.1 Heterotopic reflections

Source: https://www.freeimg.net/photo/1517158/wallpaper-black-kaleidoscope-mirror.

reflection. When surfaces are placed in the right kinds of conditions, like the precise angles inside the kaleidoscope, the result can be surprisingly beautiful. Our mentoring space has us thinking about reflection in this way because it was a space to be seen and to see, to reflect and receive each other's renderings of the university and tales of working in the university. The mentoring space was a place to be able to see yourself reflected in the experiences of others and to create something new together. The relationship and positioning between us, like the mirrors in a kaleidoscope, produced something more than the sum of the parts. Like light bouncing off surfaces and making new shapes, this is not a flat call and response kind of reflection, not just an echo. It is seeing your values being reflected back, affirming what you project and what you see. Our contributions met and bounced off each other and somehow combined to produce concert and community. Individually a mirror might almost be considered mute but when brought together, new futures and new ways become possible.

Aligning heterotopic principles: our space

Foucault (1967) offered six principles (heterotopology) that define heterotopias (Table 11.1). The table outlines the principles and maps them to the university of the past (column two) and to our created heterotopia (column four). The third column describes the rupture with a heterotopian university that characterises contemporary higher education. There was a time when the university, or perhaps the idea of the university, was perceived to be a heterotopia, where the academy as a whole displayed the characteristics we have found in our mentoring space. This heterotopic university, perhaps the university encountered in the reflection that opens this chapter, has receded and new heterotopias need to be found or made. Whether that university ever really existed may be open for some debate, but regardless there is a sense of loss for the *idea of the university* presented in column two.

Taking steps toward change: Care, courage, and collectivism

The World Health Organization defines self-care as "the ability of individuals, families, and communities to promote health, prevent disease, maintain health, and cope with illness or disability with or without the support of a health worker" (2023). In lay terms, self-care is understood as making sure we meet the needs of ourselves (so that we are better able to meet the needs of others). We consider self-care in the higher education context as a relational and political act (Askins & Blazek, 2017). It cannot solely be an individual undertaking. *Caring with* is essential to self-care in academia and involves *caring about* and *caring for*, while we are *cared about* and *cared for*. Self-care in these ways involves caring about ideas, intentions, or feelings (Askins & Blazek, 2017).

Table 11.1 The university as heterotopia: past, present, and created

Foucault's heterotopic principles	University idyll	Contemporary university	Our heterotopia
Reserved for those in crisis or deviance	A place of learning and exploration. A space to find oneself and become. 'Crisis' being the crisis of growing up and coming into the future self. The transforming self a deviance. 'Reserved' meant there was time, and nothing more to do than grow and learn.	'Hustle' culture is celebrated. Performance excellence is expected from the very beginning. For example: PhD applicants needing research publications before they are eligible for a scholarship. To earn the right to learn how to be a researcher, you have to already demonstrably be a researcher.	The wounded mentors and 'lost' mentees as deviant, in crisis, find retreat in the heterotopic mentoring space where they can regain a sense of hope and possibility.
Their function is affected as history unfolds	Purpose of the Australian university was aligned to nation building. Education was considered a public good. Being in university was valid and valued.	Over time, the idea of HE shifted towards consumer product and private benefit (i.e., with the introduction of HECS)[a] and we saw increases in international enrolments. Being in the university is not so much "valid" as self-indulgent, or elitist.	Response to the carelessness of the modern university. Trying to create space/s in the university that holds the complexity of many purposes for the university and a plurality of motivations. A response to unbundling – drawing together teacher and researcher identities.
Formed from juxtaposing spaces	University campus is the epitome of juxtaposed spaces; one can attend to different functions in different spaces. Research in your office, lab, or studio and teach in the classroom. The time and journey through spaces affords delineation and a pause for thought and being.	Modern university, and its work (during & post COVID-19), is mediated by technology. University spaces are not necessarily campus based. We may be sitting in the same room (even in our home) doing T&L, then research and then committee work without moving. This is hard on a human.	The mentoring space was a deliberate act of making a boundary around this conversation to try to resolve and bring into relief the multiple identities we carry in the university. We booked rooms for meetings – library, cafes, teaching spaces, meeting rooms +/- corporate spaces – all being put to different purposes.

(Continued)

Table 11.1 (Continued)

Foucault's heterotopic principles	University idyll	Contemporary university	Our heterotopia
Linked to slices in time	University as an idyll with time to think deeply, luxuriate in questions, plan sabbaticals, engage in retreat for scholarly purposes.	Accelerated university – fast moving and metricised, inhospitable to deep thought. Little time afforded to figuring it out. Measures must be met and the expectation is 'excellent'. Time meted out and academic work unbundled with rampant casualisation and precarity accompanying workload models and performance expectations.	The mentoring space was always scheduled, sequestered time where we could work together to reassemble the academic self. Time was given, and time was taken.
They are closed systems	An ivory tower, a refuge and protected space for thinking and being and exploring futures.	The concerns of broader society are felt inside the university. Part of the opening up of the university is that there is no refuge from corporate logics. Much time must be spent creating and holding boundaries for the thinking / being / exploring work, leading to exhaustion.	The space of the mentoring programme was a closed system. Folks were invited and admitted and the space held apart to consider the ideas of growing as a researcher and as a teacher in the university and then make those identities make sense.
Relationships with wider society	University of the past had a relationship with society. In Australia, the birth of the university was part of a nation-building exercise. Graduates and researchers needed who could work in the economy and grow Australia without continued reliance on the mother country. Public good was understood.	Through social and political changes, the social contract for universities has shifted and become contested. Contemporary debate is centred on what role and obligations HE has to society.	The mentoring space of our project is in conversation with the wider context of the university. The purpose was to empower and develop members to be effective and confident in navigating the university at large. There was also a straddling of academic and clinical identities, which informed and kept professional contexts and futures in play. Informed by 'care' – for the bigger picture (the discipline, being a steward, for the future professionals our students will become). Care on this level brings the space into connection with society.

Note: [a] HECS or Higher Education Contribution Scheme was a government administered loan scheme to eligible students (usually with citizenship) studying approved higher education courses in Australia. It is now known as the Higher Education Loan Program (HELP).

It is a mindset, a state of being, of being willing to push against neoliberal pressures and work towards change.

The mentoring space – our heterotopia – provided a place where we could *hope*, *care*, and *imagine together*, while enduring and tolerating the hyper-performative academic environment. It was a space where we could wrestle with hurt, disappointment, and frustration; but at the same time with possibilities in ways that supported, energised, nurtured, restored, even healed so we could continue to live, rather than just operate, in daily university life.

What advice do we have for others for rethinking or creating the kind of heterotopic space developed? Have courage. You can't do it alone, so find your people. Be vulnerable but have purpose when doing so. Recognise these spaces – and what emerges from them – as legitimate and something that matters.

Have courage

Being an academic in the contemporary university can be a cut-throat game pitting individuals and institutions against each other. The game is based on prestige, high expectations, oblique rules, and relentless self-promotion. Publish or perish (i.e., more specifically publish a certain number of times and via platforms that are deemed worthy). Win competitive grants where only 24% of applications are successful (Australian Research Council, 2022). Receive excellent teaching ratings from student satisfaction surveys even though widely and empirically recognised as flawed (Harvey, 2022).

Yet, it is possible to play another game to survive and thrive in the kind of university that is worth dreaming about. That game involves risk, being brave, and leading or engaging in slow tiny acts of resistance, or STARs as others have coined them (Grant & Elizabeth, 2015; Bosanquet, 2017). These acts are not resistance in the form of being obstructive or deliberately contrary, but rather, are founded on a recognition that *we are the university*, that we can create conditions that align with our intellectual values, and act with agency and self-determination, despite (and in spite of) the larger rhetoric of being an academic.

The mentoring project was not a specific part of our workload. We were not asked to do it by our managers to address a strategic direction. We began this project simply with a desire to help those wanting to join the academy. As the project unfolded, our emotional investment in exploring hope, care, and change with and for our mentees surfaced our vulnerabilities. We did not shy away from this; instead, we took deliberate steps to use our wounds in hopeful, positive ways for ourselves and others. Buoyed by what we had gained in the process, we (the mentors) continued to meet throughout the pandemic and Melbourne's six lockdowns despite that period being characterised by uncertainty and precarity. We have invested five years together (and with others) on this project. But in terms of university metrics, we might be considered to not have a lot to show for those five years. We have been promoted in that time, delivered a conference presentation (McDowell et al., 2019) with our mentees, and authored a journal article (Fortune et al., 2023) related to this project. Through a STARs lens, however, we have achieved much that does not fit the university yardstick. Our research outputs could be also considered STARs; they demanded that we engage in critique of the university, advocate for different possibilities and write in ways not typical for our disciplinary backgrounds.

Connect and collaborate: You can't do it alone

A wealth of literature indicates that to lead healthy lives we need connections. The Okanagan Charter (2015) advocates for universities to adopt health promoting approaches, maximise institutional success, and create cultures of compassion, equity, and justice to improve the health and wellbeing of people involved in university life. Health promoting actions involve collaborative action and a shared responsibility towards the university. At a grassroots level, we maintain that heterotopic spaces such as our mentoring group enable self-care, at the same time as creating the conditions for better universities. This might be achieved (for example) through the deceptively simple act of inviting others into a conversation that illuminates the likelihood that the sense of anxiety they may be feeling is not a deficit of self, but rather a legitimate response to the wounding effect of the neoliberal academy.

In recent years, there has been an increasing interest in the importance of relationships and care within learning and teaching (Burke & Larmar, 2021; Felten & Lambert, 2020; Gravett et al., 2021) and research (Khoo, 2023). We believe the importance of relationships extends to caring for the idea of the university.

... so find your people

Invite others to join you. Think about how to enact STARs "in the company of others whom we enjoy and whose thinking and conduct can teach us. Their companionship will comfort and sustain us" (Harré et al., 2017, p. 12).

Academic networks are traditionally considered instrumental to career success and are formed of academics from the same field working together (Heffernan, 2021). However, this conceptualisation of networks plays to the pressures and structures of the neoliberal university. Playing the university game cultivates competition amongst individuals but networks formed by *caring with* others subvert this. They are a platform to *care for* and *about* similar to the idea of the *comm*university (italics used in original) where people's experiences and struggles are necessary to enact change and transform the university (mrs kinpaisby, 2008; Moss, 2012).

Though research collaborators, fundamentally our relationship is built on shared interests and concerns and a way of thinking together where the priority is nourishing our being as much as, if not more than, our careers. We '*found*' each other through starting employment at the same institution at a similar time, being enrolled in a course together, and attending a writing retreat together.

There are innumerable ways to find your people. Go to the on-campus event that you're interested in, even (especially!) if you don't know anyone. Strike up a conversation with someone interesting. Convene your own event and invite participants who share your passion and concerns. Explore possibilities – not through a lecture, but through open conversation. The key thing is to be attuned to opportunities to find like-minded others and boldly invite them to join you.

Be vulnerable but have purpose when doing so

We talk about lots of things when we are together. If you were eavesdropping, you might catch us in moments of rage, dread, and despair, to instances of silliness, laughter, and wonder, and even passionately talking about our latest TV recommendations (*Succession*, *Friday Night Lights*, and *The Chair* are some worthy mentions). It is a safe space, where irreverence is welcome and oriented towards thoughtful and constructive critique. While it might sometimes sound as if our being vulnerable together is pessimistic, it brings nourishment and has purpose. As Askins and Blazek (2017, p. 1099) offer:

> we believe that insecurity is already a defining feature of contemporary academia, and working through – and with – emotions, … understanding critically what emotions are already doing, how they are working and being put to work in social relations, in our lives, and in our academic knowledge production and practices, and where care has the capability to intervene.

Grappling with feelings is part of a reflexive process of making sense of situations, necessary to the intellectual work attached to being and becoming academics (Askins & Blazek, 2017). The conditions that make that kind of sense making possible are the social act of '*caring with*', the enjoyment that comes from being with your people, and the act of engaging in scholarly thinking with others. These conditions were met in our mentoring project and in the reflexive conversations the three of us continue to share.

Recognise these spaces as legitimate

Once a place of learning and inquiry, then a place where knowledge and research became a focus, the contemporary university is now focused on industry and real-world connections, measuring performance and impact, revenue-based research, and working and learning at a fast pace (Barnett, 2011; Troiani & Dutson, 2021). Our idea of the university resists, at least to a degree, this entrepreneurial focus of the neoliberal university. We argue that there is a place – a need – within universities for heterotopias that allow academics to pause, think, and care to create better conditions for themselves and others. Or as Troiani and Dutson write, that allow: "the academic community to nurture citizens who can learn/think/work in a socially and ethically responsible manner to better the world outside the university" (2021, p. 19). These kinds of spaces, the work that happens within them, and the "social nature of offering and receiving support through reciprocal and interdependent relations" (Askins & Blazek, 2017, p. 1101) are legitimate; as legitimate as publication counts, grant income, and excellent teacher ratings. While not as easy to measure, a culture of kindness has been identified as a factor that contributes to happy, successful, and productive academic teams (Ball & Crawford, 2020). The work that happens in the types of heterotopic spaces we have been a part of speaks to a way of being in our personal and professional lives that is incalculable. It is not self-indulgent – but rather an act of warfare as Sara Ahmed (2014) describes:

> self-care is about the creation of community, fragile communities, assembled out of the experiences of being shattered. We reassemble ourselves through the ordinary, everyday and often painstaking work of looking after ourselves; looking after each other. This is why when we have to insist, I matter, we matter, we are transforming what matters.

We need to therefore: cherish that work and each other; protect and invest in that time; value the acts of creating, cultivating, and nurturing; and celebrate what grows and develops from such efforts and mindset, even if the system does not.

Conclusion

Drawing on the idea of heterotopia by Foucault and others, we described a space in which we were able to revitalise ourselves while providing support and guidance to aspiring academic doctoral researchers. Our heterotopia was a space of wonder and possibility, a space of reflection, but a space to have your passions and ideas about the university reflected back to you – as worthy, relevant, and free from restraint. Our kaleidoscope metaphor intended to do justice to the magical empowerment of the space as separate but related to an otherwise disempowering environment. Our humanity is reflected in a constellation of capacities, interests, and motivations that must find expression in personally, socially, and culturally relevant endeavours, that on balance are free from punitive external control. Creating collaborative and collective spaces to imagine and execute our desires alongside personal actions that subtly resist institutional demands for compliance may help us survive the measured university.

References

Ahmed, S. (2014). Self care as warfare. http://feministkilljoys.com/2014/08/25/selfcare-as-warfare/

Australian Research Council (2022). NCGP trends: Success rates. https://www.arc.gov.au/fundingresearch/funding-outcome/grants-dataset/trend-visualisation/ncgp-trends-success-rates

Askins, K., & Blazek, M. (2017). Feeling our way: Academia, emotions and a politics of care. *Social and Cultural Geography*, *18*(8), 1086–1105. https://doi.org/10.1080/14649365.2016.1240224

Ball, K., & Crawford, D. (2020). How to grow a successful – and happy – research team. *International Journal of Behavioral Nutrition and Physical Activity*, *17*(4). https://doi.org/10.1186/s12966-019-0907-1

Barnett, R. (2011). The coming of the ecological university. *Oxford Review of Education*, *37*(4), 439–455.

Blackmore, J. (2020). The carelessness of entrepreneurial universities in a world risk society: A feminist reflection on the impact of Covid-19 in Australia. *Higher Education Research & Development*, *39*(7), 1332–1336. https://doi.org/10.1080/07294360.2020.1825348

Bosanquet, A. (2017). Stars = slow, tiny acts of resistance. https://theslowacademic.com/2017/03/06/stars-small-targeted-acts-of-resistance

Burke, K., & Larmar, S. (2021). Acknowledging another face in the virtual crowd: Reimagining the online experience in higher education through an online pedagogy of care. *Journal of Further and Higher Education*, *45*(5), 601–615. https://doi.org/10.1080/0309877X.2020.1804536

Felten, P., & Lambert, L. (2020). *Relationship-rich education: How human connections drive success*. Johns Hopkins.

Fortune, T., Fyffe, J., & Barradell, S. (2023). Reimagining the university of our dreams: Heterotopic havens for wounded academics. *Higher Education Research and Development*. https://doi.org/10.1080/07294360.2023.2228213

Foucault, M. (1967). Of other places. Heterotopias, translated by Jay Miskowiec (1984) from Des espaces autres' lecture for the Cercle d'études architecturales on 14 March 1967. In *Architecture, movement, continuité 5*(1984), pp.46–49 https://foucault.info/documents/heterotopia/foucault.heteroTopia.en/

Grant, B. M., & Elizabeth, V. (2015). Unpredictable feelings: Academic women under research audit. *British Educational Research Journal*, *41*(2), 287–302.

Gravett, K., Taylor, C. A., & Fairchild, N. (2021). Pedagogies of mattering: Re-conceptualising relational pedagogies in higher education. *Teaching in Higher Education*. Advance online publication. https://doi.org/10.1080/13562517.2021.1989580

Harré, N., Grant, B. M., Locke, K., & Sturm, S. (2017). The university as an infinite game: Revitalising activism in the academy. *Australian Universities Review*, *59*(2), 5–13.

Harvey, L. (2022). Back to basics for student satisfaction: Improving learning rather than constructing fatuous rankings. *Quality in Higher Education*, *28*(3), 265–270.

Heffernan, T. (2021) Academic networks and career trajectory: 'There's no career in academia without networks'. *Higher Education Research & Development*, *40*(5), 981–994. https://doi.org/10.1080/07294360.2020.1799948

Johnson, P. (2006). Unravelling Foucault's 'different spaces'. *History of the Human Sciences*, *9*, 75–90.

Kinman, G. (2014). Doing more with less? Work and wellbeing in academics. *Somatechnics*, 4(2), 219–235.

Khoo, T. (2023). Creating spaces to develop research culture. *International Journal for Academic Development*, 28(2), 217–229.

Lynch, K. (2010). Carelessness: A hidden doxa of higher education. *Arts & Humanities in Higher Education*, 9(1), 54–67. https://doi.org/10.1177/1474022209350104

McDowell, C., Borkovic, S., Doroud, N., Weadman, T., Fortune, T., Fyffe, J., Bruce C., & Barradell, S. (2019). Doctoral mentees and academic mentors' experiences of a collaborative teaching development project: Exploring disciplinary stewardship through action research. [Paper presentation]. 2019 HERDSA Annual Conference – Next Generation, Higher Education: Challenges, Changes and Opportunities, Auckland, New Zealand.

Moss, P. (2012). *Taking stock in the interim: The stuck, the tired, and the exhausted*. Antipode Foundation. http://radicalantipode.files.wordpress.com/2012/10/moss-response.pdf

mrs kinpaisby (2008). Taking stock of participatory geographies: envisioning the communiversity. *Transactions of the Institute of British Geographers*, 33(3), 292–299.

Okanagan Charter (2015). Okanagan Charter: An international charter for health promoting universities and colleges. https://www.healthpromotingcampuses.org/okanagan-charter

Troiani, I., & Dutson, C. (2021). The neoliberal university as a space to learn/think/work in higher education. *Architecture and Culture*, 9(1), 5–23.

World Health Organization (2023). Self care interventions for health. https://www.who.int/health-topics/self-care#tab=tab_1

Chapter 12

Balance

How a unique student fellowship model enables proactive wellbeing

Mikayla Hunter, Jamie Pfau, Hera J. M. Casidsid, Stephaney Patrick, Emily Brownell, Anita Durksen, Nyla Comeau, and Jennifer E. Enns

Introduction

Within academia in Canada, a research assistant is typically selected from top-performing university students hand-picked by professors to work on their projects. These relationships usually have a top-down structure, with professors having specific goals in mind and tasks that the research assistants are hired to perform. SPECTRUM (Social Policy Evaluation Collaborative Team Research at Universities in Manitoba) is a research collaborative in Manitoba, Canada, that considers graduate student Fellows as equal partners. A *proactively developed work-life balance* is an integral part of the SPECTRUM Fellowship that enables Fellows to feel comfortable with setting boundaries where they need them to maintain a work-life balance and to cope with the emotions that come with doing social policy research. Through e-mail prompts, SPECTRUM's current cohort of Fellows will describe how a mentorship model grounded in experiential learning, mutual respect, and non-hierarchal leadership enables them to proactively achieve balance and wellbeing in their lives.

The Fellow authors of this book chapter are Mikayla (she/they), Jamie (she/her), Anita (she/her), Nyla (she/her), Stephaney (she/her), Emily (she/her), and Hera (she/her). Four are master's students (Mikayla, Nyla, Emily, and Hera), and three are doctoral students (Jamie, Anita, and Stephaney). Several of the Fellows are parents, and most have other familial caregiving responsibilities. Most of them identify as women, however, one openly identifies as non-binary. Two are people of colour (one immigrant, one international student), one is Indigenous, and the rest are Canadian-born Caucasians. These identities, among others, colour how they have experienced the SPECTRUM partnership and the Fellowship structure. The visual narrative chosen for this chapter is an image from Jamie, depicting how balance is integral to her role as a student and Fellow. Although this is a jointly written chapter, the Fellows agreed that this image was well suited

DOI: 10.4324/9781003457510-15

Image 12.1 Proactively developed work-life balance

to depict their narrative as it reflected many of the themes revealed through their reflection. Jamie describes this image as:

"My office with the door always open so kiddos can come in and out as they need. It's covered in artwork my kids have made to remind me why my research is so important and of course all my work scattered across the desk! When I'm done for the day, I happily close the door." – Jamie

Fellows were first asked to consider the themes presented by the publisher of this book to select the top three that they felt were reflective of their experience with SPECTRUM. The theme of balance received the majority vote. Fellows were then asked via e-mail to reflect on how SPECTRUM helped them to maintain balance in their lives and how that balance supported their wellbeing and enabled self-care. These independently written reflections were then collected and reviewed for common themes which were then presented back to the Fellows for validation. Two main themes arose regarding how SPECTRUM supported their wellbeing: balancing life and balancing resources.

Graduate students' wellbeing and mental health

Graduate students, in the Canadian context, are students who pursue the "opportunity to develop fully as a researcher and scholar under the mentorship of the supervisor, advisory committee and the department" (University of Waterloo, 2021) after the completion of their undergraduate degree. Although a career in academia is not the only option available to those who complete a master's, PhD, or postdoctoral training, these higher-level degrees can pave the way for students to become independent academics. These junior academics are at high risk for mental health concerns and, as such, proactively addressing these stressors is imperative.

Compared with the general population, graduate students are six times more likely to experience mental health problems (Robledo Yamamoto et al., 2023). A study by Evans and colleagues (2018) found that 41% of graduate students experienced moderate to severe anxiety and 39% experienced moderate to severe depression, compared to 6% of the general population. In the same study, 82% of graduate students reported excessive stress on a daily basis (Evans et al., 2018). These findings can be further contextualised by understanding who is most at risk of experiencing adverse mental health outcomes.

The transgender/gender nonconforming population are at high risk for experiencing anxiety and depression (Reisner et al., 2015) as well as suicidal ideation (Clark et al., 2017; Reisner et al., 2015). One study revealed a high prevalence of anxiety (55%) and depression (57%) among transgender/gender nonconforming graduate students (Evans et al., 2018). This is a stark contrast between the prevalence of anxiety (34% men, 43% women) and depression (35% men, 41% women) among cisgender graduate students (Evans et al., 2018). It is also important to note that women are consistently more likely than men to experience mood and anxiety disorders (Eaton et al., 2012).

Being a graduate student is one thing but being a visible minority graduate student is another. Immigrants who are visible minority experience poorer mental health than other immigrant groups (George et al., 2015). Studies suggest that visible minorities experience higher levels of racism and discrimination as they assimilate in Canada leading to poor self-reported mental health status (Hilario et al., 2014), stress (Guruge & Butt, 2015), and emotional problems (Beiser & Hou, 2016).

In addition to these mental health concerns faced by immigrants, international graduate students of colour (IGSC) must also contend with neo-racism that creates inequalities and blocked aspirations (Anandavalli et al., 2021). One in every four IGSC students has faced racism from "advisers, domestic students, faculty members, or community members" (Lee & Rice, 2007). Moreover, 40% of graduate students are reluctant to report such incidences or seek help for stress and these pose a serious risk to IGSC mental health (Lee, 2021).

Taken together, this evidence suggests that transgender/gender nonconforming, women, and visible minority immigrant graduate students are at considerable risk for mental health concerns throughout their studies. Furthermore, the graduate student experience has been described as one of being "betwixt and between" social roles within academic institutions (Grady et al., 2014). They are not entirely students nor professionals, and they are at times both instructors and learners (Grady et al., 2014). The conflicting expectations of holding multiple roles is not limited to within academic institutions but also exists within their lives outside of their studies. For example, 35.5% of all master's students and 28.4% of doctoral students have dependent children (Yoo & Marshall, 2022). The role of being a parent brings about both an important motivation for graduate students with children as well as additional strain on time, finances, and resources available to them (Yoo & Marshall, 2022). Of course, parental status is not the only factor that contributes to multiple sources of stress experienced by graduate students, but it is a highly impactful one. Graduate students who are parents also need to juggle their responsibilities as (potentially) a partner, student, and research assistant. Being a parent is one reason why half of doctoral students who are parents do not complete their degrees (Litalien & Guay, 2015).

The literature cited within this chapter is part of why SPECTRUM places utmost importance in providing support to its student Fellows through its non-hierarchical and flexible fellowship model. The SPECTRUM partnership acknowledges that graduate students are statistically at high risk for adverse mental health outcomes, especially those with intersecting marginalised identities. To best support student Fellows, the SPECTRUM partnership has developed an innovative mentorship model to proactively foster positive mental health outcomes.

SPECTRUM and the student fellowship model

The SPECTRUM partnership was established in 2018 to facilitate collaborative research and evaluation of social policies (Enns et al., 2023). This innovative approach to social policy research focuses on bringing all parties to the table early in the research process and prioritising ongoing engagement throughout. The functioning of this tripartite partnership between community organisations, government, and academia is made possible by the student Fellows (Enns et al., 2023).

Within academia, a research assistant is typically selected from top-performing university students hand-picked by professors to work on their projects. SPECTRUM, on the other hand, utilises a non-hierarchical fellowship model wherein Fellows are considered equal to other members of the partnership who also have their own valuable expertise and lived experience to bring to the table. They are not just tasked with completing what is asked of them by their mentors, but also to contribute actively to conversations and lead aspects of the work. Essentially, they are not viewed merely as hands with which to do the work, but as valued members of the team who can enrich the research process through their active and equal participation.

Fellows are relatively junior in their respective fields and can therefore bring fresh perspectives, challenge ineffective practices, and are open to imagining creative solutions. However, Fellows have competing priorities, as many graduate students do. In addition to the innovation they bring to the partnership, Fellows have multiple community, employment, and personal/familial commitments that necessitate the constant juggling of multiple deadlines and responsibilities.

SPECTRUM acknowledges that each of the Fellows has a life outside of academia and has developed a flexible work arrangement to allow Fellows to balance their lives. The flexibility of this work makes it possible for Fellows to be involved in SPECTRUM and commit to the partnership for the long term. This balance has also allowed Fellows the opportunity to become active collaborators in the growth and work of SPECTRUM. The long-term commitment has given Fellows the opportunity to maintain their involvement in SPECTRUM while still being active participants in their own lives outside of the partnership.

Balancing life

Via an e-mail prompt, each of the Fellows independently reflected on their identities and lives outside of academia as being important aspects to both how they come to the work SPECTRUM does and how they manage their stress. For some, their reasons for pursuing graduate studies and working with SPECTRUM were motivated by their personal lives. The ability to work with a research team focused on solving social policy problems that they were passionate about and being paid for it offered a sense of accomplishment and added meaning to their work.

Jamie, who is both a mother and actively involved in the foster care system, explained that "the impetus for my return to school was to help inform policy on promoting positive outcomes for children in care." SPECTRUM's first research project aimed to demonstrate the potential of the partnership and focused on elucidating the impact that going into the custody of Child and Family Services has on children. For Jamie, this overlap between her goal to promote positive outcomes for children in care, her identity as a (foster) mother, and the demonstration project facilitated a sense of wellbeing associated with accomplishing important goals.

Hera, who has been a research assistant on other projects, highlighted a similar point in her reflections. As a Fellow, she is afforded something she calls a work-passion balance.

> "Fellows can pursue their passion while being paid as Fellows. Where else can you have paid work-passion balance? Only in SPECTRUM." – Hera

Oftentimes, graduate students need to find sources of funding that may not necessarily align as strongly with their values as they might like. In that sense, there is a disconnect between the work that they participate in to fund their studies and their passion. For SPECTRUM Fellows, all are enabled to carve out pieces of work within SPECTRUM that fuels their desire to bring the necessary work in better alignment with their research and personal goals. This form of balance is one that was cited by several Fellows as contributing to their wellbeing. Not needing to sacrifice time spent working on their passions for the sake of reducing financial stress is essential for contributing to a sense of balance in their lives.

Many of the Fellows experienced significant life changes throughout their fellowship with SPECTRUM, both for better and for worse. Those who experienced loss were able to find a safe space in the SPECTRUM partnership and through the other Fellows and their mentors. In her reflections, Stephaney described how she was able to balance the demands of the grieving process without needing to worry about taking a step back from her role while she did so.

> "As I tried to make sense of it all, SPECTRUM was there, empathic, giving me the space to step back from my role and mourn. When I resumed, that first meeting with my mentors, the space was safe. As I shared my loss so did one of my mentors, and my tears came." – Stephaney

Jamie described her unique experience of being so invested in promoting positive outcomes in child welfare, while also being a foster parent. Sometimes the overlap can be overwhelming, especially during placement breakdowns, which unfortunately is a reality of foster parenting.

> "My dissertation work is following up SPECTRUM's demonstration project focusing on outcomes for children in care. At the same time, I am a foster parent and have helped to raise eight children. In the last two years, we have had three devastating placement breakdowns. I am grateful for the time, space, understanding, and empathy I have received from the Fellows and Mentors on SPECTRUM. No one else could understand my experiences." – Jamie

Some Fellows have seen their families grow during their time with SPEC-TRUM and have been supported unconditionally. Emily described how the flexible and understanding nature of SPECTRUM has enabled her to adjust how she spends her time to support her family, her studies, and her work with SPECTRUM.

> "As a graduate student and a mother, being provided with the ability to increase or decrease my time spent on SPECTRUM each month or week while still making meaningful contributions to the partnership and the different SPECTRUM teams and projects I am involved in is invaluable." – Emily

Mikayla further elaborated on this point:

> "We come to SPECTRUM as whole people. We are more than just Fellows, we're humans with thoughts and feelings. When those feelings get too heavy, or when something awful happens in the world, we're allowed to take space to take care of ourselves and come back to the work when we're able to without shame or guilt." – Mikayla

For Mikayla, her identity as a queer non-binary person and SPECTRUM's goal of creating a more fair and just society through research allowed them the opportunity to ameliorate the stress related to lack of representation in coursework.

> "Something that really took a toll on my mental health and wellbeing throughout both my undergraduate and graduate studies has been the lack of queer/trans representation. It's hard to constantly see myself and people like me not being considered in important research. It's invalidating. Through SPECTRUM, I can bring those parts of me to the table and call attention to them, to highlight the need to do something about it. What's even better is that those concerns will be taken seriously by others, and I am empowered to make suggestions about how we can do something, together as a team. That respect for my lived experience has made such a difference in maintaining good mental health through my graduate studies." – Mikayla

For Hera, being a part of SPECTRUM helped her not just balance but also navigate life in academia as a visible minority immigrant.

> "As a first-generation graduate student and first-generation immigrant, I often feel like a trailblazer venturing a place unknown. Because I am the first one in my family to attend graduate school, I had no background on what graduate school is like, or existing connections that can provide

support in being admitted to and in navigating life in academia. However, through my mentors in SPECTRUM, I was not alone in traversing life in academia. My mentors enthusiastically supported me every step of the process from applying to the program to working on my Master's thesis. They have also provided me opportunities that otherwise would not have been available to a visible minority immigrant like me. The support of my mentors has significantly helped my mental health and I am very grateful for that." – Hera

Stephaney then described her experience of racism in Canada and how SPECTRUM helped alleviate some frustration and feelings of hopelessness as an IGSC.

"I have personally experienced covert racism in the Canadian community. Unlike the United States (US) where racism is overt, Canada's racism is covert and is often difficult to articulate and prove. Coming from a country where racism is not a thing has been stressful. However, my advisor and mentors at SPECTRUM have made me feel less helpless and more empowered to make real change towards creating equity in the society for minority groups. As such, SPECTRUM offers a ray of hope in providing a safe space to discuss inherent discriminatory systemic biases and exploring ways to change them." – Stephaney

Ultimately, this model of student fellowship allows students to come to the work as whole humans who experience life outside of academia. They each have motivations for engaging in the work and experience loss and joy throughout their time working with the SPECTRUM partnership. The supportive, non-hierarchical nature of the mentorship structure allows Fellows the space to be active participants in all aspects of their lives without work-related consequences.

Balancing resources

In their individual reflections, nearly all Fellows commented on the strength of being a part of a team of Fellows compared to being the sole research assistant on a project.

"When the weight of an entire project is on your shoulders, it feels like you have no choice but to suffer through it alone. There's no one to go to for help. Telling your supervisor that you're struggling can be terrifying and so, I usually found myself struggling alone on other projects. In SPECTRUM, I know that I am safe to be honest with my mentors about what I need. What really helps, though, is knowing that at any time I can reach out to one of the other Fellows and ask them for their support. Knowing I'm not alone makes it easier to breathe, even when things are busy." – Mikayla

Hera further elaborated on this, saying:

"If one Fellow decides to take a step back, other Fellows are supportive and will take initiative to fulfill the duties of the role. There is a
sense of assurance that SPECTRUM will find a way to make it work
and that you are always welcome to come back should you wish. I do
not think the same can be said to any other Research Assistant position." – Hera

Emily provided a personal experience with this aspect of SPECTRUM:

"As a student and a research assistant, you never want to 'let the ball
drop' or let your colleagues down, and planning a year-long parental
leave can cause a lot of stress and anxiety in this area – knowing that the
team of Fellows and our mentors on SPECTRUM supported me, that
the work I had been contributing to would continue uninterrupted, and
that my position with SPECTRUM would be waiting for me after my
leave helped alleviate so much stress." – Emily.

The sense of comradery and belonging that the Fellows have with one another is a key factor in how they balance their work. By ameliorating the fear
associated with not being able to perform and the consequences of needing
to take a step back for valid reasons, SPECTRUM has allowed the Fellows to
develop a deep sense of trust with one another. Much like how the partnership seeks to balance the scales of justice in society, the Fellows work together
to balance the workload and care for each other when one cannot carry their
work for a time.

Several Fellows also reflected on how each of them brings different skills,
knowledge, and ideas to the partnership, contributing to the resources available to the wider group. No two Fellows have the same academic, occupational,
or life experiences. They each bring something unique to the table, creating
more robust research products than they could have done alone. The Fellows
felt that this wide array of skills and knowledge helped them to appreciate their
own contributions even more.

Nyla discussed how she felt comfortable acknowledging the tasks she felt fell
outside of her skill set and to instead lean into her strengths in the work that
she did. Knowing that there were other Fellows to fill the gaps where she may
not have the necessary skills helped to ease her worries and encouraged her to
offer her unique skills.

"Emotionally, I can assess my strengths and challenges, while taking
steps towards offering my skillset, which makes me feel like an integral
part of the partnership." – Nyla

Anita further elaborated:

"Each of us bring a different set of skills, experiences, and outlooks to the partnership, which in turn means that each of us experience exposure to different skills, experiences, and outlooks. We continually rub up against different ways of understanding the world, and this broadens our own perspectives." – Anita

As Nyla suggested, working as a Fellow also enables the students to balance emotional resources. The nature of the work SPECTRUM undertakes to solve social policy issues using research is an inherently emotional process. Uncovering gaps in social policies and investigating the inequities that they perpetuate can be difficult to sit with. Several of the Fellows recounted instances of sharing their emotions and shedding tears together as the gravity of research findings are made apparent. This sharing of feelings associated with the research the partnership conducts has helped the Fellows to support each other and to regain emotional equilibrium, which they felt was essential to promoting wellbeing in academia.

As discussed in the introduction of this chapter, mental health concerns are pervasive in graduate school, especially among transgender/gender diverse people, women, and IGSC (Eaton et al., 2012; Evans et al., 2018; Lee & Rice, 2007). Given that all the current Fellows fall within at least one of these identities, the likelihood of at least one of them struggling with mental health at any given time is high. However, the non-hierarchal structure of SPECTRUM and the sense of togetherness it has fostered amongst the Fellows serves as a protective factor against adverse mental health outcomes.

"I have depression and anxiety, and that alone makes academia hard sometimes. Combining that with how heartbreaking some of the research findings are and the stress of succeeding in my coursework creates a perfect storm for a downwards spiral. Of all the research teams I've been involved in, SPECTRUM has been by far the most supportive. The other Fellows are more than just colleagues, they're friends. I have no doubt that it's the way that SPECTRUM is structured that has allowed us all the chance to care for each other as people first." – Mikayla

The balancing of time, skill-related, and emotional resources allowed Fellows the opportunity to come to trust one another and build strong relationships between them. This sense of comradery and the distribution of labour based on each person's present capabilities overall contributed to a sense of wellbeing amongst the Fellows.

Strategies for wellbeing

Much of the support for wellbeing provided through the SPECTRUM model comes from the ways in which it breaks from the typical mentorship and research assistant structure. The focus on Fellows being recognised as humans with complex social needs was imperative in promoting their wellbeing. Once again prompted via e-mail, the Fellows were asked to provide suggested strategies for proactively supporting wellbeing withing academia.

Make time for personal check-ins

Creating space for a check-in with participants at the beginning of a meeting creates a culture where wellbeing is prioritised. Although it may not appear to be an efficient use of meeting time, it is important to leave space for humanity within the work that we do. Personal check-ins can also contribute to fostering a safe and understanding environment and can help build relationship between participants.

Create opportunities for teamwork and diversity

Being the sole research assistant on a project can be overwhelming. Where possible, consider hiring two or more positions to support the work to allow students to support each other through the ebb and flow of graduate coursework. Multiple assistants with diverse backgrounds can provide different perspectives which can further develop and enrich the work. This recommendation also combats the competitive nature of many graduate school settings, promoting collaboration and supportive interactions between junior academics instead.

Welcome feedback

Not all junior academics will feel comfortable with providing their input immediately. Some may need another person to make space and to invite them to the proverbial table. An intentional effort on behalf of one's mentors to contribute to the conversation can support the development of confidence and self-worth in one's work.

Acknowledge important events

We do not conduct our work in a silo. The events in the world around us can, and do, impact how we come to our work and how we engage with it. Moreover, world events impact each person differently. Create a work culture that allows space for a human response to important world events.

Conclusion

The nature of academia is one that has been well documented to perpetuate the development of mental health conditions of students. The top-down, hierarchical approach to mentorship and conducting research has not improved outcomes for graduate students to date, based on the alarming statistics presented by studies conducted on the topic. The Fellows agree that the model of fellowship implemented by SPECTRUM has contributed to the maintenance of their wellbeing by means of the balance it offers them. They are able to balance the competing demands in their lives with their work, find balance as a team in how to allocate resources, and ameliorate role conflict by being viewed as equals by the other members of the partnership. Through the dismantling of the traditional mentorship model, SPECTRUM Fellows are proactively supported to prioritise their own wellbeing and self-care as they contribute to life changing social policy research.

To conclude, Jamie's thoughts on the importance of making space for prioritising one's own needs within SPECTRUM truly highlight how this unique student fellowship model enables proactive wellbeing in academia:

> "This taking a step back is not just tolerated, it is encouraged and celebrated. When I receive notification from other fellows letting the team know they need to take a step back, my first genuine emotion is happiness and gratitude. I feel this way because SPECTRUM is built on trust, respect, honesty, vulnerability, understanding, and encouragement." – Jamie

References

Anandavalli, S., Borders, L. D., & Kniffin, L. E. (2021). "Because here, White is right": Mental health experiences of international graduate students of Color from a critical race perspective. *International Journal for the Advancement of Counseling, 43*(3), 283–301. https://doi.org/10.1007/s10447-021-09437-x

Beiser, M., & Hou, F. (2016). Mental health effects of premigration trauma and post-migration discrimination on refugee youth in Canada. *The Journal of Nervous and Mental Disease, 204*(6), 464–70.

Clark, B. A., Veale, J. F., Greyson, D., & Saewyc, E. (2017). Primary care access and foregone care: A survey of transgender adolescents and young adults. *Family Practice, 35*(3), 302–306. https://doi.org/10.1093/fampra/cmx112

Eaton, N. R., Keyes, K. M., Krueger, R. F., Balsis, S., Skodol, A. E., Markon, K. E., Grant, B. F., & Hasin, D. S. (2012). An invariant dimensional liability model of gender differences in mental disorder prevalence: Evidence from a national sample. *Journal of Abnormal Psychology, 121*(1), 282–288. https://doi.org/10.1037/a0024780

Enns, J. E., Brownell, M., Casidsid, H. J. M., Hunter, M., Durksen, A., Turnbull, L. A., Nickel, N. C., Levasseur, K., Tait, M. J., Sinclair, S., Randall, S., Freier, A., Scatliff, C., Brownell, E., Dolin, A., Murdock, N., Mahar, A., Sinclair, S., & The

SPECTRUM Partnership (2023). The full spectrum: Developing a tripartite partnership between community, government and academia for Collaborative Social Policy Research. *Gateways: International Journal of Community Research and Engagement, 16*(1). https://doi.org/10.5130/ijcre.v16i1.8433

Evans, T. M., Bira, L., Gastelum, J. B., Weiss, L. T., & Vanderford, N. L. (2018). Evidence for a mental health crisis in graduate education. *Nature Biotechnology, 36*(3), 282–284. https://doi.org/10.1038/nbt.4089

George, U., Thomson, M., Chaze, F., & Guruge, S. (2015). Immigrant mental health, a public health issue: Looking back and moving forward. *International Journal of Environmental Research and Public Health, 12*(10), 13624–13648.

Grady, R. K., La Touche, R., Oslawski-Lopez, J., Powers, A., & Simacek, K. (2014). Betwixt and between: The social position and stress experiences of graduate students. *Teaching Sociology, 42*(1), 5–16. https://doi.org/10.1177/0092055x13502182

Guruge, S., & Butt, H. (2015). A scoping review of mental health issues and concerns among immigrant and refugee youth in Canada: Looking back, moving forward. *Canadian Journal of Public Health, 106*(2), e72–e78.

Hilario, C. T., Vo, D. X., Johnson, J. L., & Saewyc, E. M. (2014). Acculturation, gender, and mental health of Southeast Asian immigrant youth in Canada. *Journal of Immigrant Minority Health, 16*(6), 1121–1129.

Lee, J. J. (2021). *Unique challenges and opportunities for supporting mental health and promoting the well-being of international graduate students.* Council of Graduate Schools. https://cgsnet.org/wp-content/uploads/2022/01/CGS_Well-being-ConsultPaper-Lee.pdf

Lee, J. J., & Rice, C. (2007). Welcome to America? International student perceptions of discrimination. *Higher Education, 53*(3), 381–409. doi: 10.1007/s10734-005-4508-3

Litalien, D., & Guay, F. (2015). Dropout intentions in PhD studies: A comprehensive model based on interpersonal relationships and motivational resources. *Contemporary Educational Psychology, 41*, 218–231. https://doi.org/10.1016/j.cedpsych.2015.03.004

Reisner, S. L., Vetters, R., Leclerc, M., Zaslow, S., Wolfrum, S., Shumer, D., & Mimiaga, M. J. (2015). Mental health of transgender youth in care at an adolescent urban community health center: A matched retrospective cohort study. *Journal of Adolescent Health, 56*(3), 274–279. https://doi.org/10.1016/j.jadohealth.2014.10.264

Robledo Yamamoto, F., Cho, J., Voida, A., & Voida, S. (2023). "We are researchers, but we are also humans": Creating a design space for managing graduate student stress. *ACM Transactions on Computer-Human Interaction, 30*(5), 1–33. https://doi.org/10.1145/3589956

University of Waterloo (2021, May 10). *Roles and responsibilities of graduate students.* Graduate Studies and Postdoctoral Affairs. https://uwaterloo.ca/graduate-studies-postdoctoral-affairs/faculty-and-staff/guide-graduate-research-and-supervision/roles-and-responsibilities-graduate-students

Yoo, H. J., & Marshall, D. T. (2022). Understanding graduate student parents: Influence of parental status, gender, and major on graduate students' motivation, stress, and satisfaction. *Journal of College Student Retention: Research, Theory & Practice.* https://doi.org/10.1177/15210251211072241

Chapter 13

Fostering an ecosystem of connection

Emily Rooney

Introduction

Oak trees are ubiquitous where I grew up. In my mind's eye, I can picture the campus where I went to college and the majestic oaks that grace the grounds. Although oaks may seem like solitary stalwarts of the land they inhabit, they're anything but isolated. Take a closer look and you'll see an interconnected ecosystem at play all housed within the span of the oak's branches and root system. For instance, take the tangly, gray, hairlike Spanish moss. It regularly rests on the oak's branches and cascades down like Christmas tinsel. Continue along the bark of the oak, and perhaps you'll be fortunate to come across my personal favorite, the resurrection fern. Also clinging to branches like Spanish moss, during times of limited precipitation the resurrection fern shrivels up, turns brown, and appears to die. However, the fern miraculously springs back to life when water is introduced to its environment. While Spanish moss and the resurrection fern share a symbiotic relationship with the oak, other organisms are not so forgiving. For instance, mistletoe clings to and infests the oak's branches depleting the tree of valuable resources.

There are numerous relationships at play within the influence of the oak; each living creature, big and small alike, is intricately and dynamically connected. The grand ecosystem of the oak is not unlike the system of higher education and the roles we as humans serve in it. Given all this talk about ecosystems and oak trees, one might fashion me as a biologist or ecologist, and yet I'm neither. However, as a clinical psychologist, I'm innately curious about the forces that unite us and the power of human connection. Connection is how I survived graduate school. Higher education is often fraught with values that are incongruent with our values as humans. Output and productivity are often valued over quality of life and curiosity. Burnout and compassion fatigue run rampant in academia. Connecting to my humanness is what enabled me to maintain and live in accordance with my values in graduate school. I did this by fostering and maintaining relationships as much as possible throughout my studies and training. I began to rely heavily on my colleagues and their shared experiences and challenges. I'd lean on supervisors and mentors I could trust to speak gentle truths to me. I

DOI: 10.4324/9781003457510-16

Image 13.1 The ecosystem of the oak is symbolic of our interconnected relationships in higher education. Some are mutually beneficially while
others are potentially harmful. We can choose to foster or cut off
relationships in order to keep our ecosystem healthy, particularly in
the realm of higher education

also learned to avoid or cut connections that were no longer serving me. Much
like the ecosystem that encompasses the oak tree, the connections we make have
implications for our wellbeing and the social network around us.

In this chapter, I'll share my lived experiences as a clinical psychology graduate student, my struggles, and some of the connections that got me through
those difficult times. Perhaps in doing so, others will realise they aren't alone
in their struggles. Along the way, we'll dip our toes into the science behind
why connection is important and the implications of the same. Finally, I'll
share steps you can take to build and foster connections that will serve you
well beyond higher education. In doing so, I hope you too can connect to
your humanness and enjoy the benefit of engaging more deeply with those
around you. My hope is that, after reading this chapter, individuals at any level
of higher education will be able to glean insight into understanding the power
of meaningful connection.

Connection in crisis

In 2005, approximately 5% of Americans reported using some form of social
media; that number steadily increased to 72% of Americans in 2021 (Pew Research Center, 2021). Globally, 4.5 billion people currently use social media,

and that number is expected to increase to 5.8 billion by 2027 (Statista, 2023). Although our world may appear more connected than ever with the increased prevalence of social networking sites and virtual meeting software, the statistics on mental health issues paint a different picture (GBD 2019 Mental Disorders Collaborators, 2022; Tham et al., 2021).

The mental health crisis is amplified when we focus on higher education. College students are at a unique age when mental disorders commonly appear (Kessler et al., 2005) and a majority of college students report above-average levels of distress, with academia ranking as the most endorsed stressor (Brownson et al., 2016). College students also consistently report rates of depression and anxiety (approximately 1 in 3 students) above that of the general population (Li et al., 2022). Perhaps not surprisingly, suicide is the second leading cause of death among college students right behind accidental injuries (Turner et al., 2013).

The power of connection becomes even more apparent when aspects of connection are taken away. During the height of the COVID-19 pandemic social distancing and lockdown requirements negatively impacted college students' mental health (Chen & Lucock, 2022; Gewalt et al., 2022; Lee et al., 2021a) and students endorsed feeling lonely (Lee et al., 2021b) and reported increased stress due to social distancing (resulting in canceled events, worsening personal relationships (Chen & Lucock, 2022; Gewalt et al., 2022).

Unfortunately, the subsequent demand for mental health services has placed a strain on the mental health field and providers. Further complicating matters, the fear of stigma and discrimination prevents many students from reaching out for help in the first place (Druckenmiller, 2022; Lee et al., 2021a; Martin, 2010). The current method of functioning in higher education isn't sustainable. More than ever, the importance of the *quality* of connection and, subsequently, *how* we connect has implications for our wellbeing.

Connection in action

My late maternal grandmother (who we fondly refer to as "Papa" or "Pa" for short) understood the power of connection better than anyone I know. Nothing made this fact more apparent than when we were at the grocery store together. Pa would often smile at shoppers as she walked by and stopped to talk to people in the aisle. Eventually, I knew whenever we'd get to the check-out line, Pa would have a full-blown conversation with the cashier. Often this unsuspecting person was not prepared for an interaction at this level. Usually, they seemed perfectly content focusing on the task in front of them scanning each item and bagging in a methodical, repetitious fashion in what I would assume could be quite meditative (or boring) at times.

Anxiety and impending embarrassment were emotions I often felt as we approached the check-out line. These emotions were particularly heightened if the cashier had a scowl on their face or any other expression that signaled

"Don't bother me". However, without fail (and I observed this experiment too many times to count) their continence didn't deter Pa from greeting them with a smile and asking, "How are you doing today?"

She would often lean in over the counter signaling her engagement in the conversation, a gesture that in the post-COVID era might be considered an evasion of one's personal bubble, and a signal that (I knew all too well) meant Pa was in no rush to get through the check-out line. The person behind the register was the most important person in the store at that moment. Pa would continue the conversation, commenting on the cashier's unique name, beautiful nails, or great hair, always finding something she admired or intrigued her about this person. And without fail, a smile would creep across the cashier's face or, even better, they would spontaneously burst into laughter and blush at the undivided attention.

Not everyone, given the same set of circumstances, could emulate these interactions and have the same outcome as Pa. What made the difference with Pa was that she was authentic in her approach. She was genuinely curious to get to know people and honest in the warmth and love she extended others. She was authentically "Pa", and no one could fault her for being herself. In fact, they loved her for it. That brings me to a point that's essential to the connections we make. For meaningful connection to work, we must be the *truest forms of ourselves*.

Meaningful connection

Early on in my journey to my doctorate, I decided to follow Pa's lead by engaging with others in a way that was authentic to me. One pivotal moment was when I met Caleb, who would eventually become my colleague and friend. Caleb and I both interviewed for the same clinical psychology programme to work under the same advisor. We got acquainted on interview day but didn't meaningfully connect until we were leaving to go back home. We flew out on the same plane and had a layover in Chicago before our final destinations. I remember getting off the plane and seeing Caleb walking ahead of me. As he stopped by a kiosk, I started to head in the opposite direction to get food and toward my connecting flight. Then I hesitated. I felt a twinge in my stomach. My husband, who was traveling with me (and has an uncanny way of reading my mind) said, "Why don't we see if Caleb wants to join us?" I called out to Caleb and the rest is history. I still have a photo my husband took of Caleb and I that day in the airport, eating together and engrossed in conversation about some psychological phenomena. We would end up being accepted into the same programme and supporting each other through graduation and beyond. Caleb and I connected in meaningful way that day in the airport.

What do I mean by *meaningful connection*? Perhaps it's best to let the American psychologist Carl Rogers do the talking. Rogers helped define the humanistic movement and introduced the glue that binds healthy relationships (often studied within the context of the therapeutic relationship): unconditional positive regard, empathy, and genuineness (Rogers, 1959). For simplicity's sake, unconditional positive regard is often referred to as *warmth* and therefore we'll abbreviate these three key components to "WEG" – warmth, empathy, and genuineness (Altmann, 1973). At a minimum, a meaningful connection must have WEG.

Warmth refers to the acceptance of a person's self and their experiences. Empathy is defined as the ability to "perceive the internal reference of another with accuracy and with the emotional components and meanings which pertain thereto as if one were the person" (Rogers, 1959, p. 210). Or as I like to think of it, stepping into someone else's shoes. Genuineness is the "unadulterated and congruent external display of an individual's actual internally recognized values, beliefs, emotions, and other perceptions of themselves including the world they exist in" (Shaw, 2017, p. 1). Or as I like to refer to it, being authentically yourself. Although any one of these three components is a great contribution to a relationship, it's the combination and the interplay between these three ingredients that create the special sauce.

Caleb and I first connected over our shared struggle to get into a doctorate programme We both tried and failed several times, having to wait a year after each failed attempt before the next application cycle. When we met, we were both disillusioned from the application process and suffering from imposter syndrome. We were also older than most of the other candidates. Thus, we empathised with each other's situation which, in turn, made us more comfortable being transparent and genuine with each other. Finally, our warmth and positive regard toward each other is what maintains our friendship. Despite our individual flaws and failings, we see the best in each other and encourage each other accordingly. I recognised early on that my relationship with Caleb as one that I wanted to foster and would help me in my journey in higher education. He's been a vital branch in my growth.

Connection as a lifeline

When I said connection saved me in graduate school, I wasn't exaggerating. Fleeting thoughts of *I don't want to do this anymore, I don't want to be here,* and *I don't want to go on* became my trusty companions throughout graduate school.

Let's pause for a moment here. I want to make one thing clear before I go any further. Going to graduate school and becoming a clinical psychologist *was* and *is* my dream. I understood the sacrifice my family, friends, and I would have to make for me to complete my degree (in fact I had a fellow friend in a doctoral programme tell me, "Don't do it"). However, before thoughts of judgment enter your mind such as, *You signed up for this, didn't you?*, I'd like to remind you of WEG, emphasis on the E for empathy. Those currently undertaking a degree in higher education may have a better understanding of the difficulties faced. It's often hard to explain the struggle of graduate school when higher education is a privilege, not a right.

Where was I? Ah yes, fleeting thoughts of leaving this Earth or evaporating into thin air culminated one day into a numb indifference. I remember waking up, going to the medicine cabinet, opening bottles, and taking handfuls of whatever pills I could find. There was no rhyme (but certainly a reason) behind the pills I took. The medication cocktail probably included an unhealthy dose of various pain relievers, allergy pills, and Zoloft. I also took a handful of melatonin gummies for good measure. At the very least, I might as well have a restful night's sleep and enjoy their blackberry taste as they went down. I didn't know if my haphazard application of medication would "do the trick" but I was at the point of not caring. I was sad, numb, and resolute all at once.

I awoke the next morning not feeling much. Not feeling good or bad, just another day that unexpectedly came. Obviously, the cocktail I created was insufficient in my subconscious intent to not experience anything anymore. I can't remember exactly what I did after waking up, but I do remember that I decided to call my brother that day.

Feeling slightly ashamed and acknowledging I'd hit an all-time low, calling my brother was not a common occurrence. I can count on one hand the number of times I've called my brother "just because". You see, my brother is a man of few words. Conversations are less a reciprocal back-and-forth volleying of ideas and opinions and more like an interview where my brother usually gives one-word responses and I'm the facilitator keeping the interview going. He's extremely introspective and private. Furthermore, adding complexity to our relationship, my brother and I didn't necessarily get along growing up.

I can vividly remember us chasing each other around the house, ready to hit whoever was the aggressor of the day with whatever random object we had in our hands. Our mutual hardheadedness is what ultimately led us to break stalemates by lashing out at each other in this manner. Our older sister deserves sainthood for her Mother Teresa-like patience, as she constantly served as the designated mediator between the two of us.

Despite our past transgressions, my intention for calling my brother that day was clear. He'd experienced graduate school in all its glory and hardship. He entered a biology doctoral programme and was lucky enough to exit stage left (somewhat intact) with his master's. Aside from blood, our shared connection is academia.

I remember sitting in my car (due to the irrational fear someone would overhear my conversation and judge me in this decrepit state) when I dialed his number. When he picked up, I explained the thoughts that had been swirling around in my head for the past month, the thoughts I'd yet to speak aloud to anyone. I also explained my feelings of hopelessness that I would never make it through my programme intact. My brother understood the assignment. He listened, validated my feelings, and withheld any judgment. He said he understood and emphasised that academia is a bubble. You often have to get out of it and come up for air to realise there's a world outside. He also said he had similar thoughts in graduate school which made me feel less alone. Whether or not he realised it, he was practising WEG. That singular phone call to my brother and receiving his support motivated me to keep going.

Ultimately, I'm grateful my impulsive decision didn't end up differently. Like the Spanish moss and the resurrection fern that rely on the oak, my loss would be felt by the ecosystem of those around me, and I wouldn't be there to notice. By reaching out to my brother, I relied on one of my many connections (my husband, mother, friends, colleagues among them) to get me through a difficult time. And as you'll soon read, going through difficulties together (rather than in isolation) is when connection thrives.

Pain and compassion

A discussion on connection is not complete without giving ample literary space to pain. Pain is the universal leveler and unifier. We all experience pain to one degree or another. Whether you call it hurt, suffering, sadness, or burdensomeness – we've experienced the weight of life. It's what makes us human.

Take 9/11 for example – a day that will go down in US history as one of the worst terrorist attacks. For those of us old enough to remember, you'll recall watching hours of news coverage, horrifically mesmerised by the scenes unfolding and the days that followed, blanketing the country with a cloud of languishing. You'll remember seeing first responders combing through wreckage for survivors and broken families trying to make sense of this senseless act. And yet, 9/11 was also a moment that united Americans. Pride in America and respect for first responders skyrocketed during this time. You didn't have to walk more than two blocks to see someone flying an American flag in solidarity with our country and in defiance of the forces that threatened it. Politicians even put aside their differences and demonstrated a united front, parading around together shoulder to shoulder at events (see the Pew Research Center article, "Two decades later, the enduring legacy of 9/11", for a reflection). How could so much suffering cultivate so much unification?

What allows us to push through or cope with pain is compassion. Recognising and empathising with someone's pain is compassion. The word compassion originates from the Latin word *compati* which means "suffer with" or "suffer together". In the aftermath of 9/11, Americans were suffering together. Pain and compassion are two sides of the same coin. You cannot have compassion without suffering, and you cannot experience compassion without first connecting to someone else's suffering. This dialectic is what makes the therapeutic relationship so poignant and our close personal relationships so meaningful.

Just as Caleb and I connected over our shared struggle to get into graduate school and how I connected with my brother over the overwhelming nature of graduate school, turning pain into compassion can be a powerful tool to strengthen relationships. I liken this strengthening to the ability of oak roots to grow and become fortified during times of drought; searching and reaching for nourishing water and relief, the same relief we receive from compassion.

Parasitic relationships

I'd be remiss not to mention that not all connections are meant to be meaningful. Some in fact, can be downright toxic to your environment, stealing your resources and zapping your energy – much like the relationship between mistletoe and oak trees. Although often viewed as a joyous symbol of winter and romance, mistletoe is, in fact, a parasite. Its roots penetrate oaks' branches to steal nutrients and water. The oak can sustain itself if only a few mistletoe plants take hold of its branches, but it can just as quickly become diseased and die given a large infestation of mistletoe. Cutting off the branches impacted by mistletoe is one way to rid the oak of this pest. Sometimes we must do the same in relationships. We must sever a tie for the greater good of our ecosystem. Other times, when we don't have the choice but to interact with certain individuals, we learn to adapt and can handle the less than pleasant relationship given our other healthy connections and resources.

I experienced my fair share of parasitic relationships in graduate school. Unfortunately, most happened to be relationships with my superiors, those who were supposed to mentor and support students. Aside from avoiding these individuals when possible and limiting communication with them, I also tried to search for opportunities to rid myself of unhealthy relationships. A prime opportunity presented itself when my programme started the search for a new faculty member. I jumped at the opportunity to be a member of the search committee by serving as a student representative. If I could voice my opinion and have a spot at the table, I was going to advocate for candidates who had students' best interests at heart and discourage the hiring of those who might not. I was going to try and prevent the mistletoe from grasping hold in the first place. During one interview cycle with a candidate, I got the sense that they were more focused on advancing their career and producing research than investing time into mentoring future psychologists. Each candidate had the opportunity to speak with students, with no other faculty present, in what we – the students – were assured was a candid conversation. I spoke up when the topic of student mental health arose. I gave my frank opinion that some faculty are understanding and supportive of our wellbeing, while others are not. In fact, sometimes students were retaliated against for sharing struggles, raising issues with the programme, or reaching out for help. (I personally witnessed students being ostracised, denied opportunities for research funding, and, in the most extreme cases, pushed out of the programme).

Unfortunately, our "candid" conversation with this candidate wasn't so candid after all. I found out that the candidate shared sensitive information from our discussion with the faculty members. This confirmed my worst fears and my gut instinct – that this would prove to be an unhealthy relationship for the ecosystem. I echoed as much in my feedback to the faculty search committee and know several of my fellow students did as well. Thankfully, in the end, this candidate was *not* hired for the position. Instead, an equally qualified and successful psychologist was hired. Most importantly they're eager to support students, a far healthier relationship for the system as a whole.

Sometimes it's not just a relationship but the environment you're in that is not conducive to flourishing. There's a reason oak trees don't grow in deserts. Given the pressure to produce and power differentials where egos abound, perhaps it's no surprise that in recent years there's been a shift to leave the often toxic environment of academia. Vacating the ecosystem will surely change your environment and might be the appropriate and healthy choice. However, we need kind and compassionate team players in higher education. Hopefully, encouraging people to maintain healthy connections and draw boundaries between less-than-healthy connections can help keep valuable team players in higher education.

Steps to foster connection

Fostering your ecosystem of connection starts with YOU. After all, you're an essential member of the ecosystem. The following are several steps you can take to help foster connection in your life.

1   Be the truest form of yourself

Don't know yourself? Then find yourself. If I had to write a prescription for "being you" it would go as follows:

- Identify your values and stick to them. Remember, higher education often has values that look different from our own. I have identified faith, relationships, and curiosity as a few of my top values. A quick Google search for "values clarification" will reveal a plethora of resources to help you identify your values. Once you identify your values, live according to them by doing things that align with your values. For instance, getting to know people by asking questions aligns with my values of relationship and curiosity.
- Know your boundaries and limits. This may take trial and error and look different for each individual and relationship. For instance, being around my close friends and colleagues gives me energy while being around distant acquaintances depletes my energy. When possible, limit time and communication with these individuals by having clear boundaries. For example, if you must have a meeting with an unpleasant co-worker, set an agenda for the meeting and make it time-limited (30 minutes max). Boundaries often equate to structure, so the more you can add structure to difficult relationships, the less you're likely to feel depleted from those relationships. One boundary that has helped me maintain space between work and my personal life is limiting communication before 8 am and after 5 pm.
- Rinse and repeat the above with healthy doses of reflection and perspective-taking when possible.

2   *Reach out for help*

What are those sayings… Rome wasn't built in a day, and it takes a village? Well, not only was Rome not built in a day, but I can guarantee you more than one person was building it. Just like people rarely encounter success overnight, people rarely achieve success alone. Thus, we must call on others when we need help.

I have a rule when I notice myself struggling on a project, when I feel overwhelmed, or find myself spiraling down a dark pit of despair. If I struggle for more than 10 minutes and can't unstick myself, I reach out to someone. Whether it be a colleague, family member, friend, or mentor, so many individuals (perhaps unknowingly) have disrupted my struggle cycle and helped me move forward. For instance, I constantly find myself struggling with papers. A quick text to a friend with a question about my topic or emailing a colleague to get some suggestions is usually all it takes to get me back on track. It's surprising how something so simple can be so powerful. I recommend you give it a try. It starts with three simple words: I need help.

3   *Turn your pain into compassion*

Use your lived experiences to connect to others going through hurt. Comfort those who need comforting. Be vulnerable. Share your lived experiences so others don't feel so alone. Sit with someone and be with them in their suffering. Even your physical presence can impact the ecosystem.

4   *Look for small opportunities to connect*

Stay aware of your surroundings. When we look down and inward, we often miss what is going on around us. Further, this tends to make the world feel smaller like we're doing life on our own. Instead, look up and around. Smile at the person next to you. Say "hello" or "good morning" to people passing by. Ask someone how they're doing and mean it. Meaningful connection doesn't mean you have to know the person for 10 years and be best friends. Meaningful connection can happen in 5 seconds with a stranger. Whether you're in the checkout line, sitting on the bus, strolling on the sidewalk, at the airport or riding the elevator, connection can happen anywhere with anyone. For example, I recently met someone who complimented my hat while we were passing each other on a hike. We got to talking, found out we lived in the same city, and exchanged contact information. Since then, we've gotten together twice and have gone hiking together with our husbands.

5   *When in doubt, practice WEG*

Warmth, empathy, and genuineness are *always* appropriate default responses.

Concluding thoughts

When you spend time pouring into your ecosystem of connection, you'll reap the benefits of strong healthy connections and meaningful relationships. My hope is that you find, even if only one piece, this chapter helpful on your journey in higher education. And perhaps it'll allow you to flourish in the ecosystem you've fostered.

References

Altmann, H. A. (1973). Effects of empathy, warmth, and genuineness in the initial counseling interview. *Counselor Education and Supervision, 12*(3), 225–228. https://doi.org/10.1002/j.1556-6978.1973.tb01555.x

Brownson, C., Drum, D. J., Swanbrow Becker, M. A., Saathoff, A., & Hentschel, E. (2016). Distress and suicidality in higher education: Implications for population-oriented prevention paradigms. *Journal of College Student Psychotherapy, 30*(2), 98–113. https://doi.org/10.1080/87568225.2016.1140978

Chen, T., & Lucock, M. (2022). The mental health of university students during the COVID-19 pandemic: An online survey in the UK. *PLOS ONE, 17*(1), e0262562. https://doi.org/10.1371/journal.pone.0262562

Druckenmiller, R. (2022, July 19). College students and depression: A guide for parents. https://www.mayoclinichealthsystem.org/hometown-health/speaking-of-health/college-students-and-depression

GBD 2019 Mental Disorders Collaborators (2022). Global, regional, and national burden of 12 mental disorders in 204 countries and territories, 1990-2019: A systematic analysis for the Global Burden of Disease Study 2019. *The Lancet. Psychiatry, 9*(2), 137–150. https://doi.org/10.1016/S2215-0366(21)00395-3

Gewalt, S. C., Berger, S., Krisam, R., & Breuer, M. (2022). Effects of the COVID-19 pandemic on university students' physical health, mental health and learning, a cross-sectional study including 917 students from eight universities in Germany. *PLOS ONE, 17*(8), e0273928. https://doi.org/10.1371/journal.pone.0273928

Kessler, R. C., Berglund, P., Demler, O., Jin, R., Merikangas, K. R., & Walters, E. E. (2005). Lifetime prevalence and age-of-onset distributions of DSM-IV disorders in the National Comorbidity Survey Replication. *Archives of General Psychiatry, 62*(6), 593–602. https://doi.org/10.1001/archpsyc.62.6.593

Lee, J., Jeong, H. J., & Kim, S. (2021a). Stress, anxiety, and depression among undergraduate students during the COVID-19 pandemic and their use of mental health services. *Innovative Higher Education, 46*(5), 519–538. https://doi.org/10.1007/s10755-021-09552-y

Lee, J., Solomon, M., Stead, T., Kwon, B., & Ganti, L. (2021b). Impact of COVID-19 on the mental health of US college students. *BMC Psychology, 9*(1), 95. https://doi.org/10.1186/s40359-021-00598-3

Li, W., Zhao, Z., Chen, D., Peng, Y., & Lu, Z. (2022). Prevalence and associated factors of depression and anxiety symptoms among college students: A systematic review and meta-analysis. *Journal of Child Psychology and Psychiatry, 63*(11), 1222–1230. https://doi.org/10.1111/jcpp.13606

Martin, J. M. (2010) Stigma and student mental health in higher education. *Higher Education Research & Development, 29*(3), 259–274. https://doi.org/10.1080/07294360903470969

Pew Research Center (2021, April 7). Social media fact sheet. https://www.pewresearch.org/internet/fact-sheet/social-media/

Pew Research Center (2021, September 2). Two decades later, the enduring legacy of 9/11. https://www.pewresearch.org/politics/2021/09/02/two-decades-later-the-enduring-legacy-of-9-11/

Rogers, C. R. (1959). A theory of therapy, personality, and interpersonal relationships: As developed in the client-centered framework. In S. Koch (Ed.), *Psychology: A study of a science. Formulations of the person and the social context* (Vol. 3, pp. 184–256). McGraw Hill.

Shaw, D. E. (2017). Genuineness. In V. Zeigler-Hill & T. K. Shackelford (Eds.), *Encyclopedia of personality and individual differences* (pp. 1–5). Springer International Publishing. https://doi.org/10.1007/978-3-319-28099-8_1475-1

Statista (2023, February 23). *Number of social media users worldwide from 2017 to 2027.* Statista. https://www.statista.com/statistics/278414/number-of-worldwide-social-network-users/#statisticContainer

Tham, W. W., Sojli, E., Bryant, R., & McAleer, M. (2021). Common mental disorders and economic uncertainty: Evidence from the COVID-19 Pandemic in the U.S. *PLOS ONE, 16*(12), e0260726. https://doi.org/10.1371/journal.pone.0260726

Turner, J. C., Leno, E. V., & Keller, A. (2013). Causes of mortality among American college students: A pilot study. *Journal of College Student Psychotherapy, 27*(1), 31–42. https://doi.org/10.1080/87568225.2013.739022

Chapter 14

A cat named Jiji

Belonging, identity, and navigating cultural displacement in academia

Bertha Chin

Introduction

In a *Wired* magazine interview, Chilean-American actor, Pedro Pascal said "Everywhere is home and nowhere is home" (Jhaveri, 2023). This quote encapsulates my complex feelings towards the concept of home, often attached to a sense of belonging, which, as Vikki Bell suggests, "necessarily incorporates the issue of how common histories, experiences and places are created, imagined and sustained" (1999, p. 3). For an academic, this sense of home and belonging are also attached to their research disciplines, and, more often than not, the peers and mentors that make up the discipline; as well as the meeting places, set within the walls of universities and conference venues. The COVID-19 pandemic, which grounded travel and kept people inside their homes for up to 3 years has given rise to questions about access and diversity in spaces where academics frequently gather, meet, exchange ideas, and socialise. The switch to virtual gatherings was celebrated as a move towards more inclusivity for academics who may not otherwise be able to attend these gatherings for various reasons, but for others, could heighten the sense of isolation (Sibai et al., 2019).

However, our sense of belonging may also exist in other ways, such as through relationships with people beyond academia, and potentially through our relationship with beloved pets. A *Times Higher Education* article remarked that the "academic-cat relationship goes back some way", tracing the role cats have inadvertently played in academic publishing since the 1400s (Wright, 2015). A search on Instagram for the hashtag #academicswithcats generated 10.9k posts, compared to the 1000+ posts of #academicswithdogs.[1] This gives an indication of the role cats play in the academic's work and personal life. Natalie Ngai (2022) declares that "pets rule the Internet", and as the Instagram hashtag suggests, academics are utilising the social media platform to share pictures of their feline companions, often as a writing companion or surrounded by books and computers. In an article on the pet–human relationship, Ines, Ricci-Bonot, and Mills (2021, p. 2) suggest that the "relationship between an owner and a companion animal may reflect an enduring tie such as an affectional bond in which the other is emotionally important as a unique individual and is interchangeable with no other".

DOI: 10.4324/9781003457510-17

Being an academic, faced with precarity enabled by a consistently neoliberal university system and the constant possibility of having to uproot for the purpose of work, can be an isolating experience. The experience of isolation is further heightened when the academic returns to their home country after spending many years abroad, confronted with cultural differences that many may just dismiss as momentary culture shock. However, this may not be momentary, as I have examined elsewhere (Chin, 2022a), and as a result, may culminate in the academic developing coping strategies that help compartmentalise between research and teaching/administrative work, in turn driving the feeling of isolation. As such, an isolated academic may also turn elsewhere to foster their sense of belonging. A beloved pet who is a constant companion can provide tangible links for academics who may be increasingly isolated due to various reasons. In this chapter, I explore, through the method of life writing, an academic's sense of belonging, of identity, and of cultural displacement through love and loss of a beloved pet cat.

The story of Jiji

Jiji was a black and white moggie; a sweet, domestic long-haired cat. Her story – or our story – began in the summer of 2006, as she wandered self-assuredly, as cats do, into the South London flat my brother and I had just moved into one afternoon as we were watching Studio Ghibli's *Kiki's Delivery Service,* and decided she was going to adopt us. We learned later that she was the neighbour's cat, and had been living outside for a couple of weeks when they adopted new kittens. Conversations with the neighbour also revealed

Image 14.1 Jiji on my laptop (2020)

that Jiji did not take too well to the kittens, and as she had a very soft meow, was often overlooked and not let back into the house because the neighbours couldn't hear her when she was at the door, meowing to be let in. After I moved to the area, she would jump into the first floor flat I was staying in via the open kitchen window when she couldn't get back into the neighbour's house. In the beginning, she would spend the day at mine and return to the neighbours in the evening. I started getting into the habit of keeping some food for her in the house.

As summer rolled into autumn, Jiji started spending longer hours at the flat, curled up next to me as I struggled over the direction of my PhD. She was a frequent writing companion, but she wasn't my cat even though I had started identifying her as 'Jiji', named after the black cat in *Kiki's Delivery Service*. One frosty autumn night, Jiji jumped through the kitchen window into the flat, cold and hungry. I fed her, and that night, she slept on a blue-checked throw blanket on my bed that till today is still referred to as "Jiji's favourite blanket". It wasn't until the next day that I realised the neighbour's flat was completely empty. They had moved out overnight, and had abandoned her on what would become one of the coldest winters in England for a while. There was no doubt after that she would be my cat. As my brother and I stocked up on cat food and a litter tray, and made appointments with the vet for her to be properly checked, my application to transfer my PhD to a different institution to work with a PhD supervisor who was better suited to the direction I wanted to go in was approved. It was almost as if, serendipitously, Jiji and I had not only found each other, but had also found a positive way to move forward.

Over the years, we developed a rhythm to our days: Jiji would stay indoors when I taught a few days a week or when I had to travel to meet my PhD supervisor; she would be curled up beside me as I wrote, whether indoors during winter or in the garden over the summer months. When my brother moved to the north of England for a couple of years, I would bring Jiji with me on the train to visit and stay for a few weeks at a time. Through it all, our routine remained: me writing, and her next to me or nearby, almost as if offering emotional support. This continued even after I was done with writing my thesis; Jiji was there through every publication, every job application sent out, every rejection received. She was a companion, but she was also a confidant, a witness through all the ups and downs of being an early career researcher at a time of great uncertainty in British academia as I struggled to secure a full-time position.

Eventually, as I made the difficult decision to leave the UK after two decades of my life there, Jiji would return with me to Sarawak. The process was long and stressful, as we had to look into how to travel and quarantine procedures (there was none needed in the end!). I wasn't just uprooting my own life, I was also uprooting her from everything that was familiar and moving her into a household with other pets (four cats and a dog). Given her history, I was concerned about how she would get along with the other cats, but from the time of her arrival in Sarawak, she surprised me with her resilience and how quickly she could adapt – much sooner than I did, for sure. While she would never let them near her, she learned to tolerate the other cats, even as she preferred the company of humans, to my surprise, and the dog. My parents would let her play in the garden in the late afternoon when the day gets cooler, and this was where she would wait for me to come home from work every day. As I struggled to find my place in an essentially foreign workplace, and remain connected to my peers, mentors, and colleagues in greater academia, Jiji continued to be a solace. A constant touchstone. Even when we had moved countries, our routine persisted. While I graded essays and continued working on publications, Jiji would stretch out beside me, like a reminder that some relationships remained the same even if things change. Her presence was a reassurance that even if I was geographically distant from friends and culture that I was familiar with, she was a constant.

More than just a solace, Jiji was an affirmation and a reminder that the knowledge and skills developed over the years as a postgraduate student, and then as an early career researcher, were a tangible connection to life and academic culture in England. She was a tangible connection to England even if I've moved away. Towards the end of July 2021, Jiji caught a bout of flu from a kitten we had recently rescued. The vet assured me that this was something that was inevitable for older cats. While I did not have her exact age, she would have been about 16 or 17 years old at the time – equivalent to 80–84 human years. As she was on the mend from the flu, she had a stroke, and deteriorated so quickly that I barely had time to process losing her. Jiji passed away in the early morning of 1 August 2021.

Losing Jiji, in the midst of a pandemic, was a shock: a mortality I was admittedly not ready to face. There was a part of me that had thought she would be around for longer, that we would have more time together. While I can now be thankful that her last year and a half was reminiscent of our time in London as I was working from home due to Malaysia's Covid-19 restrictions, it drove the feeling of isolation, of being even further away from friends whom I would have seen every year, but now impeded by a global pandemic. Jiji was an anchor to my life in England, and she was a huge part of my formative years of first being a PhD student, and then an early career researcher. Losing her made me question where I belonged, and how I view my identity (as an academic), my relationship to peers and colleagues, and my workplace, and to greater academia as a whole.

Home and belonging

When I was fresh out of my PhD, one of the frequent conversational exchanges among early career researchers revolved around whether I'd found my 'home conference'; that is, the one (or two) conference I'd return to annually (or every other year, depending on the frequency of these meetings), regardless of where in the world this was held. The 'home conference' is understood to be the conference where an academic feels most welcomed, most at home presenting and representing their research discipline. The importance of this sense of belonging is emphasised even more when the academic feels displaced within their everyday work environment.

Conferences – and travelling to these conferences – anchor academics to their community of scholars and build a sense of belonging. This is especially important for those who are situated geographically away from their peers and for those who may not be working in institutions that necessarily understand them; making attendance at these conferences all the more important as forms of connection. Hopkins et al. (2019, p. 478) argue that the ability and opportunity, despite personal costs (of long-haul travels, negotiating teaching schedules and the like), "to develop and maintain connections with international communities [is]…a critical aspect of an academic career… [where the conference space enabled] colleagues [to become] friends, blurring the social and professional networks, relationships, and identities".

The COVID-19 pandemic and subsequent grounding of air travel for two years (and more for some) changed the way we think about academic conferences as many of these events shifted to virtual modes. This shift prompted many to reflect on the possibilities of academic conferences to be more inclusive and accessible (Donlon, 2021; Sipley, 2021), particularly for scholars who are unable to be present at these conferences due to health, financial, or geographical reasons. Carrigan and Elder-Vass (2020), however, reminded that online conferences and meetings will pose a challenge to "the informal networking affordances offered at face-to-face events by meeting rooms (before and after sessions), corridors, coffee breaks, opportunities to go for dinner in interesting groups, etc.". Many of the reflections considered differing time zones as a potential ramification to virtual conferences, but few remarked on how this might further isolate the scholar, and as such, affect their sense of belonging to their peers when they are unable to fully participate for various reasons, punishing time differences being one of many other obstacles.

This was starkly felt when global lockdowns kept me in Sarawak, Malaysian Borneo, for close to three years, unable to travel back to the UK, where majority of my academic peers and colleagues are based. Prior to the pandemic, annual trips to the UK served as a return to familiar spaces and opportunities to (re)connect with friends, colleagues, and fellow academics at conferences and in other social situations. Attending conferences and meetings online, while it afforded me the ability to participate in seminars and talks I'd otherwise not be able to attend since moving back to Asia, came with its own set of challenges. Being in Southeast Asia, and having a specialisation where most peers are in the Global North, meant many such conferences were taking place with time differences that were averaging between 8 to 13 hours. This meant staying awake till 3 or 4 am to present a paper or attend a panel, but not necessarily being able to attend any of the virtual social sessions as it would mean staying up all night while still expected to be back teaching a class, or attending and chairing meetings by 9 a.m. the next day. It meant being increasingly behind with watching pre-recorded panels before they were deleted from the archives, and potentially spending a week or two being jetlagged without the long-haul air travel. I have briefly questioned who these virtual conferences privilege (Chin, 2022b), but being present at virtual conferences also meant feeling divided by expectations to be the engaged research academic at the conference and the attentive lecturer-slash-administrator at the workplace. It both challenges and reinforces the concept of the academic's sense of belonging, particularly to a conference or their chosen research discipline; and an inability to participate in the social events of a conference due to time zone differences may also drive the sense of isolation for geographically distant academics.

In a recent article, Narelle Lemon wrote about how the pandemic has caused a major disruption in the ways we think about self-care and wellbeing in higher education, not merely as a space of teaching and learning, but also as a work space. Lemon (2023) highlighted the importance of belonging as one of these lessons, writing that "[b]elonging is connected to our identity, meaning making, our relevance in the world and our life satisfaction. Our need to belong is significant and to how we bolster our wellbeing". She goes on to argue that this sense of belonging isn't just tied to a physical place (such as being on campus), but also to the relationships we build and foster with others. For me, this sense of belonging is also tied to a beloved pet who provided a tangible connection to a sense of familiarity, of shared experiences. We often explore our sense of belonging through our ties to groups of people, or to a place, but rarely do we think about the ties between an academic and their pets, often an academic's most constant writing companion, and solace from an otherwise isolating experience in academia.

The isolating academia

Elsewhere, I reflected on how repatriation or the return of the academic to their home countries after spending their formative years abroad can create a tension that requires constant negotiation, one where the diasporic academic continually struggles with the duality of being a 'local' but never really being 'local' enough for most (Chin, 2022a) – a challenge to an often-assumed close relation between "community and locality, between community and place" (Massey, 1994, p. 110). Diasporic identities, according to cultural theorist Paul Gilroy, are "creolised, syncretised, hybridised, and chronically impure cultural forms" (2000, p. 129). They are messy, complex, and do not necessarily fit into fixed ideas of a place, a community, or a culture. Sophia A. McClennen argues that diasporic subjects narrate their lives through two frameworks: "a strategy of duality, where the self is described as interacting with two oppositional social forces, and … a strategy of polyvalence, where the self is described as a hybrid that cannot be represented through dualisms" (2005, p. 171), a common thread found in the "life writing of exiles and the displaced" (McClennen, 2005, p. 171). However, our understandings of diaspora now go beyond those in exile or displaced; diaspora also relates to economic and cultural migrants who have left their home countries for various reasons, and given the consistently global and neoliberal nature of work (not just in academia), these migrants may have moved to a third country or return to their home or 'native' countries. These movements displace lives and norms and, as such, create a feeling of isolation that is potentially both self-inflicted as much as it is institutionalised.

When repatriated academics such as myself 'return' to their 'native' countries, tensions arise "between conceptions of academia (and the academic), the differences in pedagogical approaches, the conception of the researcher or academic versus teacher identity, being an arts and humanities academic in the West versus being one in (Southeast) Asia" (Chin 2022a, p. 136). The demands of the neoliberal Malaysian academic workplace are such that the academics, especially those with PhDs, are expected to do everything beyond that of teaching or research or administration. Here, the academic is also a marketer, customer service personnel, a student's study planner, and other miscellany. An academic's value to the institution is framed within the context of a rhetoric of capability, as multiple instructions for tasks would begin with "You have a PhD; therefore, you should be able to teach/do/fulfil/organise this", and these tasks are often outside the area of expertise or knowledge the academic is trained in. Research is expected to be done outside of office hours, but the problem with this rhetoric of capability is that the expectation now is that the academic's weekends and after-office hours are filled with requests and instructions from line managers, and the expectation to participate in university-centred activities such as marketing, including travelling for said marketing activities.

These are, of course, increasingly common demands of a neoliberal university dependent on the labour of academics who can perform multiple roles, but as wellbeing scholars start to question how these demands affect the academics' sense of self, I would also like to call attention to how these demands may affect diasporic academics isolated from their peers, geographically, socially, and culturally. Often, a failure to participate and perform is seen as a rejection of the institution's concept of 'we', or group identity.

As Paul Gilroy (2000, p. 99) argues:

> the distinctive language of identity appears...when people seek to calculate how tacit belonging to a group or community can be transformed into more active styles of solidarity, when they debate where the boundaries around a group should be constituted and how – if at all – they should be enforced. Identity becomes a question of power and authority.

Gilroy's argument here can be contextualised to the Malaysian academic institutions, where sameness is encouraged through use of 'uniforms' at functions (to build a communal identity and corporate brand), or as Gilroy puts it "large-scale theatrical techniques for producing and stabilising identity and soliciting ... identification" (2000, p. 103). A rejection of these practices is seen as foreign and 'Western', and this is constantly communicated through reminders that I'm no longer in the UK, and thus, the complex thinking around identity and culture is not needed nor valued in the Malaysian context. As such, the collective 'we' does not need 'that kind of academic'.

This is problematic; for while the academic workplace (situated in Malaysia) does not need complex thinking around issues of identity and culture, my research discipline (mostly situated in the UK, Europe, and North America) does. In the years since I've moved back to Asia, I have taken to compartmentalising the labour I perform for the university (teaching, administrative work) versus the labour I perform for research (publication, conferences) in order to maintain a sense of wellbeing and for the sake of mental health. As such, separate spaces need to be maintained in order for these labours to be performed, and they may not intersect, thus making the academic more isolated.

This compartmentalisation of labour – and, as such, of identity – also creates a language displacement. In this case, it is both a conscious and subconscious effort to not speak or be fluent in any of Malaysia's – or Sarawak's – local languages[2] to maintain a critical distance from local cultures. At the same time, this accentuates imposter syndrome, which Aminda J. O'Hare defines as "a phenomenon where an individual feels inadequate in their role despite external evidence that they are successful, is unsure of their abilities, and experiences stress and fear about being found out as a fraud" (2022, p. 60). This is certainly intensified at academic conferences for me, when I struggle to recall the academic language of media and cultural studies when one has gotten used to not using it in everyday vernacular, or to conceal that part of the academic identity.

Colin Davis (2006, p. 340) argued that:

> the link ... between (the loss of) language and diasporic subjectivity is important. In a key metaphor, Derrida (Derrida, 1996: 91) relates the possession of language to the protection of a *chez-soi* ... And lacking a *chez-soi* in language is also to be deprived of a *soi*, as Derrida suggests (1996: 108) in a resonant list which links place, home and subjectivity... To lack language is also to lack a place, a home, a being-at-home and a being.

As a diasporic academic, this means being constantly isolated from both, for never being local enough for the workplace, and for always feeling like an imposter among academic peers. For me, these emotions were assuaged in the company of Jiji, however. As I have mentioned earlier, Jiji acted as tangible link to life in the UK, a place where my academic and university-teaching selves do not need to diverge, and importantly, aren't viewed as a threat to the "we" of the university. As Gilroy notes, "identity ceases to be an ongoing process of self-making and social interaction. It becomes instead a thing to be possessed and displayed" (2000, p. 103).

Sense of belonging

The "question of belonging necessarily incorporates the issue of how common histories, experiences and places are created, imagined and sustained" (Bell, 1999, p. 3). This is complicated by diasporic identities whose histories, experiences, and places are now fragmented. Diasporic academics such as myself do not necessarily belong to the country that trained me; as I have written, the state of the UK's higher education is such that I am made to feel I am "the wrong race, gender and in possession of the wrong nationality. In short, I was not a good enough immigrant" (2022a, p. 136). At the same time, neither do I belong to the country of my birth, for I have not only lost the language, I am, as Gilroy (2000) puts it, too "creolised, syncretised, hybridised, and chronically impure" (p. 129) for the sameness that operates within a group identity, essentially Asian countries that prioritise the homogenous community.

For a long time, my sense of belonging is attached to my relationship with Jiji, the one constant from the days of being a PhD student, to an early career researcher, to the time I moved back to Asia. Time spent together as I write or read out sections of writing while she naps is ritualistic, which "operates to recall and reconnect with places elsewhere that, through those very movements, are re-membered; at the same time, a site of diasporic belonging is created" (Bell, 1999, p. 3). It is a belonging that connects me to my past and anchors me to the present.

Losing Jiji in the midst of a national stay-at-home order during the COVID-19 pandemic emphasised my isolation from the workplace and from academia. The anchor that connects me to my past – the training, the accumulation of academic knowledge – and to the present is now gone. To return to Narelle Lemon's (2023) piece:

> The pandemic has raised our awareness of the need for compassion, made us hungry to be on the receiving end of compassion and allowed us to reconsider how we are compassionate to ourselves and each other in higher education. The pandemic has also slapped us in the face with what we will no longer accept and that, in particular, means a lack of compassion.

In a way, losing Jiji made me more compassionate with myself, in terms of accepting that I will always compartmentalise the labour I perform for the university workplace, and for academia. But as Lemon reminded, it has also reminded me of what is no longer acceptable, which is the expectation that I will be anything but a diasporic subject who will always be culturally displaced.

Conclusion

When I began this chapter, I remarked that we often explore our sense of belonging to a place (usually a country of birth or domicile) or to groups of people. Rarely do we think about our ties as academics to our pets, even when one of the most common traits of conversation at a social gathering during academic conferences is academics sharing pictures of their pets. Numerous virtual conferences I have attended have a forum or channel set aside for the sharing of pet pictures, suggesting that pets take up a big portion of our lives, regardless of where we are geographically located.

This chapter is an attempt to link the abstract ties of belonging, identity, and cultural displacement through the narrative of loss of a beloved pet, and how that has made me question my academic identity, where I belong, and my cultural displacement. As a result of love and loss, over an especially isolating period of lockdowns during the COVID-19 pandemic, it has propelled me to think about what is and isn't acceptable in the workplace, and in academia.

Notes

1 Search performed on 27 August 2023
2 Malaysia's official language is the *Bahasa Melayu* (the Malay language) although a variation of this – the *Bahasa Sarawak* – is spoken in Sarawak. Mandarin and other Chinese dialects are also widely spoken, and used across various other mediums like advertising, while English is the country's official second language (which is also the major academic language). The use of language is extremely politicised in Malaysia, which is too complex to get into in this chapter.

References

Bell, V. (1999). Performativity and belonging: An introduction. *Theory, Culture & Society, 16*(2), 1–10.

Carrigan, M., & Elver-Vass, F. (2020, September 4). Online conferences don't have to feel like substitutes. 4 considerations for making yours better than the 'real thing'. *LSE Impact Blog.* https://blogs.lse.ac.uk/impactofsocialsciences/2020/09/14/online-conferences-dont-have-to-feel-like-substitutes-4-considerations-for-making-yours-better-than-the-real-thing/

Chin, B. (2022a). Exploring cultural identity through coffee: Steps towards self-care. In N. Lemon (Ed.), *Creating a place for self-care and wellbeing in higher education: Finding meaning across academia* (pp. 131–143). Routledge.

Chin, B. (2022b, June 27). Virtual conferences and the 'tyranny of distance'. *Coffee & Research.* https://coffeeandresearch.com/blog/virtual-conferences-and-the-tyranny-of-distance/

Davis, C. (2006). Diasporic subjectivities. *French Cultural Studies, 17*(3), 335–348.

Donlon, E. (2021). Lost and found: The academic conference in pandemic and post-pandemic times. *Irish Educational Studies, 40*(2), 367–373. https://doi.org/10.1080/03323315.2021.1932554

Gilroy, P. (2000). *Between camps: Nations, cultures and the allures of race*. Penguin Books.

Hopkins, D., Higham, J., Orchiston, C., & Duncan, T. (2019). Practising academic mobilities: Bodies, networks and institutional rhythms. *The Geographical Journal, 185*(4), 472–484. https://doi.org/10.1111/geoj.12301

Ines, M., Ricci-Bonot, C., & Mills, D. S. (2021). My cat and me—a study of cat owner perceptions of their bond and relationship. *Animals, 11*(6), 1601. https://doi.org/10.3390/ani11061601

Jhaveri, H. (2023, January 9). *Unmasking Pedro Pascal, the complicated new face of sci-fi*. https://www.wired.com/story/pedro-pascal-interview-last-of-us-mandalorian/

Lemon, N. (2023, June 24). *Post-COVID, we can no longer accept a lack of compassion*. *University World News*. https://www.universityworldnews.com/post.php?story=20230620155123571

Massey, D. (1994). Double articulation: A place in the world. In A. Bammer (Ed.), *Displacements: Cultural identities in question* (pp. 110–119). Indiana University Press.

McClennen, S. A. (2005). The diasporic subject in Ariel Dorfman's *Heading South, Looking North. MELUS, 30*(1), 169–188.

Ngai, N. (2022). Homemade pet celebrities: The everyday experience of micro-celebrity in promoting the self and others. *Celebrity Studies, 14*(4), 437–454. 1–18. https://doi.org/10.1080/19392397.2022.2070714

O'Hare, A. J. (2022). Being one with myself: Embracing the teacher identity. In N. Lemon (Ed.), *Creating a place for self-care and wellbeing in higher education: Finding meaning across academia* (pp. 60–71). Routledge.

Rowe, N. (2018). 'When you get what you want, but not what you need': The motivations, affordances and shortcomings of attending academic/scientific conferences. *International Journal of Research in Education and Science, 4*(2), 714–729. https://www.ijres.net/index.php/ijres/article/view/368/pdf

Sibai, O., Figueiredo, B., & Ferreira, M. C. (2019, January 29). Overworked and isolated: The rising epidemic of loneliness in academia. *The Conversation*. https://theconversation.com/overworked-and-isolated-the-rising-epidemic-of-loneliness-in-academia-110009

Sipley, G. (2021, March 4). The post-Covid future of virtual conferences. *LSE Impact Blog*. https://blogs.lse.ac.uk/impactofsocialsciences/2021/03/04/the-post-covid-future-of-virtual-conferences/

Wright, G. (2015, December 18). *Cats and academia: A short story*. *Times Higher Education*. https://www.timeshighereducation.com/blog/short-history-cats-and-academia

Section 4

Emerging researchers, mentoring, and finding one's self

Chapter 15

Listening to the stillness and darkness of academia

Boundaries that encircle international emerging researchers

Yue Xu and Yuqi Lin

Prelude: Where the story began

One girl gazed out of the porthole at the steadily enlarging vastness of exotic sceneries, a mixture of exhilaration and apprehension coursing through her, carrying with it the perspective of a cultural stranger in a foreign land, for the first time. *One girl* fixated on the manuscript's gradually shrinking and blurring words, her mind replete with anticipation and aspiration as she imagined herself stepping towards the pinnacle of the academic ivory tower, amidst the repetitions of summer nights. *Two girls* crossed paths at the intersection of their sojourns, oblivious at that moment as to how intricately their fates would soon become entwined.

We are two international students and emerging researchers (ERs) based in Australia. It feels somewhat odd when placing these labels onto ourselves, but please allow us to borrow them for now for the sake of "convenient" categorisation, much like what society often finds comfort in doing. As Asian students who are pursuing a research degree within western academia, we have come to realise that it is common to feel odd at times. However, instead of treating and accepting it as a norm, we aim to delve deeper into the multilayered oddness that we perceive along our research journey in the host country: What is it that made us experience those sentiments?

Identifying boundaries in academia

The academic sphere is constantly being constructed and reconstructed, giving rise to a series of invisible boundaries. Some of these boundaries serve as guardians, preserving the sanctum of our inner intellectual spaces from unwelcome intrusion. Yet, there exist boundaries that, in their intangibility, wield the power to inflict harm, even fostering alienation or segregation. Consider, for example, the predicament of doctoral students who are ensnared in a twilight zone of affiliation – neither entirely aligned with the academic establishment nor the student body (Hradsky et al., 2022). This conundrum often leaves them adrift, unable to traverse the subtle lines that demarcate doctoral

DOI: 10.4324/9781003457510-19

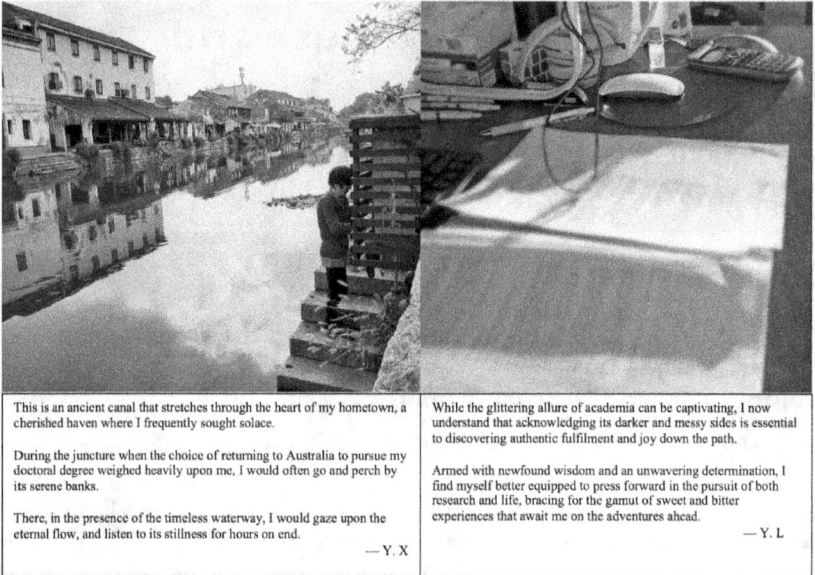

This is an ancient canal that stretches through the heart of my hometown, a cherished haven where I frequently sought solace. During the juncture when the choice of returning to Australia to pursue my doctoral degree weighed heavily upon me, I would often go and perch by its serene banks. There, in the presence of the timeless waterway, I would gaze upon the eternal flow, and listen to its stillness for hours on end. — Y. X	While the glittering allure of academia can be captivating, I now understand that acknowledging its darker and messy sides is essential to discovering authentic fulfilment and joy down the path. Armed with newfound wisdom and an unwavering determination, I find myself better equipped to press forward in the pursuit of both research and life, bracing for the gamut of sweet and bitter experiences that await me on the adventures ahead. — Y. L

Image 15.1 Stillness speaks vs. darkness inspires

students from those degree holders. For international doctoral students, this labyrinthine journey is compounded by an array of added impediments that infiltrate every facet of their daily existence (Dang & Tran, 2017). Essentially cultural strangers, they stand as outsiders, navigating unfamiliar certain social mores and codes. Enveloped as "*others*" they remain isolated and disconnected from their native counterparts (Fotovatian, 2012), shackled by these divisions that impede their meaningful integration into the scholarly odyssey. Thus, these boundaries can assume an obstructive role and lead to emotional turmoil throughout their transience.

In light of these reflections, we raise the question – how do international ERs discern and navigate the boundaries that encircle them? Furthermore, how can they exercise vigilance and nurture their wellbeing within the academic field, as they endeavour to stretch or shatter these confinements? In this narrative, we intentionally adopt the term "emerging researchers" to encompass not only the doctoral student group but also those who are impassioned by research yet do not see themselves imprisoned by the constraints mandated by a formal degree.

Contextualising emerging researcher wellbeing

It is widely acknowledged that novice academics often encounter challenges when attempting to navigate the complex and ever-evolving terrain of a new university environment (Boyd & Horstmanshof, 2013; Velardo & Elliott,

2021). This issue is accentuated by the well-documented mental health complexities faced by this group of people (Jackman et al., 2022, 2023; Sverdlik et al., 2021; Sum, 2023; Velardo & Elliott, 2021). As Lau and Pretorius (2019) point out, it becomes imperative to delve into ERs' intrapersonal wellbeing to grasp the impact of academic journeys on one's mental welfare and to stay attuned to the accessibility of support services during moments of crisis. While institutional-level support is pivotal for nurturing wellbeing (Petersen, 2011), there arises a need to explore alternative avenues outside the formal system to guide new academics through this intricate navigation (Boyd & Horstmanshof, 2013).

In the discourse surrounding wellbeing and self-care within the context of international ERs, the concept of connectedness or disconnectedness has surfaced as a major determinant (Dang & Tran, 2017; Gomes, 2017; Machart, 2017; Rosenblum et al., 2017; Tran & Gomes, 2017). This facet holds a significant association with mobility, exerting profound influence over both the wellbeing and academic performance, as well as the life trajectories of international students (Tran & Gomes, 2017). Notably, the absence of a sense of connectedness and belongingness can precipitate a search for alternative affiliations other than the higher education institution (Steven, 2017). Given that international ERs' connectedness is formed in an idiosyncratic manner, influenced by their positions, identities, and transnational social spheres (Dang & Tran, 2017), it is important to not only direct attention outward but also to introspectively examine factors that may lead to their disconnection. Following this line, we highlight the power of raising self-awareness and practising self-care when upfront confrontation with systemic barriers is not yet feasible. It is within this framework that we position the critical matters of wellbeing and self-care, contextualised within the unique landscape of international ERs.

Methodology

This chapter adopts a collective autoethnographic approach to explore the authentic experiences of two international ERs. Collective autoethnography has gained traction for its capacity to make sense of the researcher's self-reflection on personal experiences and to connect them with the broader sociocultural meanings and interpretations they hold (Chang et al., 2016; Hradsky et al., 2022; Lin & Xu, 2022). This approach stands as a conduit for us, two beginner explorers of academia, to unveil the contours of our journey – a journey that navigates the oceans of cultural adaptation, scholarly challenges, and personal growth. Through this lens, we intend to elucidate how we perceive and engage with the boundaries that lace our academic pathways within the Australian context. We reflect on the very nature of these boundaries in an attempt to discern the forces that have shaped them. Furthermore, we aim to dissect the means through which we have summoned the strength to thrive amidst the constraints imposed upon us. To this end, the following questions were used to guide our reflections:

- What aspects have you identified as boundaries or barriers to your wellbeing throughout your academic journey?
- How did you manage to flourish against the frames of these boundaries?
- What did you learn from these experiences that can contribute to your future wellbeing?

Discussion and implications on self-care

Unveiling diverse forces of expectations

The experiences of international ERs reveal a unique set of challenges they encounter in their scholarly journey. Unlike early career researchers, who may have already established more sophisticated social and academic networks, we face the task of constructing our foundations anew. As individuals who have departed from our familial support system to pursue education overseas, we inevitably carry with us a web of expectations from various stakeholders, particularly those who hold significant roles in our lives. These expectations wield a dual influence over our wellbeing. Initially, they can function as catalysts propelling us into the realm of academia:

> To my astonishment, my lecturer recommended that I consider submitting my assignment paper for publication, praising its merit for a wider audience. An overwhelming surge of honour, flattery, and excitement engulfed me, as I had never envisaged my scholarly work being acknowledged on an international stage. Fuelled by determination to meet my lecturer's high expectations, I dedicated my entire summer break to crafting the manuscript. Surprisingly, my efforts bore fruit as my work found its place in a prestigious journal. This marked a turning point that not only instilled newfound confidence within me but also painted a portrait of myself as a potential researcher. (Yuqi)

> I had not encountered any research-related elements until the final year when I embarked on crafting my dissertation... As I began drafting and refining the literature review section, my then-supervisor recognised my potential in academic writing and offered me a wealth of constructive feedback. In addition, to facilitate my revision process, she put forth a trove of suggested readings encompassing research methodologies and texts that could guide me through formulating the theoretical framework. (Yue)

However, as time wears on and when we venture further into academia, these expectations can also give rise to adverse effects on our wellbeing, thus metamorphosing into a boundary. Specifically, the weight of such anticipations can transform from motivational sparks into burdens that weigh heavily on our shoulders, casting shadows on our sense of self and causing a strain on our emotional equilibrium:

> But as with any great adventure, challenges lurked just around the corner. After the first taste of success, I started to work on publishing more papers. However, as the manuscripts flowed outward, they returned bearing the stamp of rejection, one after another. It was at that moment that I began to comprehend the true starkness of academia. The works I had painstakingly poured my heart into were inexorably tied to my very identity, making each rejection feel like a personal attack. Laden with the weight of high expectations from those around me, I found it hard to ask for help, driving myself to exhaustion through endless hours of toil and a mind consumed by publications. (Yuqi)

In this excerpt above, the taste of success in publishing kindled the flame of her ambition, but soon the bitter notes of rejection served as a reminder of the stark realities of academia. Each manuscript, a labour of dedication, became intertwined with the core of her identity, rendering rejection into a personal affront. The weight of external expectations, coupled with the struggle to seek support, fuels a relentless pursuit that risks plunging into burnout:

> The mounting pressure eventually took its toll, leading to burnout and a loss of passion for academic work. Doubt plagued my mind, the very foundations of my chosen path were shaken, leading me to question whether the quest for research was truly aligned with my purpose. (Yuqi)

It is not uncommon that ERs would experience imposter syndrome at a certain point in their academic paths (Abdelaal, 2020; Sverdlik et al., 2021). However, instead of internalising external expectations and taking them seriously, alternative perspectives offer pathways for interpreting these outward evaluations:

> With the prior publication experience, I commenced reaching out to other lecturers from the courses I had undertaken since the second year of my master's programme. Upon the culmination of each course and the reception of my grades, I initiated discussions regarding potential collaboration opportunities or guidance in transforming my assignment tasks into publishable papers. While the majority politely declined, a handful responded with expressions of interest. However, undeterred by rejections, I continued honing my academic writing skills, fortified by

the growing realisation that now that I had already been familiar with the publication process, I could venture forth independently or in collaboration with fellow peers even without the professionals' help. (Yue)

In this case, the pursuit of collaboration and guidance brings forth both acceptance and refusal from experts. In the face of refusals, resilience prevails, as the understanding of the publication process evolves, forging a path of independent exploration. Here, the expectations interwoven with ERs' academic pursuits come not only from within but from their proactive interactions with peers and mentors.

These narratives highlight the dynamic exchange between external expectations, internal aspirations, and the evolving emotional domain of academic pursuits. In the trajectory of international ERs, the challenges encountered in their scholarly journey often intersect with the notion of unhelpful expectations, potentially leading to the creation of boundaries that hinder their progress and wellbeing. This exploration underlines the need for more holistic approaches to self-care, emphasising the importance of deconstructing the underlying forces of the expectations we perceive when establishing and expanding our immediate networks to preserve our mental and emotional wellbeing.

Understanding the darker side of academia

Prior to fully immersing ourselves in academia, we often harbour fantasies of what the path might entail. However, when that idyllic bubble bursts, an inevitable encounter with its challenges looms and naturally we get exposed to the difficult side of it. Nevertheless, not everyone gets to also glimpse the less favourable aspects therein – the "ugly" side of it firsthand. The episode we are about to recount involves one of us as a direct participant, while the other assumes the role of an observant narrator who witnessed the whole duration of this experience. This duality offers a unique vantage point encompassing both the insider's (Author 2) and outsider's (Author 1) perspectives. It should be noted that this incident transpired several years in the past. The outsider to this narrative documented the event in her reflective journal at the time, serving as a testament to the occurrence. However, the insider has only recently garnered the courage to share the story, several years hence. This revelation comes now, at a juncture when we both find ourselves in a place of greater security and inner strength. We hope that the tale will shed light on the unique challenges and boundaries that international ERs face, particularly concerning the power dynamics between different parties in academia, as well as strategies to navigate these obstacles.

The insider's version of the story:

Deciding to give research another chance, I embarked on a journey as a research assistant, eager to work alongside experts in the field. However, fate had a different script in store. I soon discovered that my commitment and hard work were not being compensated fairly. Feeling torn between gratitude and justice, I sought advice from experienced individuals and realised I deserved better treatment. Summoning my courage, I mustered the strength to communicate openly with my supervisors. I knew I had to step away from the role, but as I braced myself for their reaction, little did I expect what was to come.

Rather than supporting my decision, they responded by reducing my workload, leaving me stranded in a state of limbo. Negotiations ensued, but I found myself struggling to assert my needs and desires. The pressure to keep working intensified, and I felt trapped in a seemingly never-ending battle. Days stretched into weeks, and weeks into months, the ordeal relentlessly continued. With each passing day, my hope began to wane, and the gleam of my academic dream began to dim. My yearning was simple – freedom, both for my mind and body. I longed for release from the oppressive yoke that had entrapped me.

I can still recall vividly the sensation that I longed to break free from this suffocating predicament! The sanctuary of knowledge I once cherished had transformed into a cage of expectations and disappointments. All I wanted was to spread my wings and soar away from this stifling environment. Ultimately, it was not just a confrontation with my supervisors; it entailed wrestling with my own self-doubts and insecurities. I could not ignore the fierce competition that surrounded me. Every stride forward felt weighed against countless others vying for the same opportunities. Despite being deemed one of the lucky ones, privileged to delve into academia's realm, I couldn't shake off the feelings of uncertainty and self-doubt. On the one hand, I felt grateful for the opportunities in front of me, knowing that many would dream of being in my shoes. On the other hand, I yearned for fair treatment and respect, longing to be recognised as a valued member of the academic community.

The outsider's version of the story:

After having experienced some recent incidents of my friend, I found myself inundated with doubt – does a realm of pristine academic pursuit still exist, or has it devolved into a crucible of power dynamics and material gains, merely contributing to the bureaucratic transformation of intellect and discourse?

Over the last few months, [that supervisor] took to satirising her intentionally during their weekly meetings, discrediting every piece of work she had penned, and later unceremoniously "took over" the project.

He justified this seizure by claiming access to superior "resources" for publishing. After these experiences, I could not help but question: as a collective whole, where on earth lies the path of emancipation for us Asian students if the method itself is to incarcerate or diminish our fellow beings and mould them into docile lambs? What enlightenment can possibly be derived from such an approach?

...

However, in the midst of these doubts, there is gratitude. Gratitude for having encountered some genuine scholars who staunchly defend the dignity and integrity of academia, who, from the bottom of their heart, are willing to contribute to the body of knowledge within their chosen spheres, striving to better the world in their own modest ways. Perhaps they are precisely the ones who would gladly let their own light shine and unconsciously give other people permission to do the same. I am attempting to internalise the belief that knowledge truly becomes liberating when it reaches a certain depth and breadth. Perhaps, by that time, we will be able to look upon our present struggles with disdain, perceiving an enduring light illuminating our future paths – a radiance that is brighter, farther-reaching, and capable of exposing all those veiled, unsavoury transgressions.

By delineating the full account of the same episode from both the insider's and outsider's viewpoints, a nuanced comprehension emerges concerning the multifaceted constraints that international ERs grapple with within academia. These constraints encompass not only the tangible boundaries existing between international ERs and figures of higher authority but also the subtle boundaries demarcating ethical scholars who employ their influence judiciously and those who exploit their power over individuals in comparatively vulnerable positions. This exploration underscores the imperative of acknowledging the darker facets of academia, apprehending the authentic motives that drive actions, thereby fortifying oneself against their potentially adverse effects. Ultimately, it serves as a clarion call for the cultivation of discernment, empowering international ERs to exercise their prerogative in selectively accommodating external influences. This intrinsic agency resonates as the bedrock upon which a trajectory towards self-emancipation can be meticulously charted.

Drawing forth the brighter side of ourselves

In this tale of struggle and self-discovery, we came to realise that our worth as a researcher extended far beyond the bridges we sought to preserve. Not only do we deserve to be acknowledged for our luck in "securing a spot" in academia, but also for the talent and dedication we have brought to the table. We wove a mosaic of self-affirming words into the narrative as a perpetual reminder of our inherent value:

> However, I developed the understanding that my journey was more than just about achieving success – which is defined by others. It should be more about finding the strength to stand up for myself and to forge a path that reflects my true worth. (Yuqi)

> Looking back on my tertiary experience, I can now recall many traces that might be associated with my growth in academia. From the very beginning of my studies in Australia, I never chose to "simplify" my learning process; quite the contrary, I tended to embrace more challenging paths, letting only my genuine research interest guide me. (Yue)

> These experiences, both triumphant and challenging, shaped my perspective on academia. The accolades and successes made me feel valued and encouraged me to persevere, while the darker moments cast doubt on the idyllic image of academia. Looking back, it is hard to believe how much has happened in such a short time. I have grown, evolved, and reconstructed my views through these trials, but I wonder how things might have been different if I had been aware of the potential pitfalls from the start. (Yuqi)

> Gradually, the label "Chinese student", or "international student", somehow began to elude me: there were moments when I no longer saw myself as any different from other non-international students. By that, I do not suggest denying my cultural roots but rather transcending that boundary to understand one's knowledge-building capacity from a more fundamental, global perspective. There should be no naïve presumption that there is anything that "non-native" or "Asian" learners cannot achieve in academia compared to other "white" researchers. (Yue)

> Yet, through it all, these experiences have made me braver and have given me the strength to navigate the uncertain waters of academia. They have taught me that success is not always guaranteed, but each failure may serve as a steppingstone to progress. While the glittering allure of academia can be captivating, I now understand that acknowledging its darker and messy sides is essential to discovering authentic fulfilment and joy down the path. Armed with newfound wisdom and an unwavering determination, I find myself better equipped to press forward in the pursuit of both research and life, bracing for the gamut of sweet and bitter experiences that await me on the adventures ahead. (Yuqi)

Although I have only started my Ph.D. course not long ago, I could see myself becoming more and more steadfast on this path. Equipped with a growth mindset, I now pay more attention to my self-cultivation and self-actualisation while following my own pace. (Yue)

We are two international emerging researchers from China. We may not identify ourselves as "international" or as a "researcher" all the time. But we ARE always emerging. This perpetual state of growth defines us and will continue to do so, transcending labels and boundaries of any sort.

Where the story continues

In this chapter, we explored our experiences as two international ERs, unfolding the emotional terrain we navigated and charting the course of our resilience through our academic journey in Australia. Our collective autoethnographic narratives are interlaced with insights gained through surmounting challenges along the way, which serves as the nutriment of our shared wisdom. The lessons learned from transcending both the external and internal boundaries have steered us towards enhancing our future wellbeing. This exploration underscores the urgency of confronting the shadows lurking within academia, of discerning the authentic motives that propel actions, thereby inoculating ourselves against potential pitfalls. It is our aspiration that these gleanings may serve as beacons for others navigating similar waters. By sharing our stories, we aim to encourage our peers to have the courage to discern, interrogate, and ultimately break the chains that may bind them. In pursuit of the betterment of the academic ecosystem, we recognise that certain boundaries are ripe for exploration, rupture, or dissolution. With this conviction, we envision a more inclusive, supportive, and enriching academic community through the dismantling of these boundaries.

References

Abdelaal, G. (2020). Coping with imposter syndrome in academia and research. *The Biochemist*, 42(3), 62–64. https://doi.org/10.1042/bio20200033

Boyd, W., & Horstmanshof, L. (2013). Response to Petersen on 'staying or going?': Australian early career researchers' narratives. *The Australian Universities' Review*, 55(1), 74–79.

Chang, H., Ngunjiri, F. W., & Hernandez, K. C. (2016). *Collaborative autoethnography*. Routledge.

Dang, X. T., & Tran, L. T. (2017). From 'somebody' to 'nobody': International doctoral students' perspectives of home-host connectedness. In L. T. Tran & C. J. Gomes (Eds.), *International student connectedness and identity: Transnational perspectives* (pp. 75–91). Springer.

Fotovatian, S. (2012). Three constructs of institutional identity among international doctoral students in Australia. *Teaching in Higher Education, 17*(5), 577–588. https://doi.org/10.1080/13562517.2012.658557

Gomes, C. (2017). Disconnections with the host nation and the significance of international student communities: A case study of Asian international students in Australia and Singapore. In L. T. Tran & C. J. Gomes (Eds.), *International student connectedness and identity: Transnational perspectives* (pp. 93–111). Springer.

Hradsky, D., Soyoof, A., Zeng, S., Foomani, E. M., Lem, N. C., Maestre, J.-L., & Pretorius, L. (2022). Pastoral care in doctoral education: A collaborative autoethnography of belonging and academic identity. *International Journal of Doctoral Studies, 17*, 1–23. https://doi.org/10.28945/4900

Jackman, P. C., Sanderson, R., Allen-Collinson, J., & Jacobs, L. (2022). 'There's only so much an individual can do': An ecological systems perspective on mental health and wellbeing in the early stages of doctoral research. *Journal of Further and Higher Education, 46*(7), 931–946. https://doi.org/10.1080/0309877X.2021.2023732

Jackman, P. C., Slater, M. J., Carter, E. E., Sisson, K., & Bird, M. D. (2023). Social support, social identification, mental wellbeing, and psychological distress in doctoral students: A person-centred analysis. *Journal of Further and Higher Education, 47*(1), 45–58. https://doi.org/10.1080/0309877X.2022.2088272

Lau, R.W.K., & Pretorius, L. (2019). Intrapersonal wellbeing and the academic mental health crisis. In L. Pretorius, L. Macaulay, & B. Cahusac de Caux (Eds.), *Wellbeing in doctoral education*. Springer, Singapore. https://doi.org/10.1007/978-981-13-9302-0_5

Lin, Y., & Xu, Y. (2022). An international student, a researcher, or a work-ready graduate? Exploring the self-formation of international students in coursework master's programmes. In B. Cahusac de Caux, L. Pretorius, & L. Macaulay (Eds.), *Research and teaching in a pandemic world*. Springer, Singapore. https://doi.org/10.1007/978-981-19-7757-2_10

Machart, R. (2017). International students' disconnecting from and reconnecting with diverse communities: Fluidity of the self in sojourns abroad. In L. T. Tran & C. J. Gomes (Eds.), *International student connectedness and identity: Transnational perspectives* (pp. 184–203). Springer.

Petersen, E. B. (2011). Staying or going? Australian early career researchers' narratives of academic work, exit options and coping strategies. *The Australian Universities' Review, 53* (2), 34–42.

Rosenblum, K. E., Haines, D. W., & Cho, H. (2017). Where are we, when are we, and who are we to each other? Connectedness and the evolving meanings of international education. In L. T. Tran & C. J. Gomes (Eds.), *International student connectedness and identity: Transnational perspectives* (pp. 169–183). Springer.

Steven, J. (2017). Exploring the lifeworld of international doctoral Students: The place of religion and religious organisations. In L. T. Tran & C. J. Gomes (Eds.), *International student connectedness and identity: Transnational perspectives* (pp. 61–74). Springer.

Sum, N. (2023). Solitude, sanctuary, and pseudo-mentors: A pandemic lens on an emerging transition into doing and being research/researcher. In I. F. A. Badiozaman, V. M. Ling, & K. D. Sandhu (Eds.), *Women practicing resilience, self-care and wellbeing in academia: International stories from lived experience* (pp. 57–68). Taylor & Francis Group.

Sverdlik, A., Mcalpine, L., & Hall, N. (2021). Insights from a survey "comments" section: Extending research on doctoral well-being. *Studies in Graduate and Postdoctoral Education*, *12*(2), 262–282. https://doi.org/10.1108/SGPE-06-2020-0035

Tran, L. T., & Gomes, C. J. (2017). Student mobility, connectedness and identity. In L. T. Tran & C. J. Gomes (Eds.), *International student connectedness and identity: Transnational perspectives* (pp. 1–11). Springer.

Velardo, S., & Elliott, S. (2021). The emotional wellbeing of doctoral students conducting qualitative research with vulnerable populations. *Qualitative Report*, *26*(5), 1522–1545. https://doi.org/10.46743/2160-3715/2021.4421

Chapter 16

Cultivating a daily journaling practice for wellness, self-care, and thriving in academia

Khairunnisa Haji Ibrahim

Introduction

In late 2021 I opened a new notebook and wrote my first Morning Pages entry. The notebook had a chequered blue and white cover, over which I pasted photos of my favourite K-Pop artists, and dotted pages. In that first entry, I wrote:

> *I am so excited to start these morning pages. For the next 8 weeks, will write first thing in the morning, until 3 pages are filled. Free flowing, no frills, and no-thinking writing. I woke up already thinking about this exercise and excited to begin. I know it won't always be this exciting – some days ahead I'm sure I will be regretting beginning this – or perhaps just bemoaning the fact that I have to do it. I had a thought just now, and it was fleeting and is now gone. Ah yes, I thought about why I want to do this when there are several other new habits that I've started and plan to pursue into this coming year. Besides the actual practices, I should like to be a person with a strong drive who pursues the things that she is interested in, that matter to her.*

Nearly two years later, I am still writing three pages every morning, a practice that artist Julia Cameron (1992) espouses to students and readers of her book *The Artist's Way* as key to unlocking their creativity. Cameron is often credited for popularising the Morning Pages, and she herself has kept the practice ongoing for several decades, rarely missing a day. Given her prodigious output – she has written over 40 books, numerous plays, songs, and poetry – her Morning Pages clearly works for her.

A Google search of Morning Pages yields a wealth of returns on the same theme: not only artists, but also corporate and service workers, have found the daily practice to be indispensable to their success, creative expression, and wellbeing. Alongside a raft of self-healing and maintenance strategies like daily breath work, movement, and meditation, journaling every morning occupies an exalted position among those who want to live good and meaningful lives. I started my own Morning Pages practices years after I came back from my PhD

DOI: 10.4324/9781003457510-20

training abroad. I'd left for the training with my baby son, and my husband, who'd just been diagnosed with an autoimmune disease. The combination of the overseas move, becoming a new parent, and coping with a chronic illness in the family was massively challenging. I did not know it then, but I experienced severe emotional dysregulation, ADHD, and executive dysfunction.

After three years we returned home, my PhD still unfinished. My son was diagnosed as autistic soon after. The next few years of raising him and attending to his complex needs were difficult. Fortunately, my husband responded to treatment and is now managing his condition well. I also returned to work as a lecturer, which came with a heavy teaching load and the expectation to do research and write papers regularly. I also participated in conferences every year since I have been back. While carrying out these duties felt exhilarating and satisfying in the moment, they also left me exhausted. Many days I felt overwhelmed, stumped, and unable to perform my day-to-day tasks.

Those years were shadowed by intense shame. Looking back, I had the signs of ADHD even before then, stretching back to my earliest job working as a journalist, when I dithered writing reports until looming deadlines forced my hand. The signs were there even earlier, during my childhood. I realise now that my intense hyper focus on imaginary worlds, my periodic bursts of hyper competence, my elevated anxiety in many kinds of situations, especially when I perceived my loved ones to be in some kind of danger that existed only in my mind, set me apart from my siblings, cousins, and classmates.

When I learned about ADHD, suddenly my entire life, especially my propensity to ruminate and run myself into panic over imagined scenarios, made sense. So I have ADHD. What does that mean? How do I use this knowledge to become a better version of myself? I love scholarship; it is everything else involving organisation, discipline, routine, and often mundane effort, that required my showing up every day and doing the work, regardless how I felt, that grated at my sense of competence and wellbeing in my career.

One of the hallmark traits of ADHD is that my brain thrives on novelty, challenge, and interest (Evren et al., 2018; Littman, 2022). This sounds exciting and advantageous, but on the flip side, anything that diverges from the fun, engaging and meaningful – no matter how necessary or important – becomes part of an impenetrable wall that bore down on me. I become paralysed, unable to know what to do next, or to rouse the energy needed to tackle the task. This is executive dysfunction, I learned, and it feels like a perpetual incompetence.

I understand this now. But I didn't back then, during the pandemic's peak when I first learned about ADHD through social media. It was as if the virus blazing across the world forced another kind of purging in addition to the normal way of life: it made visible the hidden suffering and pain of so many from a range of emotional and mental health issues. Today, self-care and wellbeing dominate discussions, on topics ranging from interpersonal relationships, business, careers, and in physical as well as online spaces.

Starting the Morning Pages practice just before COVID-19 emerged was a stroke of luck. It gave me a tool to manage the fear and uncertainty of the pandemic. The long and languid lockdown in 2021 and 2022 also gave me ample time to read up on the benefits of this journaling practice. These are described in the following section, which examines the scientific evidence of the rewards of journaling, which also applies to the Morning Pages.

Journaling for wellness and self-care: A literature review

I took up journaling because I was struggling with anxiety, weak self-esteem, mental block, and lack of clarity about what I wanted to do. Gradually the answers revealed themselves. Alongside the minutiae of my life, the Morning Pages also captured the epiphanies, triumphs, and failures. As I explained in the earlier sections, this is a great payoff of journaling: the gift of self-awareness. There are other benefits too, as I share below. These include improved emotional regulation, a sharpening of focus and mindfulness, and positive habit-building.

Emotional regulation

One of the gradual gifts of Morning Pages is the space to be kind to myself, but also to find grounding. Nervous system dysregulation has been associated with many modern-day maladies, particularly anxiety and depression. People with ADHD are particularly sensitive. I have come to understand that my intense fear around the safety of the people I love, difficulty in calming down and propensity to ruminate, leading to further cycles of anxiety and stress, are due this kind of dysregulation.

Studies on journaling in many settings, especially educational ones, have found that a period of consistent journaling helped to reduce stress and anxiety among those who participated in the study. The subjects, often students, ranged from those in nursing (Dimitroff et al., 2017; Goodman, 2018), medical studies (Mercer et al., 2010), to management education (Goodman, 2018). Overall, students were found to be the key demographic to benefit from journaling, primarily because college studies can be stressful and anxiety-inducing (Lumley & Provenzano, 2003; Pastore, 2020).

Sharpening focus and mindfulness

Three pages is a finite limit, and it can be filled quickly or more leisurely. Because it *must* be filled, it enforces a sort of discipline on the writer. There is not enough space to write everything, so the writer must choose what to write about. Whatever the topic is, the writer must ensure that it fills enough to reach the requisite three pages. Deliberation is involved. The concept of deliberate practice, which writing the Morning Pages certainly is, is a popular productivity technique. Psychologists use it to explain why and how training programmes in sports and specialised fields of skill and talent contribute to high performance among athletes, specialists, and creative artists.

Psychologists identify several key traits of deliberate practice, which include focused attention, repetition, monitoring and continuous refinement (Duckworth et al., 2011; Ericsson, 2004). When translated into journaling, I believe that the daily practice cultivates the kind of self-reflection that leads to continuous adjustment in the way that the pages are written. When I look back at my earlier pages and compare them to the more recent ones, I can say that the content has evolved and become richer descriptively and topics-wise. My voice in the writing has become more distinct. I used to describe events, feelings, and anecdotes in broad strokes, but over time my accounts have become more colourful and in focus.

Deliberate practice also promotes mindfulness. Much has been written about the mental and physical health benefits of mindfulness, especially in relation to its use as a stress-reduction technique. Simply defined, mindfulness is the capacity to be fully conscious and aware on a sustained basis (Siegel et al., 2009).

Finally, journaling can lead to better working memory and cognitive capacity. This is the common finding of two separate studies on expressive writing among students. According to Klein and Boals (2001), by journaling about their experiences and emotions every day, the subjects demonstrated increases in working memory weeks after the start of the experiment. The authors believe that the focus on expressing negative emotions alleviates intrusive thoughts and frees up working memory resources. A similar conclusion is reached by Ullrich and Lutgendorf (2002), but they believe that focusing solely on writing about negative emotions can be restrictive. They suggest that journaling that attempts to understand and make sense of previous experiences may be more beneficial.

Habit-building: Showing up and discipline

One of the challenges of ADHD is managing negative emotional associations around difficult or uninteresting tasks, which lead to overwhelm. An academic career comes with high standards and an expectation of continuous productivity in the form of publishing well-regarded books and articles in peer-reviewed journals. This culture of publish or perish has led to detrimental impacts on the wellbeing of academics and researchers, as documented by many authors including De Rond and Miller (2005) and Van Dalen and Henkens (2012). Writing for academic publication is one of the most arduous aspects of my job, but there is no way around it: to publish I must write from start to finish, and send the piece off for publication.

Somehow, I must contend with the tumultuous emotions created by a highly sensitive nervous system, one of the hallmark traits of ADHD. How? One common advice is to consider managing overwhelm as akin to building a muscle. The more often this muscle is exercised, the more capable one gets at dealing with fraught emotions and thoughts. In one of the most prominent studies on writing productivity among academics and researchers, psychologist Robert Boice, found that the most successful writers share several traits in their writing practices: they write regularly, in short but frequent sessions, and set realistic goals (Boice, 2015).

Doing this routine consistently builds writing stamina, but it also creates a sense of accountability. As someone who struggles with starting and especially finishing a task, every Morning Pages entry I write is a vote for my own self-worth. It makes me feel like I am someone who can, and does, write regularly. Discipline, troublesome for many but especially for those with ADHD, is fostered through the act of showing up every day.

This is one of the strengths of the Morning Pages. Abiding by this routine for many months has built my capacity for writing and dealing with its emotional attachments. Every day I fill three pages I make small but meaningful gains in self-awareness and worth. Three pages is a realistic goal, and filling them out does not take a significant amount of time. These short sessions of morning daily writing warm up but do not tax the writing muscles, priming them therefore for the actual work of academic writing.

Strategies for practising Morning Pages

The Morning Pages entry is three pages long, written by hand in the morning, about anything. This is how Julia Cameron describes the practice (Cameron, 1992/2013). She also recommends doing it as soon as you wake up, or before you do anything else, so that the writing can be as authentic and uninhibited as possible. This candour is important to reveal aspects of self that may have been hidden, denied, or wilfully overlooked.

The first condition is to write in the morning. While doing it as soon as you wake up is ideal, this might be difficult for some. I give myself grace and write at any time before noon. Some days may see me frantically scribbling three pages before the clock turns 12:00. The second condition of the Morning Pages is to write three pages. I have seen other people use three A4 or letter-sized pages; I write faithfully in an A5-sized notebook. This is what works for me, so find your own preferred settings.

What to write about? There is no right or wrong way to write. I have written about the weather a lot, about the sky and clouds. Some days I have written lists – of things I want to do, of things that annoy me, of things I like about myself – and some other days I have covered pages with poems, each line in increasingly larger script. If you find it hard to write anything, I have included some prompts later in this chapter.

Longhand writing, however, is essential. The physicality of the writing by hand, the feel of the paper, and the fact that we write by hand much slower than we can type, forces a gentler, somewhat meditative practice. In a fast-paced world, this feels like taking some moments to pause and breathe by a babbling brook on a patch of green grass, the sun gentle and warm against my skin. Even after more than 500 days of the Morning Pages, writing by hand still feels this leisurely, this calming.

Writing tools

The tools of the Morning Pages are three pages you can write on, a pen or pencil you can write with, and a place and time to write. Which pen, which venue, and when to write are all dependent on you. Each of us has our own preferences, and these may change over time.

My first few Morning Pages were written in notebooks of various brands, but eventually I settled on the ones produced by stationery brand LEUCHT-TURM1917. The hardcover notebooks contain 251 pages of creamy, dreamy pages that elevate the writing experience. I also bought and discarded many types of pens until I discovered the joys of writing with a fountain pen.

Someone reading this may accuse me of romanticising the writing experience. I would argue back: Why not make a daily practice as pleasurable as possible? Let's reap the benefits of morning writing and enjoy the process along the way. If you find fun and functional apparatuses can reduce the friction of everyday writing – especially at the beginning, when building a habit is most challenging – then I truly believe they are an investment in your wellbeing.

A place to write

It's early or late morning, and you have a notebook or three sheafs of paper to fill with a pen of your choice. The next question is: *Where* do you write? Some writers require total silence and solitude to write; others enjoy being in the midst of a crowd, among them but apart. The poet Kate Baer carved out time to produce a collection by leaving her four children at home to write in a café (Moshakis, 2021). American artist and writer Patti Smith has her own corner in a New York coffeehouse until it eventually closed. She brought back her favourite table and chair to her apartment, but she has always been able to carve out a space for herself in the many coffeehouses in New York and around the world. Once seated, she orders coffee, some bread, and writes from morning to afternoon (Smith, 2015).

I have written in a variety of places. When I first started, my country was in widespread lock down so I wrote every day in the downstairs room that holds my books, looking out the window as I pondered what to write. While

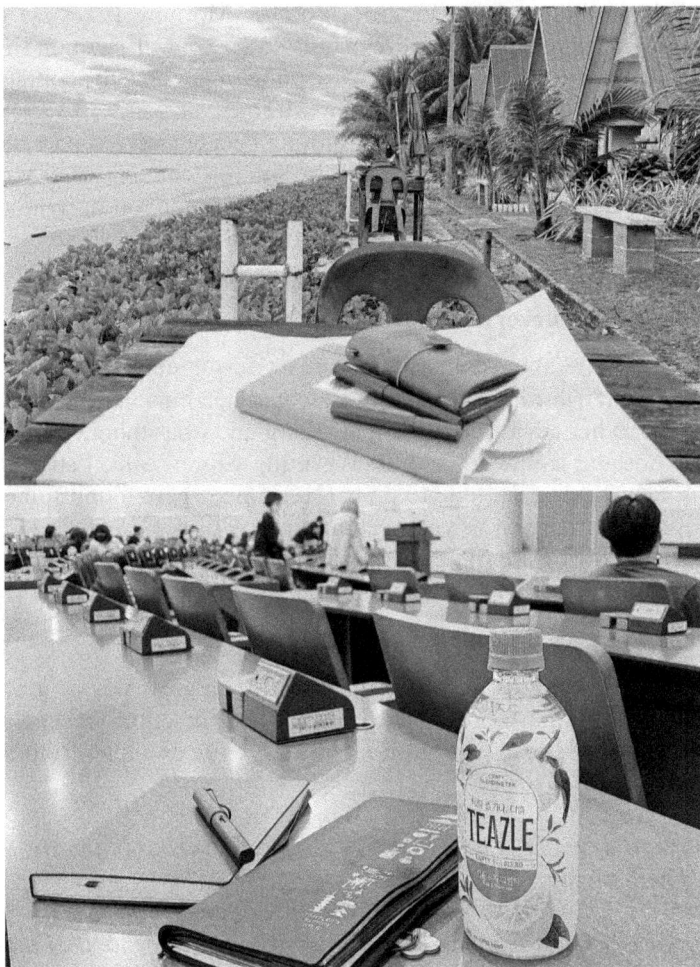

Image 16.1 In cafés, cars, in the office, and even by the beachside (top) and at conferences (bottom), I bring my Morning Pages journal wherever I go

on school run, I write in my car. I bought a portable table that hooks onto the steering wheel and filled another day's worth of three pages. Because the Morning Pages are to be written every day, I have brought my journal with me everywhere, even on vacation and at conferences, surrounded by academics and listening to keynote speeches (Image 16.1).

Write where you feel like writing. I mentioned the writers I admire above because their practices and the places they write in evoke a romantic image of the solitary writer crafting away in public. There are others who toil in the private spaces of their homes.

A final thing about writing location. Because Morning Pages are private, and can potentially reveal and unravel truths about yourself, writing them can be a vulnerable experience. I find writing in public allows me the courage to be vulnerable without being carried away by extreme emotion. Conversely, writing at home, in a place of my own, taps into a deeply reserved part of myself that I can only hear in the quiet of solitude. You may find you have your own rhythms and preferences. As long as there's a surface for you to write on, and a few minutes to get through three pages, you can write anywhere.

Write 'anything and everything'

What do you write about? Julia Cameron sets no limits to the potential of what might materialise on the page, and I would recommend doing the same. I would add to her advice on writing anything and everything, the following reminder: nothing is unworthy, and everything counts. Still, I struggle with the blank canvas fear from time to time. Over time, I have found some strategies to overcome that fear. If you need inspiration or simply an idea of where to start, the following are some of my suggestions.

1   Describe where you are and what you see around you

I begin many Morning Pages entry this way. It is a great way of going over the hurdle of starting. Another benefit is that such descriptions set the scene and mood when I re-read past entries. Here are some examples from my own journal.

> *Sitting outside the DCI at my fav. FASS bench, drinking in the air so sweetly tinged with sea salt.*
> *There is a pounding outside. Somebody is building something.*
> *Thick white smoke hangs in the air. Everywhere I turn I see it around me.*

2   Describe what you are grateful for

The connections between gratitude and wellbeing are well-established. In their extensive review of literature on the effects of gratitude, Wood et al. (2010) found that many studies have found close linkages between practising gratitude and maintaining positive relationships, experiencing subjective and eudemonic (believing that one's life is lived well and to the fullest) wellbeing, and enhancing happiness. Watkins (2004) meanwhile noted that gratitude and happiness reinforce each other in a positive cycle. Happy people are more likely to be grateful, and grateful people more often regard their life situations in a positive light. Gratitude journaling is easier than others, in my opinion. I simply begin by writing "I am grateful for..." and let the pen do the rest.

3 Make lists

One way to write what you are grateful for is to write lists. Making lists is cathartic. Psychologist David Cohen cites three reasons to love lists: "they dampen anxiety about the chaos of life; they give us a structure, a plan that we can stick to; and they are proof of what we have achieved that day, week or month" (Chunn, 2017). Alan Ziegler, an American professor of writing, points out that lists are non-discriminatory and can be about anything. Lists can be a call for action, a reminder or even a motivational tool. "Lists will reveal things you may have forgotten, drop hints, spark ideas and shape routes to accomplishment. They can also inspire things to do" (MR POR-TER, 2020). Lists can also bridge the gap between thinking about goals and actually accomplishing them, by activating the planning phase (Masicampo & Baumeister, 2011).

I have found listing things to be an efficient way to brain dump. Alongside the list of gratitude and to-dos, I have made many lists that range in complexity, from the simple grocery list and cooking ingredients, to ones that are more reflective (a list of my strengths at work) and contemplative (What will my life look like when I am 80 years old?). Whenever you are stumped and still have a long way to go before the end of the third page, make a list. They fill up a page quickly and nicely.

4 Use prompts

Writing prompts are a series of questions or suggestions to get the writing juices flowing. Google returns hundreds of results when you search for 'journaling prompts'. Some of my favourite prompts are on intention-setting (What do I want to feel at the end of the day? What energy do I want to bring to the world today?), letting go of worries (What bothers me? Why does it bother me? What would you say to a good friend if they came to you with the same problem?), and being mindful (What made me smile today? How did I feel after teaching?). One bonus of prompts is that you can write the answers in a list, and again quickly fill up the three pages.

5 Self-dialogue

This is a technique I discovered only relatively recently, after I have practised journaling for some time. Inspired by psychology and self-help literature on the inner child, the idea that our anxiety and distress arise from a wounded part of our core that is innocent and child-like, I have periodically begun to initiate a conversation between my inner child, and an inner adult that also exists within me. The inner adult is the responsible figure, the one who takes charge, takes care of others, and who does so calmly and rationally. This inner adult has also been referred to as an inner parent, the one whose task is to soothe and guide the inner child (Paresky, 2017). A dialogue between my inner child and inner adult is always helpful to process emotions. I always feel better after having this dialogue. Here is an example.

Inner adult:	*Why are you angry?*
Inner child:	*I'm angry because I think she implied she is better suited for the role.*
Inner adult:	*How so? What did she say?*
Inner child:	*She kept saying she should be the one to go there. She said it's her area of interest.*
Inner adult:	*No wonder you're mad. That sounds like she was discrediting you.*
Inner child:	*Yes! I feel like she is looking down on me.*
Inner adult:	*Next time, you can tell her that you feel she is disrespecting you by saying such things. It's not a nice thing to do.*

Conclusion

This chapter provides a simple practice for wellbeing and self-care: Write three pages every morning about anything and everything. The chapter began with my own inner turmoil and the realisation that I needed a tool to manage my ADHD, to manage my emotions, to look ahead, plan, and execute those plans, and to tap into my creativity. The Morning Pages caters to all these needs. As a form of journaling, it is a practice with many scientifically proven benefits, as I have related in the literature review. I have also shared some of the strategies I have developed to maintain a consistent Morning Pages practice, and I hope you find them useful.

If there is a caveat, though, it is this: writing in the journal can be a cathartic form of stress release, and you may find that laments and complaints can fill up three pages very quickly. This purging is periodically helpful, but I would urge you to not get stuck in rumination. Such a state keeps us helpless. Once we expend our worries onto the page, and take time to centre ourselves, it is best to look towards the future. Write about what you want the future to be like and write about where you are now. I think that you will find that, over time, the Morning Pages can help realise your dreams, and make you become the person you have always wanted to be.

References

Boice, R. (2015). *Professors as writers: A self-help guide to productive writing.* Scholarly Writing and Research.

Cameron, J. (1992/2013). *The artist's way.* Tarcher.

Chunn, L. (2017). The psychology of the to-do list – why your brain loves ordered tasks. *The Guardian.* https://www.theguardian.com/lifeandstyle/2017/may/10/the-psychology-of-the-to-do-list-why-your-brain-loves-ordered-tasks

De Rond, M., & Miller, A. N. (2005). Publish or perish: Bane or boon of academic life? *Journal of Management Inquiry, 14*(4), 321–329.

Dimitroff, L. J., Sliwoski, L., O'Brien, S., & Nichols, L. W. (2017). Change your life through journaling – the benefits of journaling for registered nurses. *Journal of Nursing Education and Practice, 7*(2), 90–98.

Duckworth, A. L., Kirby, T. A., Tsukayama, E., Berstein, H., & Ericsson, K. A. (2011). Deliberate practice spells success: Why grittier competitors triumph at the National Spelling Bee. *Social Psychological and Personality Science, 2*(2), 174–181.

Ericsson, K. A. (2004). Deliberate practice and the acquisition and maintenance of expert performance in medicine and related domains. *Academic Medicine, 79*(10), S70–S81.

Evren, C., Alniak, I., Karabulut, V., Cetin, T., Umut, G., Agachanli, R., & Evren, B. (2018). Relationship of probable ADHD with novelty seeking, severity of psychopathology and borderline personality disorder in a sample of patients with opioid use disorder. *Psychiatry and Clinical Psychopharmacology, 28*(1), 48–55. https://doi.org/10.1080/24750573.2017.1395312

Goodman, J. T. (2018). *Reflective journaling to decrease anxiety among undergraduate nursing students in the clinical setting.* University of Northern Colorado. https://search.proquest.com/openview/1b395869fb654c79bfe310871757cc50/1?pq-origsite=gscholar&cbl=18750

Klein, K., & Boals, A. (2001). Expressive writing can increase working memory capacity. *Journal of Experimental Psychology: General, 130*(3), 520–533.

Littman, E. (2022). Brain Stimulation and ADHD/ADD: Cravings and regulation. *ADDitude.* https://www.additudemag.com/brain-stimulation-and-adhd-cravings-dependency-and-regulation/

Lumley, M. A., & Provenzano, K. M. (2003). Stress management through written emotional disclosure improves academic performance among college students with physical symptoms. *Journal of Educational Psychology, 95*(3), 641–649.

Masicampo, E. J., & Baumeister, R. F. (2011). Consider it done! Plan making can eliminate the cognitive effects of unfulfilled goals. *Journal of Personality and Social Psychology, 101*(4), 667.

Mercer, A., Warson, E., & Zhao, J. (2010). Visual journaling: An intervention to influence stress, anxiety and affect levels in medical students. *The Arts in Psychotherapy, 37*(2), 143–148.

Moshakis, A. (2021). Kate Baer on the burden of motherhood: 'My book is like an angry friend'. *The Observer.* https://www.theguardian.com/lifeandstyle/2021/jul/11/kate-baer-my-book-is-like-an-angry-friend

MR PORTER (2020). Why keeping a journal is both cool and cathartic. *The Journal.* MR PORTER. https://www.mrporter.com/en-us/journal/lifestyle/how-to-keep-an-isolation-journal-1233660

Paresky, P. B. (2017). Finding your inner adult. *Psychology Today.* https://www.psychologytoday.com/intl/blog/happiness-and-the-pursuit-leadership/201705/finding-your-inner-adult

Pastore, C. (2020). Stress management in college students: Why journaling is the most effective technique for this demographic. https://soar.suny.edu/handle/20.500.12648/1512

Siegel, R. D., Germer, C. K., & Olendzki, A. (2009). Mindfulness: What is it? Where did it come from? In F. Didonna (Ed.), *Clinical handbook of mindfulness* (pp. 17–35). Springer Science+Business Media.

Smith, P. (2015). Patti Smith: 'It's not so easy writing about nothing'. *The Observer.* https://www.theguardian.com/music/2015/sep/27/patti-smith-m-train-extract-its-not-so-easy-writing-about-nothing

Ullrich, P. M., & Lutgendorf, S. K. (2002). Journaling about stressful events: Effects of cognitive processing and emotional expression. *Annals of Behavioral Medicine,* *24*(3), 244–250.

Van Dalen, H. P., & Henkens, K. (2012). Intended and unintended consequences of a publish-or-perish culture: A worldwide survey. *Journal of the American Society for Information Science and Technology, 63*(7), 1282–1293.

Watkins, P. C. (2004). Gratitude and subjective well-being. In N. R. Silton (Ed.), *Scientific concepts behind happiness, kindness, and empathy in contemporary society* (pp. 167–192). Oxford University Press.

Wood, A. M., Froh, J. J., & Geraghty, A. W. (2010). Gratitude and well-being: A review and theoretical integration. *Clinical Psychology Review, 30*(7), 890–905.

Chapter 17

Does belonging affect wellbeing?

A researcher's experiences of transition from a conflict-affected country to Australia

Abdul Qawi Noori

Introduction

In an increasingly interconnected world, students pursuing a research degree in higher education face different challenges as they navigate social, cultural, and educational landscapes, mainly when the students hail from conflict-affected countries (Sherry et al., 2010), including marginalisation, language barriers, cultural differences, discrimination, problems in mental wellbeing and self-care, and the search for a sense of belonging (McClure, 2007). Such students often feel disconnected from their societies when seeking educational opportunities abroad due to their exposure to trauma, war, and social and political instability in their home countries (Stark et al., 2021; Noori, 2021; Noori et al., 2022).

In conflict-affected countries the prolonged conflicts created problems for students but also adversely affected societies and caused disruptions in education (Noori, 2023). For example, Afghanistan is one of those countries in Asia that has experienced decades of conflicts that have resulted in a low quality of education (Noori et al., 2023). The first administration of the Taliban (1996–2001) brought devastation, as most schools and universities were closed, and gender violence pervasively increased (Noori et al., 2020). Some advancements were made during the two decades of republic administration, but weak governance and corruption worsened the situation (Noori et al., 2023). The darker time started when the Taliban regained power in August 2021 and imposed restrictive measures on women and society at large, including banning girls from going to school and university and working in governmental and non-governmental organisations (Orfan & Samady, 2023). As a result, thousands of people were affected by the situation and left the country searching for a new life and education in other countries (Orfan et al., 2023), leading to challenges and disruptions that can impact their self-care and wellbeing.

Australia is one of the main destinations for individuals seeking higher education (Sherry et al., 2010), including students from Afghanistan. Studies show that Australian universities provide a high-standards teaching-learning and research environment for students to promote their academic achievement

DOI: 10.4324/9781003457510-21

(Gleeson, 2022; Dally et al., 2019; MacLeod, 2020). But there are limited studies about how students from conflict-affected countries develop a sense of belonging and cope with their wellbeing and self-care problems in the Western world (Flaherty et al., 2020). This chapter explores the personal experiences of a researcher who has moved to Australia from a conflict-affected country and examines the journey, search for a sense of belonging, challenges, and overcoming the challenges with the use of several strategies. Through contextualising the broader sociocultural and educational landscapes of Australia and Afghanistan, the study offers insights that can inform academic institutions, policymakers, and individuals involved in supporting the integration and wellbeing of individuals, especially international students from conflict backgrounds.

Belonging

The concept of belonging is one of the primary needs of humans and refers to the feelings of being connected, accepted, and included within a particular group, community, or social environment (Allen et al., 2021). It is a profoundly subjective and emotional journey that influences how individuals see themselves and connect with others (Myhre et al., 2020). The sense of belonging significantly enriches the social fabric of communities and societies, cultivating a profound sense of unity and interconnection among individuals (O'Connor, 2017).

Belonging has been a topic of interest in psychology since the 1940s when Abraham Maslow identified it as one of the essential human needs (Maslow, 1943). Maslow emphasised that the need to belong and connect with others is a crucial aspect of human social development. Other psychologists, like Carl Rogers, further explored the idea and described it as a subjective and positive experience of connecting with others, highlighting its role in shaping a positive sense of self and others (Rogers, 1956).

As research on belonging expanded in the 1960s, scholars like Vygotsky focused on the social-cultural aspects that influence cognitive and psychological belonging (John-Steiner & Mahn, 1996). Other researchers, such as Bronfenbrenner (2000) and McClelland (1987), explored the impact of the environment and social interactions on a person's sense of belonging and social identity. They stated that the physical environment impacts humans' values, lifestyle, and interactions. They also believed that human ecology plays a pivotal role in facilitating the development of individuals' sense of belonging and social identity. Additionally, Schlossberg (1981) highlighted the significance of support and strategies in facilitating students' successful transitions and fostering a sense of belonging. She concluded that a sense of belonging adds to the value of students' wellbeing and self-care in higher education (Schlossberg, 1981).

Baumeister and Leary ((1995[2017])) delved into the role of belonging in human behaviour and motivation. They pointed out that belonging is the main driver of human motivation which plays the fundamental aspect of individuals' thinking, feeling, and interaction with the environment. In addition, Vallerand (1997) emphasised that belonging is an essential human need and overall wellbeing. Furthermore, Deci and Ryan (2000) stated that belonging is a vital emotional need of humans that impacts mental health, wellbeing, self-care, performance, and identity-building.

Belonging is important for the motivation and wellbeing of humans (Walton & Cohen, 2007). A sense of belonging profoundly influences how people perceive themselves and their place in the world, fostering a positive sense of identity and purpose (Allen, 2020). When individuals feel a strong sense of belonging, they are more likely to exhibit higher levels of self-esteem, resilience, and life satisfaction, leading to improved mental and emotional wellbeing and self-care (Yıldırım et al., 2023). Conversely, a lack of belonging can result in isolation, loneliness, and decreased overall satisfaction with life (Lim et al., 2021). Therefore, fostering a sense of belonging is essential for building cohesive societies, promoting mental health, and enhancing individuals' overall quality of life (Arslan et al., 2022).

Sense of belonging is a crucial aspect of student development in higher education and is influenced by various factors (Sari, 2012). Firstly, academic achievement and motivation (Tice et al., 2021), along with positive social relationships with peers and teachers (Ahmadi et al., 2020) and the school's physical environment (Ackah-Jnr & Danso, 2019), play a pivotal role in shaping students' sense of belonging (Tice et al., 2021). Moreover, their personal characteristics, such as self-efficacy and emotional regulation, also directly impact their feelings of connection and attachment (Grobecker, 2016). Additionally, engaging in extracurricular activities fosters a sense of belonging and contributes to skill development (Vaccaro & Newman, 2016).

Furthermore, belonging is a significant factor that enhances mental health and emotional wellbeing among students (Khatri & Duggal, 2022). Haim-Litevsky et al. (2023) stated that the sense of belonging contributes to wellbeing and self-care in daily participation. Waller (2020) added that a sense of belonging is a fundamental human need and has a significant impact on our psychological wellbeing and lack of belonging causes anxiety, depression, and hostile behaviour, an increased risk of mental illness, and social isolation (Hunt & Eisenberg, 2010).

Wellbeing

The concept of wellbeing is multidimensional and refers to the overall quality of an individual's life (Lara et al., 2020). It is used to understand satisfaction levels, mental and physical health, social connection, and meaning in life (Clair et al., 2021).

The term wellbeing has a long history and was used in different philosophies and schools of thought. Plato, the famous Greek philosopher, interchangeably used different words such as living well, being successful, and doing well to refer to wellbeing (Badhwar, 2014). He believed that wellbeing is a multidimensional state of flourishing and fulfilment that goes beyond mere physical pleasure or satisfaction (Compton & Hoffman, 2019). In his philosophy, wellbeing was closely tied to the pursuit of virtue, the cultivation of wisdom, and the alignment of one's soul with the ultimate truths of reality (Fletcher, 2015). Socrates focused on pursuing virtue, self-knowledge, and moral integrity as essential components of wellbeing (Moore, 2015). He argued that wellbeing is a matter of objective fact, discoverable by the wise (Rosen, 2022). Aristotle defined wellbeing as a state of flourishing or a happy life (Fletcher, 2015). Epicurus believed that wellbeing is the pursuit of pleasure and the minimising of suffering from pain and fear, leading to a good life (Joshanloo & Weijers, 2019).

Confucius, a Chinese philosopher, believed that wellbeing is not only an individual pursuit but it is also a foundation for a stable and flourishing society (Fletcher, 2015). Stoicism is a popular philosophical school of thought and believes that one can achieve a state of wellbeing by actively developing virtuous qualities, using rational thinking, and maintaining a calm and peaceful attitude, dealing with the difficulties and situations in life that are outside of our control (Salzgeber, 2019). Daoism believes that wellbeing is living in harmony with nature, embracing simplicity, and cultivating a balanced and peaceful life (Wong, 2015). Buddhism believes that wellbeing is about ending suffering, finding inner peace, and reaching enlightenment, which frees us from the cycle of birth and death (Fletcher, 2015). From the Christian perspective, wellbeing encompasses spiritual, physical, emotional, and relational aspects (Rosmarin & Koenig, 1998). It involves a close relationship with God, adherence to moral and ethical principles, and a sense of purpose and fulfillment rooted in faith (Mutalib et al., 2022). From the Islamic perspective, wellbeing refers to the spiritual, material, existential and social elements, including the relationship with Allah, good manners and respect, good physical and mental health, family and social relationships, peace, justice, and fairness, and seeking knowledge (Shaikh & Seedat, 2022). In recent centuries, wellbeing has continued to be a multidimensional concept, encompassing the physical, mental, emotional, and social aspects of a fulfilling life (Keyes, 2006). It includes factors like good health, positive mental states, meaningful relationships, a sense of purpose, and overall life satisfaction (Walton & Cohen, 2011).

Methodology

I employed an autoethnographic approach to share my experiences of transition from a conflict-affected country to Australia. Autoethnography, as a qualitative research method, places the researchers at the centre of the study (Chang, 2016), allowing them to conduct a deeply personal and introspective examination of their lived experiences (Starr, 2010; Chang, 2016). This is a process to let the informants tell their stories (Pretorius, 2024), personal experiences, and reflections (Pretorius, 2023) and share them with a broader readership.

In this study, the researcher serves as both the subject and the primary source of data for the research. The researcher's first-person account of his journey through the lens of a sense of belonging will be the foundation of the study, allowing for an authentic and introspective exploration process (Xue & Desmet, 2019). As the participant in this study, I went into the deeper context of my memories in search of a sense of belonging to enhance the richness of the chapter in the self-explanatory process (Chang, 2016). This empowered me to reflect on my experiences of transition from a conflict-affected country where I experienced decades of conflict. Accompanying my voice, photo elicitation was used to visualise the data and support my journey in the search for a sense of belonging. Eberle (2018) believed that photo elicitation represents images to reflect visuals and emotions to present narrative stories. The photo was taken after my transition to Australia in one of the spaces on the campus. It represents how I struggle with the navigation of my academic journey.

In this chapter, I present stories of my transition, the challenges I encountered, and the strategies I used to cope with the challenges. I elaborate on my experience, searching for a sense of belonging and how it affected my wellbeing to engage the reader intellectually and emotionally through the authenticity of first-hand accounts (Le Roux, 2017). I extend a warm invitation to the readers looking through this piece of writing from a researcher in search of a sense of belonging. This chapter also reflects the social, political, and cultural context of experiences of challenges in the new environment; these may resonate or be of reflective value.

Data analysis in this autoethnographic piece of writing involves a rigorous and iterative process of reflection, interpretation, and photo elicitation. As the researcher, by identifying recurring themes, emotions, and patterns related to my sense of belonging, I systematically reviewed my reflective journal entries (Bhattacharya, 2017). Through constant comparison and thematic analysis, I gained a deeper understanding of my sense of belonging in the cultural context of Australia, communicated in this chapter.

I applied the reflective prompt technique outlined by Pretorius and Cutri (2019) to revisit my past experiences. This method allowed me to articulate the events, analyse my emotions and thoughts both at the time and in retrospect, and assess how these experiences shaped my learning practices. As I delved into the manuscript writing process, I further pondered my mindset during the recounted experiences. This introspection triggered memories of additional childhood incidents that significantly influenced my identity. This expanded reflection deepened my understanding of my own experiences, contributing to a more comprehensive exploration of the manuscript.

Image 17.1 Search for a sense of belonging (taken at the Monash University's campus). This photo reflects my multifaceted quest for a sense of belonging. It captures my emotional and psychological response to future uncertainties, highlighting the interplay between social inclusion, wellbeing, and the challenges of adapting to a new environment

Search for a sense of belonging

Fuelled by a strong desire to continue my PhD studies, I moved to Australia from a conflict-affected country. However, the transition has presented significant challenges, especially considering my personal experiences enduring prolonged periods of conflicts and political instabilities. These experiences have carried poignant narratives of conflicts and transitions. This juncture represents a crucial turning point, offering me a precious opportunity to search for a profound sense of belonging and to refine my personal skills.

Aspiring scholars pursuing advanced research degrees aim to achieve significant milestones and establish an identity and sense of belonging. Upon transitioning to university life, I entered a space where I was expecting a sense of freedom and self-reliance, fully welcoming the exciting start of a promising new phase in my life. During this phase, I sought to establish connections with peers, fellow students, friends, faculty members, and the broader community. I was striving to create a transformative opportunity that would foster personal growth, nurture essential skills, and empower me to shape the precise pathways I envision for my future. Prominent psychologist, Nancy Schlossberg (1981), highlights that during transition periods, individuals often seek a sense of belonging and connection. Schlossberg emphasises the importance of connecting with others, such as friends and the community, to navigate successfully during this period of time. So, she suggests that if students are supported and valued as individuals adapt to new environments, their transition offers opportunities for personal growth and skill development.

Despite the opportunities for development, challenges related to belonging, mental wellbeing, and stress have adversely affected my productivity and posed considerable problems to my smooth integration into this new environment. The oppressive restrictions imposed by the Taliban on education and intellectual pursuits exacerbate my worries, leaving me with a deep sense of uncertainty as I ponder the opportunities and constraints awaiting me on this academic journey. Notwithstanding these obstacles, I remain determined to persevere and seek avenues for growth and development wherever they may lead me. I have been concerned about navigating family stress and searching for a sense of belonging, as I constantly ponder thoughts of my family and the place where once I called home. The question of where I truly belong looms large, leaving me unsure of my identity. I would like to know if my dream of searching for a true sense of belonging will come true and whether I will be embraced with open arms as a regular individual in this new learning environment.

Challenges faced before, during, and after the transition

My dream to pursue a higher research degree in Australia was fraught with numerous challenges. Providing an English language proficiency certificate was the first challenge because almost all organisations left Afghanistan after the Taliban took power in August 2021, and I needed to travel to another country to fulfil the initial requirement. After submitting my application to the university, receiving an offer of admission, and launching my visa application, I encountered additional hurdles, as biometric and medical checks were requested by the department concerned. I had to navigate logistical and safety concerns while undertaking these steps to submit the required documents. Furthermore, despite obtaining the student visa issued by the Australian government, the Taliban's ban on online visas from Kabul airport posed a significant hurdle. I tried to go to a neighbouring country to fly to start my educational journey, but my attempts to get a visa from neighbouring countries like Iran and Pakistan proved to be difficult due to various political policies and protocols. After several days of struggle, I found a way to fly, but I needed help finding a connecting flight to Melbourne and discovered the flight tickets were unaffordable. I therefore needed help securing the necessary funds to purchase a ticket, relying on assistance from a relative living in another country. Finally,

I managed to begin the first step of my educational journey. When I arrived in Melbourne I had an exhausted budget, and was contemplating how to initiate the integration process and acquaint myself with the intricacies of academic life. I had a problem finding accommodation; I had landed at midnight and waited at the airport for hours to maintain a WIFI connection and find a network to help me with my temporary lodging. Luckily, with the help of a friend, I could adapt and start my life in search of a sense of belonging in academia.

Navigating academic life and adjusting to a new culture and educational system brought a set of complexities. I had to adapt to the unfamiliar atmosphere and actively engage in educational ventures. I was seeking opportunities to connect with fellow researchers and friends. During my first visit to the campus, I found a few open-hearted friends who familiarised me with the campus and welcomed me. I also benefited from a university staff member who helped me with my initial integration. Later, I strengthened my networking and made new friends. These connections infused me with a sense of hope for belonging. They played a promising role in integrating me to my academic journey, which underscored the essence of a sense of belonging at the start of my academic journey.

Upon commencing my studies at the Faculty of Education, Monash University, I was trying to navigate the challenges of transitioning to a new country and academic life. However, I also needed to think of my personal and familial problems. Embarking on my education journey, I had left behind my family, whose worries intensified as the days passed. These concerns were valid as the Taliban's restrictions on women's education had a direct impact on my family. Not only did they lead to my wife losing her job, but the Taliban also imposed severe limitations, including the prohibition of women leaving their homes without a mahram (male guardian). These stringent measures created substantial challenges for our family, highlighting the harsh realities we had to navigate. The situation deteriorated when my second son began expressing his feelings to his mother. He bemoaned the absence of his dad to take him to the park or the supermarket, recalling a poignant reminder of the absence of my fatherly presence and not being able to go out with his mother. These challenges would deeply affect my emotional wellbeing, self-care, and academic productivity since it was challenging to handle my studies and cope with these heartbreaking complications. After a few months, the situation became even more challenging as my wife struggled with the loss of support resulting from my absence. The constant worry for my family's safety and wellbeing in the conflict-affected country weighed heavily on my mind, adding to the psychological burden of my own transition to a new country.

The sense of forlornness and longing intensified my emotional struggles during this period. I considered inviting my family to join me as additional support while pursuing my studies. However, I encountered several challenges, including difficulties in applying for their visa. Despite seeking assistance from the university, my efforts to resolve the problem were unsuccessful.

Simultaneously, I explored taking a campus job to assist me with logistical matters. These challenges prompted me to engage in deeper introspection, searching for ways to overcome these obstacles while also considering the well-being of both my family and myself.

Overcoming adversity: A journey of resilience

Even though my life was adversely affected by the mentioned worries, they could not stop me from achieving my goals. Being passionate, not accepting failure, and believing in the power of education helped me overcome negative thinking. I was able to improve my self-care and wellbeing, and work towards improving my interpersonal, professional, and academic skills. To do this, I employed various strategies to ensure the wellbeing of both my family and myself. One effective approach was to maintain regular online meetings with my family members. These virtual connections helped us stay emotionally close, allowing for meaningful conversations. This, in turn, inspired my wife to take proactive steps in caring for our children. She engaged them in various indoor games and activities, fostering their creativity and promoting their self-care. We have celebrated the discovery of what is possible in sharing this way of being together, even if not physically in the same place. These interactions became crucial for maintaining our family's overall wellbeing during challenging times and improved my self-care as well.

I did not lose hope when I initially couldn't secure a part-time job on campus. Instead, I explored alternative opportunities to thrive. My journey began by exploring alternative opportunities and finding an entry-level job for a short period of time, which helped me understand the working culture and organisational dynamics. I then focused on refining my resume and actively started seeking better job opportunities. Through leveraging my network and conducting my job searches, I eventually found a position matching my background. This not only provided income but also supported my family, who were facing their own financial hardships.

Being a research student and working in academia can be stressful and isolating. To enhance my self-care and wellbeing I incorporated a 30-minute daily outdoor running and sports routine. Engaging in physical activity and spending time with friends not only allowed me to temporarily set aside my academic challenges but also rejuvenated my mind, enabling me to return with a fresh perspective. These practices significantly contributed to improving my academic productivity and enhancing my ability to focus on my studies.

Approaching friends and strengthening my networking was useful in finding strategies to advance my knowledge and skills, manage stress and wellbeing, and improve my relationship to search for a sense of belonging. For example, I found a scholar whom I had never met before. I reached out to him and asked for a possibility to meet. During our meetings, I carefully listened to his fatherly advice; his kind words were valuable and drew a map in my mind and for my academic journey. He also presented me with some books that helped me to engage myself in reading, learn some philosophical concepts, and improve my interest in seeking more resources that advanced my knowledge. Being involved in clubs and communities was also advantageous in developing a sense of belonging to improve my wellbeing and self-care.

Conclusion

I aspire not only to share my personal journey but also to offer a guiding light to those embarking on a similar one. May it bring to light the powerful impact that education can have, the enduring relationships formed through belonging, and the journey to embrace the changing world in search of a sense of belonging.

In pursuing a sense of belonging, my journey from a conflict-affected country to Australia has been fraught with challenges and complexities. Fuelled by a strong desire to continue my PhD studies, I faced obstacles ranging from the political upheavals in my home country to the logistical hurdles of transitioning to a new academic and cultural environment. These challenges, from obtaining an English proficiency certificate to overcoming visa restrictions, have tested my resilience and determination. The impact on my family, separated by the Taliban's restrictions, intensified my emotional struggles. However, I navigated these adversities, maintaining family connections through virtual meetings and finding solace in physical activities and supportive networks.

Beyond my individual experience, this chapter offers valuable implications for educators and students worldwide. It sheds light on strategies to enhance students' sense of belonging and wellbeing, fostering a more inclusive and supportive educational environment. While limited to my personal experience, this work motivates and informs individuals facing challenges in other countries and in conflict-affected regions in particular, illustrating the resilience required to achieve one's goals.

References

Ackah-Jnr, F. R., & Danso, J. B. (2019). Examining the physical environment of Ghanaian inclusive schools: How accessible, suitable and appropriate is such environment for inclusive education? *International Journal of Inclusive Education*, 23(2), 188–208. https://doi.org/10.1080/13603116.2018.1427808

Ahmadi, S., Hassani, M., & Ahmadi, F. (2020). Student- and school-level factors related to school belongingness among high school students. *International Journal of Adolescence and Youth*, 25(1), 741–752. https://doi.org/10.1080/02673843.2020.1730200

Allen, K. A. (2020). *The psychology of belonging*. Routledge.

Allen, K. A., Kern, M. L., Rozek, C. S., McInerney, D. M., & Slavich, G. M. (2021). Belonging: A review of conceptual issues, an integrative framework, and directions for future research. *Australian Journal of Psychology*, 73(1), 87–102. https://doi.org/10.1080/00049530.2021.1883409

Arslan, G., Yıldırım, M., Tanhan, A., & Kılınç, M. (2022). Social inclusion to promote mental health and wellbeing of youths in schools. In C. Boyle & K.-A. Allen (Eds.), *Research for inclusive quality education: leveraging belonging, inclusion, and equity* (pp. 113–122). Singapore: Springer Nature Singapore. https://doi.org/10.1007/978-981-16-5908-9_9

Badhwar, N. K. (2014). *Well-being: Happiness in a worthwhile life.* Oxford University Press.

Baumeister, R. F., & Leary, M. R. (2017). The need to belong: Desire for interpersonal attachments as a fundamental human motivation. In B. Laursen & R. Žukauskiene (Eds.), *Interpersonal development* (pp. 57–89). Routledge. Originally published in 1995 in *Psychological Bulletin,* 17(3), 497–529.

Bhattacharya, K. (2017). *Fundamentals of qualitative research: A practical guide.* Taylor & Francis.

Bronfenbrenner, U. (2000). *Ecological systems theory.* Oxford University Press.

Chang, H. (2016). *Autoethnography as method* (Vol. 1). Routledge.

Clair, R., Gordon, M., Kroon, M., & Reilly, C. (2021). The effects of social isolation on wellbeing and life satisfaction during pandemic. *Humanities and Social Sciences Communications,* 8(1). https://doi.org/10.1057/s41599-021-00710-3

Compton, W. C., & Hoffman, E. (2019). *Positive psychology: The science of happiness and flourishing.* Sage Publications.

Dally, K., Dempsey, I., Ralston, M. M., Foggett, J., Duncan, J., Strnadová, I., Chambers, D., Paterson, D., & Sharma, U. (2019). Current issues and future directions in Australian special and inclusive education. *Australian Journal of Teacher Education* (online), 44(8), 57–73. DOI:10.14221/ajte.2019v44n8.4

Deci, E. L., & Ryan, R. M. (2000). The "what" and "why" of goal pursuits: Human needs and the self-determination of behavior. *Psychological Inquiry,* 11(4), 227–268. https://doi.org/10.1207/S15327965PLI1104_01

Eberle, T. S. (2018). Collecting images as data. In Flick, U. (Ed.), *The SAGE handbook of qualitative data collection* (pp. 392–411). Sage.

Flaherty, M. P., Sikorski, E., Klos, L., Vus, V., & Hayduk, N. (2020). Peacework and mental health: From individual pathology to community responsibility. *Intervention Journal of Mental Health and Psychosocial Support in Conflict Affected Areas,* 18(1), 28–36.

Fletcher, G. (Ed.). (2015). *The Routledge handbook of philosophy of well-being.* Routledge.

Gleeson, M. (2022). Is supporting the needs of emergent bilingual learners in mainstream classes a cultural or linguistic issue? How do policy, curricula, and secondary teacher education programmes in Australia and New Zealand compare? *International Journal of Bilingual Education and Bilingualism,* 25(8), 2962–2975. https://doi.org/10.1080/13670050.2021.1997900

Grobecker, P. A. (2016). A sense of belonging and perceived stress among baccalaureate nursing students in clinical placements. *Nurse Education Today,* 36, 178–183. https://doi.org/10.1016/j.nedt.2015.09.015

Haim-Litevsky, D., Komemi, R., & Lipskaya-Velikovsky, L. (2023). Sense of belonging, meaningful daily life participation, and well-being: Integrated investigation. *International Journal of Environmental Research and Public Health,* 20(5), 4121. https://doi.org/10.3390/ijerph20054121

Hunt, J., & Eisenberg, D. (2010). Mental health problems and help-seeking behavior among college students. *Journal of Adolescent Health,* 46(1), 3–10. https://doi.org/10.1016/j.jadohealth.2009.08.008

John-Steiner, V., & Mahn, H. (1996). Sociocultural approaches to learning and development: A Vygotskian framework. *Educational Psychologist*, *31*(3–4), 191–206. https://doi.org/10.1080/00461520.1996.9653266

Joshanloo, M., & Weijers, D. (2019). A two-dimensional conceptual framework for understanding mental well-being. *PLOS ONE*, *14*(3), e0214045. https://doi.org/10.1371/journal.pone.0214045

Khatri, P., & Duggal, H. K. (2022). Well-being of higher education consumers: A review and research agenda. *International Journal of Consumer Studies*, *46*(5), 1564–1593. https://doi.org/10.1111/ijcs.12783

Keyes, C. L. (2006). Subjective well-being in mental health and human development research worldwide: An introduction. *Social Indicators Research*, *10*(77), 1–10.

Lara, E., Martín-María, N., Forsman, A. K., Cresswell-Smith, J., Donisi, V., Ådnanes, M., Kaasbøll, J., Melby, L., Nordmyr, J., Nyholm, L., Rabbi, L., Amaddeo, F., & Miret, M. (2020). Understanding the multi-dimensional mental wellbeing in late life: Evidence from the perspective of the oldest old population. *Journal of Happiness Studies*, *21*, 465–484. https://doi.org/10.1007/s10902-019-00090-1

Le Roux, C. S. (2017). Exploring rigour in autoethnographic research. *International Journal of Social Research Methodology*, *20*(2), 195–207. https://doi.org/10.1080/13645579.2016.1140965

Lim, M. H., Allen, K. A., Furlong, M. J., Craig, H., & Smith, D. C. (2021). Introducing a dual continuum model of belonging and loneliness. *Australian Journal of Psychology*, *73*(1), 81–86. https://doi.org/10.1080/00049530.2021.1883411

MacLeod, L. (2020). Shaping professional development of educators: The role of school leaders. In M. A. White & F. McCallum (Eds.), *Critical perspectives on teaching, learning and leadership: enhancing educational outcomes* (pp. 189–217). Springer.

Maslow, A. H. (1943). A theory of human motivation. *Psychological Review*, *50*(4), 370.

McClelland, D. C. (1987). *Human motivation*. Cup Archive.

McClure, J. W. (2007). International graduates' cross-cultural adjustment: Experiences, coping strategies, and suggested programmatic responses. *Teaching in Higher Education*, *12*(2), 199–217. https://doi.org/10.1080/13562510701191976

Moore, C. (2015). *Socrates and self-knowledge*. Cambridge University Press.

Mutalib, M. A., Rafiki, A., & Razali, W. M. F. A. W. (2022). *Principles and practice of Islamic leadership*. Springer. https://doi.org/10.1007/978-981-19-0908-5

Myhre, A., Råbu, M., & Feragen, K. J. (2021). The need to belong: Subjective experiences of living with craniofacial conditions and undergoing appearance-altering surgery. *Body Image*, *38*, 334–345.

Noori, A. Q. (2021). The impact of COVID-19 pandemic on students' learning in higher education in Afghanistan. *Heliyon*, *7*(10), e08113. https://doi.org/10.1016/j.heliyon.2021.e08113

Noori, A. Q. (2023). Job satisfaction variance among public and private school teachers: A case study. *Cogent Education*, *10*(1), 1–18. https://doi.org/10.1080/2331186X.2023.2189425

Noori, A. Q., Orfan, S. N., & Noori, N. (2023). Principals' transformational leadership and teachers' emotional intelligence: A cross-sectional study of Takhar high schools, Afghanistan. *Leadership and Policy in Schools*, 1–16. https://doi.org/10.1080/15700763.2023.2176780

Noori, A. Q., Orfan, S. N., Akramy, S. A., & Hashemi, A. (2022). The use of social media in EFL learning and teaching in higher education of Afghanistan. *Cogent Social Sciences*, *8*(1), 1–12. https://doi.org/10.1080/23311886.2022.2027613

Noori, A. Q., Said, H., Nor, F. M., & Abd Ghani, F. (2020). The relationship between university lecturers' behaviour and students' motivation. *Universal Journal of Educational Research*, *8*(11C), 15–22. https://doi.org/10.13189/ujer.2020.082303

O'Connor, P. (2017). *Home: The foundations of belonging*. Routledge.

Orfan, S. N., & Samady, S. (2023). Students' perceptions of gender equality: A case study of a conflict-stricken country. *Cogent Social Sciences*, *9*(1), 2225819. https://doi.org/10.1080/23311886.2023.2225819

Orfan, S. N., Perry, J. A., Daqiq, B., Seraj, M. Y., & Noori, A. Q. (2023). "Hey American! What is up?" At-risk men's experiences before and while waiting for evacuation flights and after returning home. *Journal of Human Rights and Social Work, 8*, 412–423. https://doi.org/10.1007/s41134-023-00268-x

Pretorius, L. (2023). A harmony of voices: The value of collaborative autoethnography as collective witnessing during a pandemic. In B. Cahusac de Caux, L. Pretorius, & L. Macaulay (Eds.), *Research and teaching in a pandemic world: The challenges of establishing academic identities during times of crisis* (pp. 25–33). Springer Nature Singapore. https://doi.org/10.1007/978-981-19-7757-2_3

Pretorius, L. (2024). "I realised that, if I am dead, I cannot finish my PhD!": A narrative ethnography of psychological capital in academia. In M. Edwards, A. Martin, & N. Ashkanasy (Eds.), *Handbook of academic mental health*. Edward Elgar Publishing. In Press.

Pretorius, L., & Cutri, J. (2019). Autoethnography: Researching personal experiences. In L. Pretorius, L. Macaulay, & B. Cahusac de Caux (Eds.), *Wellbeing in doctoral education: Insights and guidance from the student experience* (pp. 27–34). Springer. https://doi.org/10.1007/978-981-13-9302-0_4

Rogers, C. R. (1956). Client-entered theory. *Journal of Counseling Psychology, 3*(2), 115–120. https://doi.org/10.1037/h0046548

Rosen, M. (2022). *The shadow of God: Kant, Hegel, and the passage from heaven to history*. Harvard University Press.

Rosmarin, D. H., & Koenig, H. G. (Eds.). (1998). *Handbook of religion and mental health*. Elsevier.

Salzgeber, J. (2019). *The little book of stoicism: Timeless wisdom to gain resilience, confidence, and calmness*. Jonas Salzgeber.

Schlossberg, N. K. (1981). A model for analyzing human adaptation to transition. *The Counseling Psychologist, 9*(2), 2–18.

Shaikh, S. D., & Seedat, F. (Eds.). (2022). *The women's khutbah book: Contemporary sermons on spirituality and justice from around the world*. Yale University Press.

Sari, M. (2012). Sense of school belonging among elementary school students. *Çukurova University Faculty of Education Journal, 41*(1), 1–11.

Sherry, M., Thomas, P., & Chui, W. H. (2010). International students: A vulnerable student population. *Higher Education, 60*, 33–46. https://doi.org/10.1007/s10734-009-9284-z

Stark, L., Robinson, M. V., Gillespie, A., Aldrich, J., Hassan, W., Wessells, M., Allaf, C., & Bennouna, C. (2021). Supporting mental health and psychosocial wellbeing through social and emotional learning: A participatory study of conflict-affected youth resettled to the US. *BMC Public Health, 21*(1), 1–14. https://doi.org/10.1186/s12889-021-11674-z

Starr, L. J. (2010). The use of autoethnography in educational research: Locating who we are in what we do. *Canadian Journal for New Scholars in Education/Revue canadienne des jeunes chercheures et chercheurs en éducation*, *3*(1).

Tice, D., Baumeister, R., Crawford, J., Allen, K. A., & Percy, A. (2021). Student belongingness in higher education: Lessons for Professors from the COVID-19 pandemic. *Journal of University Teaching & Learning Practice*, *18*(4), 1–14. https://doi.org/10.53761/1.18.4.2

Vaccaro, A., & Newman, B. M. (2016). Development of a sense of belonging for privileged and minoritized students: An emergent model. *Journal of College Student Development*, *57*(8), 925–942. https://doi.org/10.1353/csd.2016.0091

Vallerand, R. J. (1997). Toward a hierarchical model of intrinsic and extrinsic motivation. *Advances in Experimental Social Psychology*, *29*(19), 271–360. https://doi.org/10.1016/S0065-2601(08)60019-2

Waller, L. (2020). Fostering a sense of belonging in the workplace: Enhancing well-being and a positive and coherent sense of self. In S. Dhiman (Ed.), *The Palgrave handbook of workplace well-being* (pp. 1–27). https://doi.org/10.1007/978-3-030-02470-3_83-1

Walton, G. M., & Cohen, G. L. (2011). A brief social-belonging intervention improves academic and health outcomes of minority students. *Science*, *331*(6023), 1447–1451. https://doi.org/10.1126/science.1198364

Walton, G. M., & Cohen, G. L. (2007). A question of belonging: Race, social fit, and achievement. *Journal of Personality and Social Psychology*, *92*(1), 82–96. https://doi.org/10.1037/0022-3514.92.1.82

Wong, E. (2015). *Being Taoist: Wisdom for living a balanced life*. Shambhala Publications.

Xue, H., & Desmet, P. M. (2019). Researcher introspection for experience-driven design research. *Design Studies*, *63*, 37–64. https://doi.org/10.1016/j.destud.2019.03.001

Yıldırım, M., Turan, M. E., Albeladi, N. S., Crescenzo, P., Rizzo, A., Nucera, G., Ferrari, G., Navolokina, A., Szarpak, Ł., & Chirico, F. (2023). Resilience and perceived social support as predictors of emotional well-being. *Journal of Health and Social Sciences*, *8*(1), 59–75. https://doi.org/10.19204/2023/rsln5

Section 5

Taking a closer look at leadership

Chapter 18

Expansive education leadership

Two viewpoints on learning, and leaning into, spacious leading

Deena Kara Shaffer[1] and Alice J. Hovorka

Introduction

What are the dimensions of expansive leadership? Of "expansion" more broadly? To understand *cognitively* this word that feels so right *intuitively*, we are inclined to explore its opposite; to understand expansiveness by what it is not, what it moves away from, and what it is unlike. Before turning to any dictionary, we want to turn to our own feeling-into, our own exploring-through-words. At first attempt, its counter somatically lands as "constriction", "compaction, "containment".

In bringing this notion and word of "expansive" and placing it aside "leadership", the road we do *not* want to go down is what *more* leadership could come to encompass. It is not "expand*ed*" leadership. It is not about asking leaders to do, hold, or take on more. It is not even really an urging for definitional expanding *about* "leadership". These, themselves, feel small. These feel like tasks. We are after a quality or tone or tempo of leadership, an approach or aspiration or different-actioning of leadership. Not different to-dos, but *doing* it differently.

Leadership that feels expansive is leadership that has space – leadership that *does not* feel restrictive, spatially boundaried, or narrowing. To wordsmith "expansive": synonyms like "open", "inclusive", and "broad" appear; so do more relational elements, as when a person is described as "expansive", denoting "communicative".

The words that leaders use matter. Languaging, perhaps it is banal or overly obvious to say, is a keystone of what sets, shapes, and shifts the tone of team culture, vision, and potential harmony (or, assures the opposite). We think of these as the words *in* leadership. But we want to make the point that the words we use *about* leadership matter. They help us think through what leadership can (and maybe even ought to) include, what leadership can gravitate towards, and the ways leadership can make less harm.

In education spaces, what do leaders have to, at present, *do*? They must hold complex, intersecting information and issues all at once, create change in response to demographic changes, tend to so-called gaps of all kinds,

[1]Corresponding author

DOI: 10.4324/9781003457510-23

establish vision, nudge feelings, shift behaviours, translate policies, provide direction, cope with ambiguity, manage others, collect and interpret data, and respond to crises (Santamaría & Santamaría, 2012, p. xii), all within a stratified structure. Our particular leadership locations are as higher education administrative leaders (who wrestle with current, formal meanings and models of "leadership").

Enter the authors (and their leaderships, their wrestlings)

In the workspaces, Alice is a Dean and a Professor. Deena is a Director and a founder.

We see leadership as necessarily a site of social justice, of dismantling, of reckoning, of reimagining – *or* of excluding, denying, or missing out on these. The potential is, however, always there. Why? Because in traditional places of work, which most higher education institutions most certainly are, leadership is married to a hierarchical structure, to a stratifying, level-making structure bound with power. Leaders then *do* their leadership in ways that go *with* this power and architecture, or *against* it – and also in a hundred different ways that straddle both. This is either/or, but leadership is lived out. It is lived – and enlivened – in what is done, and undone.

We see that

> educational administration and social justice have nothing in common at this time. Educational administrators are trained, hired technicians of the status quo who generally believe in, benefit from, and often coerce teachers and students into supporting unjust state and corporate agendas (Chomsky, 2000; Rapp, 2001a, 2001b, 2002b). Leaders for social justice, on the other hand, resist, dissent, rebel, subvert, possess oppositional imaginations, and are committed to transforming oppressive and exploitative social relations in and out of schools (McLaren, 2000; Rich, 2001; Zinn, 1997).
>
> Rapp (2002, p. 226)

We are engaged and eager participants in this *going against*: in this inquiring and rethinking, in this reckoning and reimagining, in this living and enlivening, and in doing and undoing. All the while knowing and naming *both* that "school administrators are increasingly forced to manufacture consent for global capitalism ... [and] forcefully fight injustice from platforms of constitutional authority and civic responsibility in locations around and outside of schools" (Rapp, 2002, p. 227). We have unique specificities, as well as notable overlaps. We share, here, our leading journeys to lay bare our lenses, and our biases, undergirded by our collective, lifelong, committed efforts to undo and unhook them.

What leadership has come to mean to Alice

I had many aspirations as a recently hired tenure-track Faculty member. One such aspiration was to secure a prestigious research fellowship at an international institution. I met with the head of department, brimming with excitement, and imagined how the fellowship would bolster my intellectual growth and bring prestige to our academic unit that prided itself on research excellence. Sharing this with my head of department, I was taken aback when he simply said: "We hired you to teach" and ended the conversation. There was no acknowledgement of my ambition, nor celebration of my accomplishments that led me to believe the fellowship was in reach. There was no patient explanation of how my absence might impact colleagues, students, and our departmental teaching schedule. There was no consideration as to how my ambitions might be realised despite these constraints. I felt unheard, shut down, and like cog-in-a-wheel.

Reflecting on this moment, I am struck by how differently I have chosen to approach my role as an academic administrative leader. I choose to listen to the aspiration and the excitement around it, to acknowledge the ambition, to celebrate the accomplishments that led to this possibility, to patiently explain its potential unintended consequences on others and how institutional expectations might not align, and to brainstorm other avenues through which to realise this ambition. I choose to be demonstrative and communicative, and wide-ranging in imagining and facilitating possibilities for individual and collective success in academia. I choose to embrace a leadership style that is necessarily expansive.

My decanal approach aligns with that which Leduc and Morley (2015) term interactive and participatory. An interactive approach to leading-as-Dean embraces collaboration and high levels of openness when issues and problems are presented for debate by those prepared and able to engage; a participatory approach to decanal leadership emphasises deep support for and engagement in Faculty governance.

In terms of the former, I tend to share decision making with Faculty members who express an interest in engaging in formal and informal dialogue. Moreover, I actively seek out those whose voices might not be foregrounded in collegial discussions, such as early career Faculty or members of equity-deserving groups. I embrace Faculty governance practices that are flexible and even informal by taking a hands-on approach whereby I offer everything (most things) for discussion and insist (ask) to be involved. There is a fine balance here between such engagement and micromanaging. I take cues from Faculty colleagues as to when this line might be crossed. In moments there can be an ambiguous, or even uneasy, relationship between my open leadership style (I have been described as "a Dean [employer] that acts like a chair [colleague]"). There can also be lingering elements of earlier traditional styles generating Faculty suspicions (such that as Dean I am perceived as simply "a neoliberal arm of senior administration").

In terms of the latter, I support Faculty governance activities with public engagement and debate on (again almost) everything. Moreover, I use collegial governance entities, such as Faculty Council or staff meetings, to share issues among various people and bodies and who incorporate the outcomes into policy and action. I also take extended periods of 'process sessions' that take place through open forums or ad hoc settings designed to encourage discussion and provide general access to decision making related to important issues. In moments this means long time periods to achieve consensus decision. My comfort with decentralised and heterarchical forms of leadership means that I can insert myself in these moments by stipulating a 'Dean decision' to facilitate an active decision-making moment among the collective.

What leadership has come to mean to Deena

In some ways, leadership has been elusive in my professional journey. At least in so far as what leadership often is taken to look like. In my body, in my life, leadership has, at different times, felt icky or unappealing, fraught or outright fraudulent. I did not seek out a hierarchical climb, I turned down opportunities for title when they presented values-conflict, and I wrestled in spaces that contained both the friction of influence without positional power.

Why has leadership felt so, well, loaded for me? Because too often, along the way, I heard things like, "you should get close to that colleague because they're going places", or "you shouldn't say things like that, it's not strategic", or "mimic what *they* do, *that* is how you get ahead". It amounted to: say this, don't say that, dress this way, hang out with those people, fake this, pretend that. All to "get somewhere" – all to acquire some kind of particular naming of a job, some size of a team to supervise, some orientation of a physical office, some volume of portfolio. It was a freeing moment indeed when my friend and anti-oppressive leadership coach reminded me, "don't forget, when everyone else goes right, *you* can go left".

In truth, I kept moving "left", *away* from formal "power", having seen it used in ugly, egoic, or confusing ways. I saw, again and again, the continuation of leadership that hurts, instead of dismantling it. Barriers maintained or fortified, instead of broken down. So, instead, I created programmes and interventions that had *lateral* impact. Programmes of non-ownership, programmes that were shared freely, programmes of scale, programmes of influence, but never had "fancy" titles; I created (a company, books, initiatives), but never went "up". And, underneath it all, I fundamentally bristled against "power", "title", and "up".

Now, in my three main professional spaces – Director (at York University), (just) two-term Past President (of the Learning Specialists Association of Canada), and Owner/Founder (Awakened Learning) – I have a new, more embodied understanding of leadership. In these roles, I am a leader in a defined institutional space, directly responsible for hiring, operations, and the like; I am a leader in a national non-profit space; and, as an ethical entrepreneur, I am the maker of a space. Together, these have me feeling that leadership is about not just speaking truth to power, but enacting it. It is about seeking less and less permission, and growing into and changemaking the spaces I get the privilege to stand in. Uplifting, more than upholding.

In these ways, leading from a stance of expansiveness, in and from this body, is not leading informed by pushing out but rather about pushing back. Instead of shying away from "power", I am ever happier to lend my voice, title, signature with the word "director" in it when it means more humanity for the team of humans whose contracts I get to transform into full-time continuing, the students for whom I get to find emergency funding, the professional development opportunities I get to facilitate for "my" staff. It means offering radical learning opportunities for the membership I serve. And it means, in my own business leadership, creating processes and pathways that are encoded with care, humanity, and expansiveness.

Encounters in expansive leadership

Below, we follow that forever fiction-writing advice here: "show, don't tell!" As such, we want to share some of what has come to inform our individual leadership dispositions, leanings toward, and movings away from. It is one thing to describe one's leadership style, it is another to practice it and to be fully 'in it' with positive results.

Expansive leadership as collaborative (Alice)

Over the past five years of my role as Dean, countless Faculty members have come to me with their aspirations: mounting a course that falls outside of the formal curriculum; pursuing a book project or empirical research that requires intense focus on a particular schedule; or, like my own aspirations, hoping to apply for a prestigious research fellowship whose timing cannot be easily predicted. I embrace these moments, even when they are, in practicality, difficult to support. These are moments where Faculty express their passions and confide in me their hopes of building upon previous accomplishments or coming into their own as academics. I choose to listen, match their enthusiasm (genuinely), and celebrate this moment with them. I absorb the moment rather than simply saying 'no' because I recognise that the institutional boundaries or my own commitments to transparency (no deal making) and equity (offering the same opportunities to all) will now allow it. So instead, I ask for context, I empathise with the individual, I reflect on what this means for the Faculty broadly, the precedents this will set, how I could justify to the collective. And I embrace a creative spirit of 'let's brainstorm together' if the original vision is not possible.

Expansive leadership as humane (Deena)

Ten weeks pregnant, nervous about a second pregnancy loss, aware of my changing needs and physical appearance, I told my then boss I was pregnant. His reaction was "fuck!"

Why, "fuck"? I was, and continue to be, a kind of full throttle, high energy, all the way in kind of person, at work, as everywhere else. In that role and its many hats, that 110% was what exuded, no less so with that growing belly.

The precarity of my contract is what nudged me to tell him in my tenth week. No matter the excellence of my work, resonance with students, and support to the team, I was in a stratified institution with set systems, and was hourly with zero job security. I needed to know whether the full-time posting for the role, mentioned and dangled for months, was going to solidify.

His "fuck" was about him. What he was going to lose.

Where would help come from? Who would serve as his right-hand person in short order? How would things that were getting done continue to get done in six-and-a-half-month's time?

There is no expansiveness to my reply in that moment – I was stunned, and no closer to secure work. Expansion did not come right then and there. But, in that interchange, the seed was planted for being a leader *with* and *for* others. Of ensuring more space for the human.

A post circulated fast and wide the year prior to the pandemic. Paolo Gallo and Vlatka Hlupic's article, "Humane leadership must be the Fourth Industrial Revolution's real innovation" (2019), brings together the current and alarming state of leadership, including the pay ratio between top-level executives and low-ranking workers, the distressing health impacts of work stress, and the shortening life expectancies of businesses. Their call to action is for humanity-driven leadership to take the stage. As they outline, this looks like leaders becoming more awake to their "beliefs, conduct, ways of handling people and understanding of strategy" (para. 13), and to shift away from viewing an organisation as "an internal set of assets" to a "dynamic entity" (para. 13).

Amid writing this, a stellar staff member gave her notice. It is a loss to our team, and to me. In carrying that "fuck" with me ever since that exchange, my response was one of congratulations, of celebration. This is a good move for them. They are happy. And so, the space I make as a leader is one not centred on my loss, but on their joy. I think of it as holding enough space to lead with a staff's good news instead of any operational discontinuity. Humanity over workflow.

Expansive leadership as welcoming pushback (Alice)

Leaning into disagreement, disgruntledness, and conflict requires a lot of oneself. Notably, it requires stepping back from one's own ego or intended approach and genuinely embracing other perspectives and possibilities – not easily done when these moments come flooding in or when you have been carving a deeper and deeper path in a particular direction. One moment stands out for me.

An email arrived in my inbox that was clearly born out of frustration expressed in a passive aggressive manner. This Faculty member had taken on – wholeheartedly and from their own initiative I thought – an experiential field course that was loaded with logistics and enrolment issues and lots of new course preparation. The biting email came a year or so after the course was initially mounted, and a second iteration was to take place. I also encountered an in-person moment where various quips emerged regarding the course and its associated burden. Finally, a second biting email arrived.

So, I reached out and invited the Faculty member for a chat. My first question was: "What is going on for you with this course? I am sensing some frustration from your emails…". The Faculty member shared that my (The Dean's) directive to take on this course was simply unrealistic – students do not wish to take this course and offering such a course requires a substantive amount of labour from a Faculty member that cannot be accomplished without support. "The Dean's directive?" I asked. "Yes, I heard that you wanted me to do this course, so I did". What the what?! I had not.

But I realised that my directive as Dean had been interpreted as such by the Faculty member (given their expectations and previous experiences with decanal leadership). I explained that my intention was to encourage all Faculty members to *consider* taking on such courses to enhance our Faculty's experiential education mandate. There was no expectation therein and my directive was to encourage and invite conversations to explore possibilities. I realised that this Faculty member had stepped in to be a team player because they had interpreted the directive as a done deal. My response was to say thank you for taking the course on, on behalf of me as Dean and especially on behalf of the Faculty. And I suggested that the Faculty member step back from the course and simply not offer it (we could make other arrangements). Their relief was palpable.

Expansive leadership as a healing (Deena)

Two months prior to the final draft of this chapter, I came to a meeting with Dean Alice to talk about all things retention. And I blew it. I mean wildly and epically blew it.

Alice had shoulder-tapped me early on in my arrival to York University's Faculty of Environmental and Urban Change to mull over retention. That has been an alive focus for me through my professional journey in post-secondary student affairs, from co-creating the Thriving in Action programme at Toronto Metropolitan University to co-authoring *Thriving in the Classroom*. It matters to me, so much, that students who are invited to join an institution are shown the ways to stay (if they want to stay).

I had not thought so acutely about the deep hurts we carry from prior bosses into encounters with current ones. Nor had I thought about leadership as being a relationship with the potential for healing. Annemarie Caño reflects how, for her, it was "only after moving to a new institution and becoming a Dean during a global pandemic that I've realized how healing can be brought into many aspects of work, including academic leadership" (2021, para. 2).

How had I failed in an early morning Monday meeting with Alice? I had overwhelmingly overprepared. Why? It is what I had been expected to do *prior*. I was serving a past boss in my current context.

In advance of our meeting, I had: deep dived into retention research, surveyed a national community of post-secondary educators about successful retention programmes, posted on a US-wide student affairs site requesting retention insights. From there, I videoed a Miro board with ideas for possibility at York University. Finally, I emailed Alice with bulleted takeaways, possible discussion questions, and a light agenda. It was friendly; it was comprehensive; and, it was too much.

When we met at 9am, the first words Alice spoke were: "okay, that was a lot." From there, "you don't have to do any of that."

I was stunned.

At first, I felt an ouch. I had done a bad job. (And no one wants to do a bad job at a *new* job.) From there, I felt an *ohhhhh*! I saw it, I got it, I understood what I had done. I had superimposed one boss' needs onto a different one. Alice then reassured me by saying, "I just want to shoot the shit with you, hear your ideas, that's all". I was being respected, not reprimanded.

"The metaphor of 'healer'", Caño notes, "provides a lens through which we can see the value of specific skills that effective leaders can practice. For Caño, these skills include being able to watch and gather: the initial "act of a healer is to assess how people are thriving and to spot any injuries, wounds, or infections that may need healing" (2021, para. 4). Caño also encourages leaders-as-healers to affirm others' experiences (and not just insert advice), check-in with staff community wellbeing (offering availability of time and heart), prioritise equity (to form fully inclusive, all-voices-welcome teams), seek integrative responses (turning to holism rather than the violence of siloed systems), and to pursue our own personal healing (particularly for folks experiencing many forms of injustice).

The expansive space that Alice allowed me to fumble, and then reflect back to her what I understood was happening – a toxic ripple carried forward – enabled a healing that I had not fully understood I needed. In the past, it had been an aggressive assumption that no meeting was worthwhile unless it was accompanied by a ranked agenda. In the present, it was my presence that was being invited.

Caño (2021, concl. para.) reflects that

some academic leadership will think that a healing approach to leadership is unnecessary or even too 'soft'. But if part of our job is to develop and sustain the vitality of our units, then we also need to care about the health and wellness of our people as they work to create a healthy future for themselves and others.

Expansive leadership as embracing competing desires (Alice)

In moments of collective friction, a leader has a choice to push forward or to absorb the pushback by listening and potentially shifting process or outcome accordingly. A pivotal moment in this regard occurred a year into my first term as Dean. Colleagues were in the final stages of selecting a name for our newly established Faculty, which was to cement our identity and collective vision for ourselves. We were mulling over three options borne out of much brainstorming and deliberation.

In preparation for our 'final vote' meeting, I chose one of the three options and put it forward as our 'final decision'. My intention was to see how it resonated with colleagues, and I was transparent with them at the meeting: "When you see our final proposal, does our new name resonate?"

For a vocal minority of Faculty members, the name did not work. An intense conversation of pushback ensued, which unsettled the whole group. I asked whether the two other alternative names suited us better – this raised more concerns, and more unsettled discussion. I realised that we were not in a position to finalise our name that day. So, I proposed that we step back, go through one more round of brainstorming and deliberations – albeit an accelerated version. Again, the sense of relief was palpable, and we moved forward with that approach.

I am struck by this moment because Faculty members shared with me that they had expected me to push ahead with the name I presented on our Faculty proposal (that was their expectation of decanal leadership). My goal was to ensure a collective decision was to be made. Interestingly, a few weeks later we reconvened with the same name front and centre. The vocal minority remained unhappy with the name but appreciated the extended process. We did not reach full consensus but rather we achieved a process of deliberation and decision-making that colleagues could embrace given its transparent, consultative approach. For me it was a moment to navigate the true spirit of interactive, participatory approaches to leadership.

Forward, future leadership

The language of "expansive" is not one thing, nor is it solely identical to or conflatable with spaciousness. From a lens of decolonisation, "expand" is part of a settler-colonial project, taking over and taking up the places and spaces of so many. Expansiveness is sometimes utilised to mean "a drive to excel" (Diamante & London, 2002, p. 405), or conflated with "influence" (Diamante & London, 2002, p. 405).

To decolonise and uncolonise leadership is to "encourage the expression and embodiment of knowledge that has been passed on through the land, living creatures, spiritualities, cultures, histories, and ancestors" (Shah, 2022, para. 7). Here, we take expansion inwards, not outwards. This is not about taking more, or about taking over, but rather about taking inventory. It is about understanding when, where, and how to use one's voice, but never to trample on the voices of others. And, in leadership, using one's voice to amplify the voices of others.

On the "The UnLeading Project" podcast, host Dr. Vidya Shah explores what leading is, is not, and what it can be, particularly in spaces of formal education. Shah plumbs the question, what might leading be when disentangled from power and control, from ignorance and so-called innocence, and what has harmfully rippled out "to students, families, and communities" (2022, 01:36) as a consequence of how leading gets performed? In response, Shah invites an "undoing, unlearning, and unleading" (2022, 01:42).

To expand what leadership looks and feels like, to feel expansive *as* a leader, to cultivate a sense of expansiveness in leadership, and to make and take up space, requires some imagination. Or rather, some re-imagining. "[W]hether we call it decolonization, demystifization, or destroying", this unleading, this re-imagining of leadership, "involves a thorough, honest commitment to shed ... to 'detox' ... to awaken our imaginations to new possibilities for ... a better world" (Rapp, 2002, p. 238). For us, this is embodied in outstretched arms, unfurling a wingspan, shedding expectations or too-tight leadership models.

We see expansive leadership, interactive and participatory, as underpinned by feminist values that have long informed both of our scholarly work and framings of the world. Specifically, feminist leadership in higher education foregrounds shared decision-making, community-building, collaborative relationships, holistic assessment, and equity (Barton, 2006; 2007; Rosser, 2003; Welde et al., 2019). There is a clear relational approach that centres on people – as individuals, as of and in community(ies) – (even within) an academic environment. It is not about a Dean or Director having power and getting to make the decisions. It is not about impotent complicity in upholding, in "the activities of students and educators ... the irrational criteria of efficiency, profit, and quick returns rather than being inspired by a vision for a just society" (Rapp, 2002, p. 229). Rather, relational leadership is about mentoring the careers and development of Faculty and staff, and trying to put in place opportunities and supports that help individuals realise their potential and be successful as defined on their own terms (Barton, 2006; Welde et al., 2019).

This is a care-full leadership approach that requires fostering authentic relationships, understanding the subjective experiences and needs of others, and

Image 18.1 Wingspan/arms outstretched

being genuinely responsive to these. This care orientation means not adjudi-cating between competing rights but rather identifying creative ways of si-multaneously fulfilling competing responsibilities to others (Gilligan, 1982). Feminist leaders are conscious of not just individual issues and concerns but of the staff and Faculty communities – the collective academic whole – as well as what is happening in society at large. This leadership invites attention to nu-anced relational dynamics at the micro-scale and considering how best to serve the community or context in which the institution is located (Barton, 2006). Ultimately, feminist leadership is inclusive and attuned to systems of oppres-sion; feminist leaders are motivated by fairness, transparency, justice, and work toward equity for all constituents. This action is implemented through a pro-cess of deconstruction – a constant reflection on one's decisions and one's own power and personal biases – and the intended and unintended consequences therein – considering the individual, the community, academia, and society (Barton, 2007; Welde et al., 2019).

And what about the "spacious" part of this piece? Our subtitle is perhaps the true heart of this chapter. To be expansive suggests a kind of starting place of fixedness with movement and momentum reaching out from a certain place; spacious being around all that is not fixed. It means to lead with uncer-tainty and humility, to lead with teariness and messiness, to lead with more questions than firm decisions, to lead with more listening than telling. It is also about making inner space for the many parts of us to also be welcome into the leadership mix. Each of us as sometimes rebels and resisters, as sometimes pacifiers and diplomats, and as oftentimes hand-wringing worriers just as often as optimists.

We borrow from the languaging and spirit of mindfulness leadership literature. Mindful leaders are often described as "inspiring hope and offering compassion for all they serve and lead" (Wells, 2015, p. 2). We inquire into our own leaderships here. We see a constellation of approaches (interactive, participatory), values (shared decision making, community building, collaborative relationships, holistic assessment, and equity), and performances (ethic of care, emotion/vulnerability, creative balancing of individual, collective, institutional interests). The outcomes have been moments of embraced aspirations, response to pushback, and co-creation of alternative visions.

And perhaps truest of all is that expansive, spacious leadership is a space for consilience – for threads and models and frameworks and knowledges to coexist. Not as amalgamated, appropriated, or stripped down, but for there to be enough space for feminist leadership, humane leadership, healing leadership, conflicted leadership, friction-full leadership, mindful leadership, and above all justice-prioritising leadership.

References

Barton, T. R. (2006). *A feminist construction of leadership in American higher education*. Unpublished doctoral dissertation, The University of Toledo, Ohio, USA.

Barton, T. R. (2007). Feminist leadership: Building nurturing academic communities. *Advancing Women in Leadership Journal, 22.*

Caño, A. (August 11, 2021). Today's academic leaders must be healers. *Inside Higher Ed.* https://www.insidehighered.com/advice/2021/08/12/how-be-healing-leader-during-these-difficult-times-opinion

Diamante, T., & London, M. (2002). Expansive leadership in the age of digital technology. *Journal of Management Development, 21*(6), 404–416.

Gallo, P., & Hlupic, V. (2019). Humane leadership must be the Fourth Industrial Revolution's real innovation. *World Economic Forum, 15.* https://www.weforum.org/agenda/2019/05/humane-leadership-is-the-4irs-big-management-innovation/

Gilligan, C. (1982). *In a different voice: Psychological theory and women's development.* Harvard University Press.

Leduc, T. B., & Morley, D. (2015). *Five decades of FES [Faculty of Environmental Studies] at York: The praxis of environmental studies.* ABL Group.

Rapp, D. (2002). Social justice and the importance of rebellious, oppositional imaginations. *Journal of School Leadership, 12*(3), 226–245.

Rosser, V. J. (2003). *Feminists in student affairs: Negotiating the process of change.* Unpublished doctoral dissertation, Bowling Green State University, Ohio USA.

Santamaría, L. J., & Santamaría, A. P. (2012). Applied critical leadership in education: Choosing change. https://www.researchgate.net/publication/287248235_Applied_critical_leadership_in_education_Choosing_change

Shah, V. (2022, August 11). *Decolonizing & uncolonizing leadership*. UnLeading. https://www.yorku.ca/edu/unleading/podcast-episodes/decolonizing-leadership/

Welde, K. D., Ollilainen, M., & Solomon, C. R. (2019). Feminist leadership in the academy: Exploring everyday praxis. In V. Demos, M. T. Segal, & K. Kelly (Eds.), *Gender and practice: insights from the field* (pp. 3–21). Advances in Gender Research, Vol. 27. Emerald Publishing.

Wells, C. M. (2015). Conceptualizing mindful leadership in schools: How the practice of mindfulness informs the practice of leading. *Education Leadership Review of Doctoral Research*, 2(1), 1–23.

Chapter 19

The reverse bungee

Balancing rapid changes in perception and academic leadership

Mark Freeman

Introduction

An academic career rarely unfolds in a neatly linear pathway. Spend some time in this bizarre ecosystem and the true trajectory of our careers is revealed like some discursive, meandering map filled with loops and reversals and unexpected surges forward. Anticipating a path like an ascending staircase means it comes as a surprise when that path involves standing on a flat, even landing for an extended period of time with no upward mobility, followed by fast escalators that hurl you upwards. The instability of academic career progression demands fast thinking and long term strategising as we attempt to manage our own expectations of our career, while we simultaneously stagger through the staccato trajectory of our work lives. It can be frustrating, exciting, debilitating, and exhilarating all within the space of a year. It's therefore an absolute imperative that career progress comes with a healthy dose of reflection, recalibration, and re-imagining what our career path might be. This in turn also requires a negotiation and understanding of who we are as a colleague or as a leader while the academic world throws challenges and opportunities and obstacles in our way in what feels sometimes like a random, haphazard series of events. It is a career that demands intense self-reflection as our pathways change, but also requires a keen understanding of the expectations of the institution and the way we are perceived by our colleagues. In achieving a position of balance between the multiple forces that propel us it requires 360 degree perspective of ourselves, and the community within which we learn, grow and progress.

In this chapter I aim to navigate how we can best balance those perceptions of self under the microscope of rapid academic change. How do we reconcile our own sense of self, our own approach to new challenges and academic positions, when we are thrust – through clear-eyed planning or random luck – into a position of authority and leadership over others? As our roles change, and new leadership opportunities present themselves, we are forced to find a balance in repositioning our relationship to work and to our colleagues but also how we present ourselves to the work community. We may present as one

DOI: 10.4324/9781003457510-24

Image 19.1 A reverse bungee – a period of stasis on firm ground and then a
rapid, disorientating ascent where balance and perspective can be
significantly shaken

kind of colleague on the ground, fulfilling a desirable, cohesive role as part of
a team, but find this same persona does not work as we adapt more substantial
leadership positions across our career. Considering the new position, how do
we best represent ourselves within the demands of the new role, and how do
we navigate the expectations of those we have worked with? The experience
of finding a level of equilibrium in this rapid change is something like the
experience of a reverse bungee: a period of stasis on firm ground and then a
rapid, disorientating ascent where balance and perspective can be significantly

shaken. Yet at the apex a sense of balance and clarity can be attained, an expansive view of the world and your relationship to it comes more sharply into focus. Using a recent example of a period in my own career, this chapter aims to propose a process of orchestrating a balance of leadership and self, following an intense period of rapid leadership change, as a pathway towards a more stable and successful perspective on an academic career.

Surrendering, confronting, and shifting assumptions

With this concept of finding a balance of self and leadership, forging a pathway towards some kind of self-actualisation can pose numerous challenges and offer multiple options to reach an effective outcome. There is no one correct way, and this investigation proposes just one out of many approaches. Primarily if we think about a leader as someone "who identifies needs, focuses thinking, and influences others to create change through coordinated action toward a common purpose or shared set of goals in a complex environment" (Clark, 2017. p. 4), then that at least is a helpful first step to focus the newly promoted academic to grapple with their new responsibilities, as well as identifying the goals and approaches the role demands. Approaches to leadership are as particular and idiosyncratic as we all are as individuals, which makes finding the most suitable trajectory both a personal and professional imperative. Clark (2017) describes the confrontation with this process as about "learning to manage change in one's self and environment while also learning to consider and involve others ... [including] developing a personal capacity to orient and align people within an ever-changing environment towards shared goals" (p. 6). Learning to manage change in both one's self and one's work environment is a central skill, and perhaps the most pressing concern following a sudden elevation into a position of significant responsibility. Promotion into a new role demands focus, an approach to goal-centred leadership, a mode of uniting the team to achieve the goals set. This change in position forces in the academic an immediate confrontation with the role they have played in the past – their function within the academic community, but also the persona they have developed across time in their relationships with others within the team. It is a common problem when we move from one context to another: changing roles necessitates changing responsibilities and the consequential realignment of the way we are perceived by others. How do we as academics find the presentational mode that was going to fit the role, without sacrificing our natural personality, and at the same time showcase the skills that were the very qualities that made us right for the position in the first place?

The first obstacle that an academic in such a situation may have to confront is a deep seated belief that we are not equipped to the task, that we have stepped beyond some invisible barrier into a space we don't belong. We often surrender to the assumption that in the new work environment with new responsibilities, we are an obvious imposter stomping around campus in an ill-fitting suit like a grandiose child playing dress-up. To truly find a pathway towards an actualised leader with some level of oversight and understanding of the surrounding environment as Clark had suggested, then the first hurdle to be crossed may be the pervasive destroyer of self-belief: imposter syndrome. This is a concept pioneered by Pauline Clance and Suzanne Imes in 1978 and their study focused specifically on the phenomenon in highly successful women who struggled with leadership and success within a context of patriarchal rule. The argument suggested by Clance and Imes (1978) was that despite "praise and professional recognition from colleagues and respected authorities … [they] do not experience an internal sense of success"(p. 241). They attribute this to the contrast between the low social expectations and the acquisition of significant achievement – the belief that they have stepped above their position without earning it, that the elevation is due to a fluke, an accident, an act of omission or error (p. 244). Bothello and Roulet in their 2019 investigation into this phenomenon focus strictly on academic life and argue that academia possesses a specific set of frameworks to intensify that sense of dislocation from academic role and self. They claim that academia is an occupation "where the induction rituals – both formal and informal – are in many ways misaligned with the multi-dimensional roles of our profession" (p. 854). Their analysis of the ways a series of systematic, ritualised markers of career progress may not cohere with an actual career trajectory is another method to work through the very specific sense of embarrassment or shame we may feel when we move from one position to the next in academia, especially if that ascension comes without the traditional formalities we associate with promotion.

This disjunct, then, between what we imagine our career path to be, and what actually can occur in an academic institution, may place us in a position of feeling as if we have duped those around us. We can fall into the trap of disavowing our own histories, and our own skills, for an imagined, ritualised set of standards that we can never meet. This is a set of circumstances which forces the dissonant perception that acknowledges ascendence as credible, coherent, true if based on cast-iron merit and the unexpected opportunity as false, fake, reliant on luck or happenstance, but never skill. Fundamentally at the core of this dissonance is a conflict between changing schemas, what Day, Harrison, and Halpin (2008, p. 107) identify as 'mental models', highlighting the discordance between self-perception and workplace function. Within the workplace/leadership realm Day et al. argue that one central guide is the normative schema, which covers perceptions of the current state of systems the person must deal with – essentially, the tasks we are required to complete. This operates in conjunction with a prescriptive model, which takes into account the person's history and experience and self-awareness (Day et al., 2008, p. 107) – the way we perceive ourselves and our abilities. Placed in a leadership role, this schema offers us a guide by which we can best execute the demands of the new position and the new leader can begin to formulate strategies that integrate both models. That sense of being an imposter, however, lies squarely in a mistaken belief that the personal schemas are in direct conflict with the normative. Our sense of who we are feels immediately at odds with what the role itself demands – we are essentially, out of balance. The first steps an academic must make to resolve this crippling sense of alienation is to recognise the confluence between these schemas: the capacity for the role and the person to work in unison. With a perspective that we prefer to envision ourselves as possessing a concrete, coherent self-concept, Day et al. (2008) argues that as leaders we are also "motivated to act in accordance with this identity" (p. 187). Consequently, an essential part of reconciling an academic identity is to put aside the *circumstances* of the appointment, and the entrenched self-denial of skills and experience, and look purely at the assets that are brought to the position. Bringing balance to a sense of self within this new role context forces the academic to confront the abilities and experiences they do, in fact, possess, and embrace the knowledge that those skills are essential to the construction of a new leader-identity.

To reconcile this knowledge is a significant first step to finding a leadership equilibrium by acknowledging the academic's suitability for the role. To put aside the sense of being an imposter and to own the role you inhabit clears space for the most important of the tasks in grappling with new leadership: understanding the demands of the job, the goals required to achieve success, and the leadership style that would encourage the team to achieve those goals. Searching for a very practical guide to approaching a leadership style is a daunting prospect. There are multiple models for exploring an approach to leadership development, covering writers from David Day to Patricia O'Connell and Robert Hogan to Craig Gruber and endless business-focused writers exploring ways to maximise leadership potential. But in considering in very practical terms how to present oneself within this new context, the work of Robert Hogan writing with Rodney Warrenfeltz (2003) and Robert Kaiser (2005) provides a helpful taxonomy of approaches that opens up pathways to grapple with this necessary change. Their clear delineation of the tasks and skillsets required for effective leadership cover some of the external factors of leadership, but also devote time to addressing the issue we sometimes most overlook in this arena: the problem of an academic's relationship with themselves.

Exploring the balance of self and leadership

Hogan and Warrenfeltz (2003) propose four central domains of effective workplace leaders – Business, Intrapersonal, Interpersonal, and Leadership. Working through each of these domains and the skills required for success proposes a practical, achievable framework for an adaptation to new leadership circumstances. The first mode proposed is the Business domain, which requires "abilities and technical knowledge needed to plan, budget, coordinate, and monitor organizational activity" (Hogan & Kaiser, 2005, p. 173). Of the four central domains identified, the Business domain is recognised as "the easiest to teach, the most cognitive … and the least dependent on the ability to deal productively with other people" (Hogan & Warrenfeltz, 2003, p. 79). Relying on a connected team and mentors, seeking assistance to navigate the labyrinthine connections that run through various administrative bodies is essential for anyone entering a new work context. To not ask for guidance, to attempt to 'fake it till you make it' is not the strategy here. Reliance on the support systems around you is essential in those early months, and recognition in this domain of the importance of "organizational effectiveness … [in] a talented management team, with talent defined in terms of the domain model" (Hogan & Kaiser, 2005, p. 178). Matthew Clark (2017) also singles out this necessity for organisational development through a reliance on support, which he argues is "the main element that maintains motivation and persistence despite the presence of the adaptive challenges" (p. 9). With experience in taking on new tasks, with new workflows, any new leader learns quickly to reach out, get advice, get feedback, and entrench the new processes until they adapt to a system of automated pathways, a clear set of decision making processes and strategies. Courtney Gosnell's (2017) research found that "those who perceive more social support available to them also tend to pursue more positive coping styles, which includes things like finding ways to adapt or change or seeking the help of others" (p. 283). By asking the questions, clarifying the procedures with those who had been working with them every day, this very functional domain can be readily achievable so that systems and processes and outcomes can be dealt with efficiently and effectively.

The first serious challenge for the newly appointed academic is grappling with what is described as the Intrapersonal domain, which is focused largely on how the leader carries themselves, their capacity to control and use their intellect, their emotion, their patience and perseverance (Hogan & Kaiser, 2005, p. 173). Maintaining a level of personal credibility is essential in leadership formation. Hogan and Kaiser describe the importance for a leader to foreground "keeping one's word, fulfilling one's promises, not playing favorites, and not taking advantage of one's situation" (Hogan & Kaiser, 2005, p. 173), which seems on the surface to be readily achievable. But as Hogan and Warrenfeltz (2003) noted, also identifying issues of self-esteem was absolutely necessary for effective leadership within this domain (p. 78). Overcoming that sense of being an imposter is one thing – truly seeing oneself as deserving is another. Gosnell (2017) argues that if "leaders cling to an initial identity and are never willing to make adjustments or challenge themselves, there would be little growth or development" (p. 276). This strikes at the core of many people in academia: this belief that if we stay static, that the person we are in the workplace somehow stays in an unchangeable, unaffected condition across the breadth of our career. Yet an inability to adapt to changing circumstances doesn't foster perfection, it creates stultification. The importance of individual growth as workplace expectations change is a career imperative: it opens us up to self- improvement as well as career advancement. Simon Dolan's (2007) work in the arena of self-esteem is particularly instructive on this matter. He discusses the connection between self-esteem and confidence, and that, removed from excesses such as arrogance or conceit, a level of "organizational confidence" (p. 65) offers an effective synergy between members of a team, aligning leader and team with goals, and enabling the navigation of change. Grappling with this Intrapersonal domain forces an academic to do the self-awareness work, identifying frankly and honestly the skills acquired, the assets a person can bring to a position, and acknowledging other features that may need to be minimised or shelved. A clear-eyed understanding of yourself is the cornerstone of effective leadership in balancing out the personal and the professional.

The Interpersonal domain focuses on "social skill, building and maintaining relationships ... listening and negotiating, oral and written communications, ... approachability (Hogan & Kaiser, 2005, p. 173). This domain and set of skills perhaps lie closest to the sort of workplace relationship building academic staff engage with at any level – a willingness to listen, to provide support or solutions, and to communicate with our colleagues to avoid any issues being confused or misconstrued. This truly is foundational leadership: without the ability to talk effectively with your colleagues or your team, then leadership is almost impossible. The ability to "put oneself in the place of another person, to try to anticipate how that person sees the world" (Hogan & Warrenfeltz, 2003, p. 79) is a skill central to interpersonal leadership, requiring a disposition that can see perspectives beyond their own. Chris Long (2017) explores issues of trust and authority in this area of leadership and argues that interpersonal relationships in a leadership setting demand "that they share their values and are focused on attending to their individual needs. Leaders do this by taking an active interest in their employees' personal welfare, by accommodating their employees' personal interests when they take actions or make decisions" (p. 168). As Clark has suggested, the shaping of leadership comes from adaptability, and adapting personal interactions to a new position of responsibility requires a recognition of a person's position in the chain of command, and acting in accord with wider university administrative structures. But if the relationships are there, and the communication skills are already in line, then the Interpersonal domain tends to require minimal transformation. Long (2017) suggests that focusing professional relationships in terms of taking "employees' interests into account through their words and actions helps leaders forge stronger value congruencies between themselves and their employees" (p. 176). As a leader, a recognition of the points of similarity between the leader and the team broaches what some can consider a divide between general academic and leader/administrator. An initial sense of separation from colleagues that may be experienced due to the movement into a leadership position can increasingly fade away as the confluences between team leader and team member became more apparent.

Identifying the last domain as Leadership, Hogan and Kaiser suggest this covers "influence and team-building skills ... communicating a compelling vision ... hiring and staffing strategically; motivating others; building effective teams" (Hogan & Kaiser, 2005, p. 173). This can be characterised best as leadership from the table, not the pulpit, and fostering the freedom for people to speak freely, to identify issues and solutions, and to craft a vision for the direction of the team. In this arena team building is the primary focus and pushes to the forefront the ability of the leader to shape the vision for the future. This demands adjustments to delivery also in that, as a leader, the academic is able to surrender a level of focus and transfer some of that power over to the team. Wodak, Kwon, and Clarke (2011) have explored approaches to this domain, and argue for a series of activities which foster team building and community to achieve the larger goals of a workplace community. Leadership styles for this domain require fostering "participation of other speakers to explore new ideas and/or develop synthesis with existing ideas related to current topic of discourse... to enhance other speakers' sense of participation and therefore their 'buy-in' to the eventual outcome" (p. 18). They suggest this opening up of discussion also must work in tandem with a capacity to direct, rephrase, and "to bring the discussion toward closure and resolution by reducing the equivocality of ideas" (p. 19). Utilising this strategy is closer to conducting an orchestra than fronting the team and giving orders. While there are goals to be achieved, and a destination that needs to be reached, the style is much more about allowing the team to work through ideas, building on discussion, and stepping in to keep the discussion on track and offer feedback in terms of logistics. Here the aim is to open up and shape the discussion, minimising discursive tangents, restating arguments for clarity, but allowing all to contribute to the central vision of the team. Listening in these wide team-focused situations is the most important skill to be demonstrated: to listen and to guide. Craig Gruber (2017) makes the point that "by engaging in the listening portion of the conversation, leaders can listen and internalize what individuals need. For those working with effective leaders, they feel listened to and appreciated" (p. 101). Within this Leadership domain, the capacity to allow the conversation to follow where it must is crucial, Indeed, it is this grand roadmap that guides the leader to understand where the team's strengths lie, where obstacles are positioned, and to encourage adaptability to sit within a larger goal-focused framework that helps the other modes of leadership fall into place. Leading the team by identifying strategic advantages, and relying on the expertise of the team to offer solutions to obstacles, creates not just strong bonds within the team, but allows the leader to identify the strengths and dynamics that could propel the team forward. Surrendering the focus fosters greater insight into the team leadership, and allows the new leader to identify the nuances necessary to facilitate effective team outcomes.

Operating on these guidelines granted specific, applicable approaches to the experience I was met with, where due to a series of unexpected events I found myself swiftly appointed to a senior leadership position. It was a tremendous chance to learn new skills, interact with new people, and be a better academic. But this sudden acceleration upwards into a position of significant leadership beyond any previous experience forced a confrontation with finding a balance between my new role and demands of the job. As Hogan and Warrenfeltz had suggested, the immediate demands of the Business domain were able to be swiftly brought under control through consultation with those with greater experience and a reinvigorated approach to calendar organisation. But what was missing was a reckoning with the interpersonal and intrapersonal. This prompted one of the more intense periods of self-reflection and growth as I was forced to grapple with a crisis of the most existential kind – who was I as a leader, as an academic, as a team member? How could I balance the new leadership expectations that had been placed on me, and still remain fundamentally the person I had been?

As a first step I had to truly understand who I was as an academic, and identify the elements that worked in tandem with the new role and those that would need to take more of a back seat. I knew I had long served as the 'jokester' of the team, affable, personable, self-deprecating, and these were qualities that worked in a social, team member context. As a team leader though, I ran the risk of appearing flippant, too casual, too self-deprecating to bolster confidence in a team. It became apparent that a strategy of restraint was necessary – there were personal impulses that had to be tamed, but not totally discarded. I sought to strike a balance between maintaining the broadly affable persona that came naturally with something more process and outcome focused, so that the priorities and goals of the position became the focus and the quips, while still a feature of my style, took a very secondary position as a sidebar moment, rather than the main focus for my approach to leadership. That self-analysis of who you are, but more importantly who people perceive you to be, is one of the most significant self-reflection strategies an academic can conduct. This intrapersonal work forces a self-reflection that identifies the strengths and weaknesses we all possess, and grappling with those honestly and frankly opens up a clear methodology for adapting an individual persona into new academic contexts across our careers.

On an interpersonal level I aimed for a level of ubiquity of presence, trying to be as available to staff as possible, reinforcing relationships with the team through incidental, corridor conversations, the sort of 'interstitial' moments between everyday events and activities. It is worth noting that investigating a range of these facets of leadership style, what becomes apparent is that although the initial impact of a change in responsibilities seems substantial in the early stages, adapting the leadership presentation of one's self is actually more about shifting fine points of delivery rather than wholesale transformation. The personable, open persona that had worked as a team member now became a significant asset as staff relied on that prior understanding and were open to discussions across pedagogical, personal, and administrative lines,

which allowed for more effective leadership outcomes: so many issues were re-
solved and curtailed before they became larger issues due to this approachability. There were other strategies that worked following some slight adjustments
concurrent with the demands of the new position – an open door policy for
team discussions, problem raising and solving opportunities for individuals,
and forward planning to circumvent any potential issues further down the line.
The efficacy of these approaches, by relying on my relationships with the team
itself, felt the most innate, the most natural, and produced excellent results.

For the big picture, leadership focus leaning into open forums for broad,
but contained discussions brought a stronger vision of the goals for the team,
and the steps necessary to achieving them. I adopted a strategic approach of
acknowledging the inevitable constraints placed on academics when planning
long terms goals, or resolving short term issues. It is necessary for staff to
find ways to express their frustrations, but adopting a position whereby those
frustrations were redirected towards achievable solutions ensuring a level of
productivity rather than purely an expression of pain. A whole team meeting
mapped out the expectations across teaching, research, and administration,
confronting long terms goals and immediate pressure points to centre the
team on both immediate relief and future planning. Bringing together a newly
focused understanding of my own position as an academic and as a leader
worked to bring into focus the goals and future trajectory of the team itself.
This was only possible, however, because of the search for the balance between
the expectations of the team, the demands of the university, and an unflinch-
ing interrogation of my own personal qualities that created an effective and
successful leadership style.

Reconciling personal and professional identity

Having worked through these multiple modes of presentation, and really in-
terrogating the necessity for change, there was a sense of reconciliation with
the new role, and a discovery of the balance required between what came
naturally to myself, and the learned expectations of the academic role undertaken. Identifying the domains, and the skillsets and personal traits necessary
for each, offered an easier, more compartmentalised strategy for understanding the ways that adapting to career change could open up and enhance my
skills, my presentational style, and the simple efficacy of my leadership. It fostered a growing sense of security in a position that initially felt alien and awkward. David Day and Hock-Peng Sin (2011) describe this as the process of
"internalization … in which one's private self-concept is aligned with visible
public behavior over time" (p. 547). Relying on self-awareness and a willingness to adapt, learn, and grow, I recognised the necessity of leaning into some
aspects of my personality and the skillsets that had worked to my advantage
in the past, and reign in the more impulsive traits that could undermine or
erode the impression I was crafting. This approach had never felt like a lie – it

was me, but a select section of me, a workplace me, Leadership Me. I felt this most keenly when I moved from seeing myself as reactive – this is happening to me and I have to solve this – to planning ahead, identifying the trajectories of projects, staff, policy. Leadership truly lies in the ability to look forward, to plan and strategise as you see the issues emerge on the horizon. By truly understanding who I needed to be for me and for the team I was leading, I found an adaptation of my natural self that acknowledged my history, my skills, and my personality, that could lead with confidence and focus and assurance to the benefit of both me, and my whole team.

References

Bothello, J., & Roulet, T. (2019). The Imposter Syndrome, or the mis-representation of self in academic life. *Journal of Management Studies*, 56(4), 854–861.

Clance, P., & Imes, S. (1978). The Imposter Phenomenon in high achieving women: Dynamics and therapeutic intervention. *Psychotherapy: Theory, Research and Practice*, 15, 241–247.

Clark, M. G. (2017). Deconstructing leader development: An introduction. In M. Clark & C. Gruber (Eds.), *Leader development deconstructed*. Annals of theoretical psychology, vol. 15. Springer

Day, D. V., Harrison, M. M., & Halpin, S. M. (2008). Section 4: Learning-based approaches to leadership. In *An integrative approach to leader development*. Taylor & Francis.

Day, D. V., & Sin, H.-P. (2011). Longitudinal tests of an integrative model of leader development: Charting and understanding developmental trajectories. *The Leadership Quarterly*, 22(3), 545–560.

Dolan, S. (2007). *Stress, self-esteem, health and work*. Palgrave Macmillan.

Gosnell, C. L. (2017). Leading with support: The role of social support for positive and negative events in leader development. In M. Clark & C. Gruber (Eds.), *Leader development deconstructed*. Annals of theoretical psychology, vol. 15. Springer.

Gruber, C. W. (2017). Leadership in dialogue: How courage informs. In M. Clark & C. Gruber (Eds.), *Leader development deconstructed*. Annals of theoretical psychology, vol. 15. Springer.

Hogan, R., & Kaiser, R. B. (2005). What we know about leadership. *Review of General Psychology*, 9(2), 169–180.

Hogan, R., & Warrenfeltz, R. (2003). Educating the modern manager. *Academy of Management Learning & Education*, 2(1), 74–84.

Long, C. (2017). Conflict management in leader development: The roles of control, trust, and fairness. In M. Clark & C. Gruber (Eds.), *Leader development deconstructed*. Annals of theoretical psychology, vol. 15. Springer.

Wodak, R., Kwon, W., & Clarke, I. (2011). Getting people on board: Discursive leadership for consensus building in team meetings. *Discourse & Society*, 22(5), 592–644.

Appendix: Titles in the Wellbeing and Self-care in Higher Education series

Wellbeing and Self-care in Higher Education
Editor: **Narelle Lemon**

Healthy Relationships in Higher Education
Promoting Wellbeing Across Academia
Edited by Narelle Lemon
In this edited collection, authors navigate how they view relationships as a crucial part of their wellbeing and acts of self-care, exploring the "I", "We", and "Us" at the centre of self-care and wellbeing embodiment.

Creating a Place for Self-care and Wellbeing in Higher Education
Finding Meaning Across Academia
Edited by Narelle Lemon
In this edited collection, the authors navigate how they find meaning in their work in academia by sharing their own approaches to self-care and wellbeing.

Creative Expression and Wellbeing in Higher Education
Making and Movement as Mindful Moments of Self-care
Edited by Narelle Lemon
This book focuses on the lived experiences of higher education professionals working in the face of stress, pressure and the threat of burnout and how acts of self-care and wellbeing can support, develop and maintain a sense of self.

Reflections on Valuing Wellbeing in Higher Education
Reforming our Acts of Self-care
Edited by Narelle Lemon
Designed to support readers working in higher education, this volume focuses on individual and collective practices of creativity, embodiment and movement as acts of self-care and wellbeing highlighting how connection to hand, body, voice and mind can be essential to this process.

Practising Compassion in Higher Education
Caring for Self and Others Through Challenging Times
Edited by Narelle Lemon, Heidi Harju-Luukkainen and Susanne Garvis
Presenting a collective international story, this book demonstrates the importance of compassion as an act of self-care in the face of change and disruption, providing guidance on how to cope under trying conditions in higher education settings.

Women Practicing Resilience, Self-care and Wellbeing in Academia
International Stories from Lived Experience
Edited by Ida Fatimawati Adi Badiozaman, Voon Mung Ling and Kiran Sandhu
Through a lens of self-care and wellbeing, this book shares stories of struggle and success from a diverse range of women in academia, illustrating the ways that higher education institutions can be more accommodating of the needs of women.

Writing Well and Being Well for Your PhD and Beyond
How to Cultivate a Strong and Sustainable Writing Practice for Life
Katherine Firth
Prioritizing wellbeing alongside academic development, this book provides practical advice to help students write well, and be well, during their PhD and throughout their career. Relevant at any stage of the writing process, this book will help doctoral students and early career researchers to produce great words that people want to read, examiners want to pass and editors want to publish.

Prioritising Wellbeing and Self-Care in Higher Education
How We Can Do Things Differently to Disrupt Silence
Edited by Narelle Lemon
This book illuminates international voices of those who feel empowered to do things differently in higher education, providing inspiration to those who are seeking guidance, reassurance, or a beacon of hope.

Navigating Tensions and Transitions in Higher Education
Effective Skills for Maintaining Wellbeing and Self-care
Edited by Kay Hammond and Narelle Lemon
With a focus on skills development, this book provides guidance on how to navigate transitions between career stages in higher education and how to maintain wellbeing in the process. Written with all career stages in mind, this book will be an essential resource for new and experienced researchers alike.

Sustaining Your Wellbeing in Higher Education
Values-based Self-Care for Work and Life
Jordan Cummings
This book provides an evidence-based approach to sustainable self-care, anchoring these strategies in individual academics' core personal values. It teaches readers how to use their values to leverage self-care strategies into a workable, individualised, and effective map to wellness.

Passion and Purpose in the Humanities
Exploring the Worlds of Early Career Researchers
Edited by Marcus Bussey, Camila Mozzini-Alister, Bingxin Wang and Samantha Willcocks
In the spirit of guiding emerging researchers in higher education, this book features twenty unique essays by emergent scholars who weave their personal lives into their research passions, offering a window into the experience of researchers in both professional and personal developments.

Exploring Time as a Resource for Wellness in Higher Education
Identity, Self-care and Wellbeing at Work
Edited by Sharon McDonough and Narelle Lemon
Bringing together international perspectives, this book demonstrates the importance of reframing time in higher education and how we can view it as a resource to support wellbeing and self-care. Whether it's making time, having time, or investing in time, this book explores strategies and reflections necessary to grow, maintain, and protect wellbeing.

Innovative Practices for Supporting and Promoting Wellbeing in the Higher Education Sector
Institutional and Individual Perspectives of Wellbeing Initiatives and Innovations in Action
Edited by Angela R. Dobele and Lisa Farrell
This book examines academic wellbeing from both institutional and individual perspectives, highlighting innovative approaches to support and promote the psychological health of faculty in an increasingly volatile higher education landscape. Featuring evidence-based practices and firsthand accounts, the book equips readers with practical ideas and strategies they can implement to become wellbeing champions within their own workplaces.

Understanding Wellbeing in Higher Education of the Global South
Contextually Sensitive and Culturally Responsive Perspectives
Edited by Youmen Chaaban, Abdellatif Sellami and Igor Jacky Dimitri Michaleczek
This volume presents an alternative conceptualization of wellbeing in higher education, grounded in the socio-cultural context of the Global South. By delineating a contextually-sensitive and culturally-responsive perspective, the edited book challenges dominant Western notions of wellbeing and invites readers to explore the complexity and multi-dimensionality of this construct across diverse educational settings.

For more information about this series, please visit: www.routledge.com/Wellbeing-and-Self-care-in-Higher-Education/book-series/WSCHE

Index

Note: Page locators in *italic* refer to images and page locators in **bold** refer to tables.

For Product Safety Concerns and Information please contact our EU
representative GPSR@taylorandfrancis.com
Taylor & Francis Verlag GmbH, Kaufingerstraße 24, 80331 München, Germany